Oh, The Mad Caradoc!

Betty.

With all best wishes

Ken Alexander

Ken Alexander

Pen Press

First published in Great Britain by Pen Press

All paper used in the printing of this book has been made from wood grown in managed, sustainable forests.

ISBN13: 0-9539013-1-9

Printed and bound in the UK
Pen Press is an imprint of
Indepenpress Publishing Limited
25 Eastern Place
Brighton
BN2 1GJ

A catalogue record of this book is available from the British Library

Cover design by Jacqueline Abromeit

Acknowledgements

I wish to express my thanks to Mrs K. Vyrnwy-Clarke of the Diss Town Council for her very kind help in supplying information necessary to the writing of the early chapters of this book. Thanks are also due to Sergeant Major Wood and Marine Pickford of the Royal Navy, Portsmouth for their help in verification of details about H.M.S. Victory.

My gratitude is also extended to my wife, Deborah, for her invaluable assistance in the examination of the Log, notebooks, diaries and photographs from which the book was compiled. Mention must be made here of Jim's grandchildren, Christopher, Louise and Fern, for the help and interest they gave to this project!

Above all my thanks are given posthumously to the following and many others too, who were able during their lifetimes to supply information to fill any gaps about Jim's life and personality:

Nora (Jim's wife, my mother)
Auntie Vi and Uncle Charlie
Great Aunt Esther
Uncle Cec & Auntie Win
Uncle Bernie
Alf & Alice Moorman, (my Maternal Granddad and Grandma)
Frank & Kitty Whittam and their son, Frank.

Foreword

My late father died at the age of forty-one when I was only twelve and my sister was three. My memories of him are fond ones. He was the most patient and understanding man I have ever encountered; a rare patience that encompassed not only the intricacies of any machinery, large or small, but also the more complex intricacies of the minds of his family and contacts. If ever a man gave himself unselfishly to the ideals of true family life it was Jim. The great love and understanding of which he was capable was perhaps all the more remarkable because of the unhappiness he suffered in his own childhood and the separation in his early years from the one person he loved at that time, his sister, Vi. So much of Jim's short life was spent in trying to find Vi again and his patience in that long search was finally rewarded.

His great contribution to those whom he loved was his encouragement of communication within the family unit, without which there can never be a proper basis for expressions of love. His sense of humour, ever present, lifted him above the level of the puritanical Christian, however, and added that magical touch to the atmosphere of love, which makes for happiness. The greatest testimony was that of my mother for although she was widowed at the early age of thirty-four and had a hard struggle in providing for her children, she never remarried. She remarked that she had been fortunate enough in this life to meet Jim and to share those wonderful years with him and that the memory of that love was hers and was sufficient.

During his service in the Royal Navy, particularly that aboard HMS Caradoc, with characters like Wiggy Bennett, John Murray, Frank Butler, Bert Featherstone and all the others of that great crew, Jim saw action in the Atlantic and the North Sea during the Great War and later, following the Armistice, the actions in the Black Sea against Bolshevism. Because so little was known of the part played by the Royal Navy in support of the Volunteer Army, it was my late father's intention to incorporate the information from his Log, diaries and other records into a book. Alas, his other responsibilities and commitments had to take precedence and the book was never completed by him. However, his original introduction bearing his signature is included in this foreword.

The work of collation and the completion of Jim's story were spread over a long period of time. The first stages were begun well over twenty years ago but the distractions of my Practice made it difficult to devote the attention required for a book of this sort to really capture the essential character of my father and those contemporaries of his whom he loved so much. The historical detail was available in the records—that was no problem, but to do justice to the characters was quite another undertaking. If the book has accomplished this aim, only the reader can judge. I hope that it has but if not, I extend my sincere apologies to my father, to Caradoc's crew wherever they are now and to whoever reads the book!

Ken Alexander

The original "Readers' Introduction":

This book has been compiled in the hopes that it may instruct and elevate those who have no other means of picturing, otherwise than Newspapers, the doings, movements, and happenings of one of the ships engaged in the Black Sea operations against Bolshevism.

I hope that, whoever happens to read this book will bear with any errors in spelling as the writer does not claim to be a present-day scholar.

Hoping that the reading will help to pass away an hour pleasantly,

I beg to sign myself

James R Alexander, AB
H.M.S. "Caradoc".

Chapter One

On the twenty-eighth of April in the year 1901, James Robert Alexander took his first breath of Norfolk air and about that same time his mother took her final breath. It had been a difficult time for her as she had been dogged with ill health throughout her life. Jim's father was left with a young daughter of three and a little baby to care for so it was, perhaps, inevitable that he took in a housekeeper whom he eventually married.

Jim's father, a Scot, was a strict Christian in every sense—strict with himself and with his household, a disciplinarian. Violet, his daughter went to Church regularly every Sunday morning at St. Mary's and attended a Sunday school every Sunday afternoon. When Jim was old enough to walk he went with his sister to the Sunday school regularly too. From a young baby he had accompanied both his father and sister, and later his stepmother, to the Sunday morning services at the Church of St. Mary.

He was enthralled by the singing of the hymns and psalms and attempted to join in as soon as he could make his own sounds. This amused young Violet very much. She would hold her little brother's hand and giggle at the youngster's attempts to join in the songs of praise. Whilst Jim's noises did not concern his father at all, the giggling from Violet was quite another matter. It displeased her father and her stepmother and the pair of them would frown fiercely at her or give her arm a tug to indicate their displeasure. Later, when the family group had left the sanctuary of the church and returned to the pink-washed cottage in which they lived, Violet was severely chastised.

It was not a happy home and their step-mother, having no children of her own and being past child bearing age, probably resented bringing them up at all. Whether there was any love between Jim's father and his second wife, or whether the marriage was one of mutual convenience, only they knew. Jim's stepmother seldom, if ever, smiled or displayed any sign of affection for her stepchildren or indeed for their father. She dressed in black, tied her hair tightly back in a bun, and with her thin lips pressed firmly together presented to the children a picture of the archetypal witch! There was very little comfort from their natural father who busied himself with his work and seemed to have very little spare time left over for his children. He was an aloof man with an unsmiling face, which looked even fiercer since he sported a thick grey moustache, waxed at the ends. Folk said that he resembled Bismarck.

Jim was only two when his sister started school. They had been such close companions up to that time, playing together in the back garden on fine days, or in the cottage on wet days. Violet's instincts towards her young brother were quite maternal and he adored her. He could not understand why he had to be left alone when she set out daily for the Church School without him.

It must have been the happiest day in his life for Jim when he was old enough to go to school himself. Brother and sister, hand in hand, walking together up St. Nicholas Street past the Corn Hall. It would have proved quite a walk for Jim on that first day when Violet went past St. Mary's into Market Place and Church Street and along the Entry where the school was situated. His walks up to that time had usually terminated at St. Mary's. Perhaps there was a tear or two when the children were separated in school, Violet to go to her classroom with the other eight year olds, and Jim to the Infants' classroom with his contemporaries!

Jim liked school. He did well at his lessons excelling in Arithmetic and Religious Instruction. Frequently he received prizes from both the Church School and the Sunday School which were usually in the form of classical or semi-classical books bearing inscriptions on their inside covers—James Robert Alexander, aged 5, 6, 7, 8 (and so on) for his exemplary conduct and full attendance throughout the year. It seemed that sickness was never encouraged in the home by either his father or his step-mother so school, church and Sunday school were attended faithfully through colds and coughs and most other temporary disabilities by both Jim and Violet. Possibly their father having witnessed the ill health of his first wife could not bear to witness any frailty in his offspring and they were not likely to have received much sympathy or comfort from their step-mother. Whatever the motivation the fact remained that neither Jim nor his sister missed any of their schooling. The very lack of parental affection forged a bond of strength between Jim and his sister who were very devoted to one another in spite of the three years difference in their ages. They grew up sharing a love for one another that left no room for petty differences, squabbles or jealousy and what one achieved became also a joy for the other.

Jim's library in those days consisted of his Bible, "Dog Crusoe", "With Axe and Rifle", "Old Jack", "Treasure Island", "Kidnapped", several Charles Dickens novels and a few religious books bought cheaply in the Market. In the winter months he read aloud to Vi as the rain pattered against the windows but in the summer sun he would enjoy acting out with her some of the scenes from the adventure books, either in Rectory Meadow or along the bank of the Waveney. Sometimes they were joined by their friends from school and when they tired of acting out the adventures Jim and the other boys would climb trees or attempt to catch fish in the river while the girls would play ball or skipping. When play was over they usually made their way back by Denmark Street, past the *Cock Inn* or by way of Mere Street and Market Hill into St. Nicholas Street, which boasted two public houses, *The Greyhound* and the *Two Brewers*. The public houses fascinated Jim as there was always a collection of what he believed to be adventurous characters using them—sheep farmers, labourers and very old men with beards who were, he thought sure, sailors who had travelled the world but had become too old to follow their calling.

When Vi was fourteen she left school and was placed in service by her father and stepmother. It was a desolate time for eleven-year-old Jim when Vi was taken away from the cottage by an opulent and somewhat portly middle aged gentleman to serve in his household as a kitchen maid. When Vi had gone Jim was left with no one with whom he could share his troubles and triumphs. At first he shut himself away in his room. He blamed his father and stepmother for sending his sister away. As time went on and it became obvious that Vi would not be coming back, he plunged himself into his school and church work, winning from the teachers the praise and affection he needed. He joined the church choir and as he had a fine voice the local vicar warmly welcomed Jim's contribution to the choir.. For his part Jim was glad of those extra attendances at choir practice, which took him out of the home environment. If anything his stepmother seemed to have preferred Vi to him although in truth she was not really fond of either of them. Although Jim's father was quite incapable of showing any real affection he was not displeased by his son's interest in the church. Perhaps Jim's stepmother was jealous of even that scant attention. Be that as it may, she became increasingly strict in her attitude and picked on the boy for every fault she could find, adding a few more that did not exist for good measure. Jim became more and more unhappy. He hated his stepmother and longed for the companionship of his sister. He vowed that when he was old enough he would leave and go in search of Vi and the two of them would then be together always.

When Jim reached his teens he was a handsome young lad, quite tall for his age, strong and already displaying something of adulthood. His voice had broken early and although this had presented a few problems in the choir at the time, he stayed on. His bass voice was a very useful contribution to the choir.

His father had noticed that Jim displayed considerable ability working with wood and thereupon decided that such natural aptitude should be exploited. So arrangements were made for Jim's apprenticeship with a carpenter in Norwich, some twenty miles away. Shortly before his fourteenth birthday Jim left school and started work in Norwich. Because of the distance involved it was arranged that he should stay with an aunt in Norwich, travelling home occasionally at weekends.

Such absence from home did not worry Jim. He was no longer subject to the unhappy atmosphere of his former life and his separation from his father and stepmother was a relief. It was true that he missed his school friends but realised that the demands of work life would have made that inevitable whether he had remained in Diss or not. His only real regret was in leaving the choir and the kindness shown him by the good folk connected with St Mary's. However his being with Aunt Esther more than compensated for the loss. Jim liked her very much. She was a distant relative on his mother's side of the family and quite a motherly person in her way. Jim had a room of his own in her house in Norwich and settled in quite happily to his new way of life, particularly his aunt's home cooking. He developed quite a taste for tripe and onions, garnished with a sprig of parsley and served up with jacket potatoes—one of her favourite dishes.

"Nutritious and not too expensive neither!" as she put it. "Just the right combination to keep a body healthy—good wholesome food for a growing lad like you, young Jim."

She baked her own bread and cakes too so there were usually some appetising smells coming from her kitchen. She had no singing voice, being tone deaf; much to Jim's amusement for she usually burst into song when happy at some domestic chore. Her grey hair bunched up on top of her head and held in place by a series of pins, her bright blue eyes and glowing red cheeks above a somewhat matronly figure, all presented a picture of domestic bliss to young Jim. He was reasonably content with his work too and earned praise from his employer who seemed quite pleased at the speed with which Jim mastered the tools and the skills associated with his trade.

Although he was not unhappy at work and in his new environment he was very unhappy whenever he had to return to his own home. At such times he constantly thought about Vi, wondering what had become of her. Any attempt at communicating his anxiety for his sister was met by rebuffs from both his father and his stepmother. He had not seen Vi for over three years and he wondered what she looked like. He had only pictures in his mind of a fourteen year old girl dressed in a dark grey top coat and black flat-heeled shoes, her hand gripping tightly the handle of a small suit-case hastily packed with her few belongings; her blue eyes expressing doubt and anxiety. She had never written to him—but then writing had never come easy to her. Although three years her junior Jim recalled how often he had helped her with writing and spelling as well as reading to her. Neither his father nor his stepmother had ever helped her and if she had ever written to them, which seemed unlikely, they had never mentioned the fact.

As he found the atmosphere in the cottage stifling, he would usually go for walks, rain or fair, along the banks of the Waveney where he and Vi had spent many happy hours together. At other times he would make his way slowly along St. Nicholas Street towards St. Mary's. The old church stood sentinel there as it had done for centuries, seemingly untouched by the passage of time. His new way of life had forced him to leave the church choir but whenever he was home he dutifully attended the Sunday morning service with his father and his stepmother, looking forward to his journey back to Norwich after the Sunday lunch. During lunch, after Grace had been said, his father would ask the inevitable questions about how he was progressing at work and he would dutifully answer that things were going very well, thank you. After those brief exchanges the meal was usually eaten in silence save for comments on the tenderness of the lamb or otherwise, the only contribution to conversation ever made by his stepmother. Sometimes on his walks he would meet school friends and exchange a greeting or two with them. Unlike him most of the youths worked in the immediate area and were in frequent contact with one another. He shared no common interest with them any more. He felt this strongly and in a way resented it.

One day he met John, a lad older than himself, who had been in Vi's class at school.

Although John was wearing a khaki uniform, which didn't fit him very well but of which he was obviously very proud, Jim easily recognised him. Under that khaki cap would be crinkly ginger hair and beneath the shadow of the peak's cap were those grey-green eyes, which always seem to be cast in Vi's direction, like the eyes of a faithful spaniel. Jim did not like John particularly, not only because of his obvious infatuation with Vi, but because the lad had tended to foist his company upon them whenever he could on their walk home from school.

In August the previous year war had broken out between Great Britain and Germany. Like John, some of the young men in the village had enlisted. Other people he knew from his work contacts in Norwich were also leaving their homes and jobs and joining the army or the navy. The wave of patriotism was high and Jim began to identify with it.

He had always been intrigued by stories of the sea, which gripped his imagination more than any other books of adventure. He had listened many times to a retired sailor who lived nearby. "Old Uncle Jack" everyone called him. This old man had served many years in the Royal Navy and was only too happy to share his experiences with anyone who had the patience to listen. He found a very attentive audience in young Jim who would sit enthralled as the old man related his tales. When he had started his career in the Navy the old man had served in sailing ships and he painted wonderful pictures of these majestic vessels and sold the paintings whenever he could find a buyer. With the advent of steam he had studied the later ships of the fleet and from memory had drawn and painted pictures of these too. He enjoyed best painting pictures which showed both steam and sailing vessels, which he told Jim with a chuckle represented "HMs Ancient and Modern!"[1]

"When you are old enough, lad," he told Jim one day, "You could do a lot worse than make a life in the Navy. I know that I never regretted it and I'd still be there if I weren't so old."

"Why when you love the sea so much do you choose to live in *Diss*?" Jim asked him.

The old man tapped one side of his large nose with his forefinger, a gesture he made whenever he decided to leave a question unanswered, implying that there was some special secret that he was not prepared to share.

On this occasion Jim was persistent: "If I wanted to draw or paint pictures of the sea and of ships, I would want to be where they are. I'd find it so much easier seeing them there in front of me."

"Maybe so but *I* don't need to see them in front of me."

"Why?"

"Because they're all in here, that's why." The old man placed one gnarled hand to his forehead and the other on his chest to emphasise his meaning.

Jim admired Old Uncle Jack and loved listening to his stories of the sea. It flashed across his mind that he wanted to be with him as soon as he could get away from John in his ill-fitting khaki uniform.

---

1 One of these was bought by Jim and hung above the fireplace in his house at Sanderstead.

In his mind's eye he saw the little stone cottage with its flaking green painted door and windows, tobacco-yellowed ceilings and its shabby furniture. Bidding a hasty farewell to John and wishing him all the best Jim hurriedly made his way to old Jack's cottage.

The old man was surprised but pleased to see him. He shook Jim's hand warmly and invited him into the cottage as he had done on many occasions before. The front door opened directly into the living room; a room untidily well lived in, filled with souvenirs from all over the world, half finished sketches and paintings and smelling strongly of pipe tobacco. Over in the corner near the window was that wooden stand with a connecting chain between it and one of the legs of a grey parrot, a bird that had the most evil eyes that seemed to follow Jim's every move. The bird had a habit too of suddenly letting out ear piercing screeches as it shifted its feet, one at a time, a few movements to one side of the wooden perch, then after a pause, a few steps to the other side.

Old Jack was a heavily built man with a weather-beaten face that was nearly the colour of the old worn leather tobacco pouch that he kept always close at hand and about as lined and cracked too. His speckly-grey hair, once black, was thick and wiry, save for that small patch of pink near the crown of his head. Long grey eyebrows of uneven length at times almost obscured his grey-green eyes. Eyes that always reminded Jim of the fathomless depths of the sea; eyes that became half-closed whenever their owner spoke about his travels, just as if the action helped transport him back in time.

"Well now, young Jim. It's so really good to see you. And how are things with you today?"

Ignoring the screech from the parrot, Jim told him that he was now living in Norwich most of the time with his Aunt and was learning carpentry. The old man listened to him attentively. Then he filled his pipe very slowly and carefully, pressing the tobacco firmly into the bowl of the pipe. Jim watched in fascination as the old man carefully swept up some small strands of tobacco that had fallen onto the newspaper on his lap; a manoeuvre that was performed rapidly, one cupped, gnarled hand sweeping the strands into the palm of the other hand. Then the strands were carefully, almost lovingly, tipped back into the pouch. Jim continued to watch as the old man puffed away until he had the bowl glowing like a small red coal. When at last Old Jack was satisfied that his pipe was as it should be, he broke the silence:

"A useful trade," he remarked. "I knew a ship's carpenter once..."

He then half closed his eyes and related an experience that had taken place back in '55. It was a yarn that Jim had heard before but he settled himself in a chair opposite Jack and listened attentively while the tale unfolded. When Jack had finished he tapped out his pipe ash and proceeded to refill the bowl with some of the dark tobacco from the well-worn leather pouch. This manoeuvre seemed to call for great concentration and was executed in perfect silence.

"How old were you when you enlisted in the Navy?" asked Jim, breaking the silence.

Jack relit his pipe carefully from a scrap of paper, torn from the newspaper on his lap and plunged the hastily made spill between the bars of the kitchen range. A shower of sparks and charred pieces of paper descended on the faded Persian rug, the pattern of which bore numerous scorch marks and several black holes with brown edges. The old man studied Jim for a few moments and then, taking the pipe from his mouth pointed the stem towards Jim.

"About your age, I guess."

"I'm fourteen," said Jim.

"Well, then I must have been a bit older than you, if that's the case. I thought you were about seventeen, lad."

Jim stood up. At fourteen he was five feet six and a half inches in height, had started to shave, and his shoulders were beginning to broaden out. Perhaps it was not surprising that the old man had taken him to be seventeen.

When Jim left the cottage to make his way back home he was deep in thought. Jack had taken him to be seventeen and whatever that shrewd old man thought it was very likely that others who did not know him might do the same. He decided that he could not wait until he was seventeen to join the Navy but would pass himself off as that age.

That weekend he packed his belongings in a canvas bag after carefully deleting anything that gave any clues to his correct age. All the school prizes were packed away with other personal things including some very early photographs of Vi and himself. With the Country at war he figured that he might not be asked too many questions.

As dawn was breaking he crept out of the cottage leaving a note propped against the French clock on the mantelpiece for his father. The note simply stated that he had decided to make a new career for himself but otherwise leaving no clue about his real intentions. In his pocket were some fifteen shillings and sixpence saved from his meagre earnings and from his choir days. He felt excited but a little nervous as he left the cottage on his way back to Norwich. He decided that he would have to take Aunt Esther into his confidence; he owed her that for her kindness.

He looked back once at the pink-washed cottage. Rain was beginning to fall and he watched fascinated as the rain spots gathered on the windows where many times, as young children, Vi and he had pressed their noses against the glass, looking out at the wet street as the rain pattered against the panes. He doubted that he would ever return to that cottage again.

Chapter Two

When Jim arrived at Aunt Esther's house he found her sitting in her chair by the kitchen range warming her hands by the fire. It was not cold but she kept a fire burning for much of her cooking and frequently relaxed by it in the evenings, winter and summer alike. She smiled at Jim and beckoned him to sit down in the chair opposite.

"Well, it's good to see you again, Jim," she said. "And how are your family?"

"All right, thank you," replied Jim, adding after a pause, "It's good to see you again."

Aunt Esther seemed to sense that Jim had something on his mind and that he was about to unburden his thoughts. She was quite a psychologist in her way and friends and neighbours very often used her to help sort out their problems.

"Auntie, I went to see that old sailor I told you about when I was in Diss. We had quite a long talk together."

"That was nice."

Jim noticed that Aunt Esther was wearing her carpet slippers. She looked so gentle and motherly that he felt encouraged to explain what was really on his mind.

"Old Jack thought I was seventeen. He was quite surprised when I told him how old I am. Do you think that I look seventeen?"

Aunt Esther gave the impression of studying him most carefully. This examination lasted for what Jim considered to be several minutes at least. At last, satisfied with her study of him, she gave her reply.

"Well now…" she began, "You are quite tall and I suppose that you could pass as seventeen. You have a deep voice too. Yes, I think that you do look seventeen. Although why on earth you want to look older beats me! When you get to my age you won't want to look older, let me tell you!"

Jim did not answer her. Her reassurance had pleased him.

"Old Jack told me that he had enlisted in the Navy when he was about my age. That's what I want to do, Auntie."

Aunt Esther bent towards the fire again, holding her hands a few inches from the red glow. She said nothing for a few moments as if deliberating. At last she turned and faced Jim again.

"If this war goes on much longer I dare say that you will, Jim."

"I didn't mean that. I mean enlist *now*!"

It was out! The thought that had been on his mind for so long was no longer his alone but had been shared. He waited anxiously for his Aunt's reaction.

"I see. And what does your dad think of it all?"

"I couldn't discuss it with him. I left a note for him, that's all."

Aunt Esther had a worried look on her face.

"I think you should have discussed it with him," she said.

Jim thought that she looked rather cross. Her face appeared to have reddened and he did not think that it was caused by her proximity to the fire.

Jim felt very uncomfortable.

"What about your job?" Esther asked him. "How will Mr. King take it if you up and leave him? You know that he is pleased with your work. What about that?"

"I think he might understand," Jim answered. He knew that Mr. King was a very patriotic man. He had told Jim often enough that were it not for his age, and the fact that his right knee was weak and always giving out on him, he would have joined up himself as soon as the first bugle call had sounded!

"Well, perhaps he will and perhaps he won't!" Aunt Esther retorted. "The thing is, how will your father take it?"

The two of them sat in silence for a time during which break in the conversation Jim formed mental pictures in his mind of confronting his father. He felt a little shaky even thinking about it but he was prepared to do anything to get into the Navy. He broke the silence by telling his Aunt so.

The pair of them talked together well past Aunt Esther's normal bedtime and once or twice he noticed that her eyelids drooped and she gave a sudden jerk. At last she stood up from the chair and glancing at the clock on the mantelpiece exclaimed that it was very late and time to climb the 'wooden hill'. This was one of her favourite expressions, which had amused Jim very much when he had first heard her use it. Now it had become the accepted phrase for either of them to use.

"It seems to me," his aunt said as she filled the kettle for the morning, a nightly ritual with her, "You should have a talk with Mr King in the morning and tell him that you want to make a career in the navy. If you are honest with him he can start looking around for another lad to take your place. Mind you, whether he will release you is another matter. Whatever the outcome you will have to have a talk with your father too. There's one other thing, Jim. Don't pretend that you are seventeen to enlist. Tell the truth and shame the devil."

Jim smiled. He had heard her use that expression several times too and she always said it with such vehemence.

Aunt Esther set out the cups, saucers, plates, knives and forks for breakfast. She always turned the empty cups upside down in the saucers.

"I'll do as you suggest," Jim told her. "Although I'm not so sure about giving my age away. How can I get in the Navy at fourteen?"

"Gladys Ranger's boy was about your age when he went off for training," she answered. "I'll speak to Gladys in the morning if you like and find out all about it for you. Of course, that was before the war started when he did his training and he's away at sea now."

Jim thanked her and could not resist giving her a kiss on her cheek.

"Now get up that wooden hill, young Jim! If we don't get some sleep soon neither of us will be fit to do anything in the morning and that would be a fine kettle of fish, no mistake!"

In spite of the fact that it was late and he felt tired Jim had some difficulty in getting off to sleep. He felt too excited but also had doubts in his mind about the reactions from Mr King and his father.

The back bedroom, which Jim occupied, faced east. He awoke in the morning with the early morning sun's rays shining through the window. He could hear the birds singing in the garden and the sounds of his aunt's movements in the kitchen below. There was an appetising smell of bacon and eggs too and he realised that he felt quite hungry. The brightness of the sky sparked off in him a feeling of optimism. Somehow he knew with an inner certainty that everything would work out all right.

When he left for work Aunt Esther handed him his lunch box and told him that she had packed him cheese sandwiches and an apple. He thanked her and gently reminded her that she would be seeing Mrs Ranger that day.

"I haven't forgotten, young Jim!" she said in admonishment but he noticed the twinkle in her eyes. "Now run along or you'll be late for work!"

When he arrived at the workshop Mr King was showing the other apprentice, Bob Tanner, the intricacies of dovetailing. Bob Tanner was about a year older than Jim. He was nearly six feet in height but rather thin. He had somewhat sharp features and a spotty face. Mr King called him "One and Six" whenever he was in a jovial mood. Bob was in the second year of his apprenticeship and entrusted with many of the more complex jobs although Mr King kept a close eye on things. The workshop was kept tidy and all the tools were on shelves and racks above the benches. The smell of sawdust and shavings was always pleasant to Jim.

The apprentices took their mid-day break in the workshop, sitting on one of the benches. Mr King lived in the house adjoining the workshop and always "went across home" for his. Sometimes Jim would smell onions on his employer's breath as he leaned over to show Jim how to hold the plane firmly and make smooth strokes over the wood.

There had been little opportunity to discuss his plans with Mr King during that morning but in the afternoon Mr King left the bench where he had been working with Bob, and came over to see how Jim was progressing. He hardly heard what Mr King was saying. He was pre-occupied with how best to broach the one subject paramount in his own mind.

"You haven't come on very fast with that job, lad," he remarked.

He then added, kindly. "Not working up to your usual standard. Don't you feel too good?"

"I'm well enough," answered Jim.

He looked so worried that Mr King could not help but put a hand on Jim's shoulder.

"What's on your mind, lad?" he asked, kindly.

Encouraged by the friendly tone of his employer's voice Jim decided to use the moment to best advantage. He explained as carefully as he could that he liked his work and appreciated all that was being done for him but really he wanted to become a sailor. Jim was conscious that his employer was listening to him intently for he made no attempt at interruption. When Jim had talked out what was on his mind Mr King, touched by the sincerity in the young apprentice's voice, gave a fierce nod of his head and beckoned Jim to follow him. The two of them left the workshop and with Mr King leading the way with Jim just behind him, crossed the yard to the house.

It was not the first time that Jim had been to the house. On one or two occasions Mr King had sent him over to the house with messages for Mrs King or to collect some spare pencils. Usually these trips had ended at the door, however, while Mrs King's matronly figure blocked most of his view of the interior of the house. When he had asked for pencils she had gone into a room just beyond the kitchen but was back with the pencils before he had much time to study the kitchen very well. It looked clean and cosy and had a variety of cupboards, obviously the handiwork of his employer. Mrs King was asleep in an elegant Windsor chair stuffed with cushions. She had obviously been reading a book before dozing off as the book was on the floor where it must have fallen. Her plump face looked even plumper in repose. Mr King put a finger to his lips to convey silence to Jim and ushered him into the room where the pencils were kept. Jim thought that he had never seen such a fine room. In one corner beside the window was a very attractive dark oak bureau. A matching bookcase occupied a position the other side of the window. In the centre of the room was a large oak table with four chairs. Several good paintings adorned the walls. The floor was covered with a thick Indian carpet of striking colours. That he had been privileged to enter the best room of the house Jim had no doubt.

"Sit yourself down, young Jim," invited Mr King, closing the door. Jim was not sure whether this gesture was intended to ensure privacy or whether Mr King was afraid of disturbing his wife. He sat down at the table; Mr King sat down opposite him.

"I've brought you over to the house Jim," he said, "because I thought it better not to talk in front of Bob. What I have to say is for your ears only."

Jim waited expectantly while Mr King fiddled with the table runner pinching it between his thumb and forefinger and then releasing it. He was a slightly built man and shorter than Jim. He had thick dark hair just beginning to grey. His face was rather sallow which seemed to make his bushy eyebrows and prominent nose stand out more. He had very light blue eyes, which Jim thought were almost out of place with his colouring.

"Let me tell you that I believe you will make a very good carpenter one day, Jim. I have watched you closely since you have been with me and I think you have a natural aptitude for the work. For that reason I would not want you to go."

Jim sighed and Mr King was quick to notice this.

"Hold on a minute!" he exclaimed. "I am not going to make you stay if it's in your mind to make a career for yourself in the navy. God knows we need all the soldiers and sailors we can get if we are going to win this war. How I wish that I could join the army myself. I can't and that's that but I would never stand in the way of anyone who has a mind to!"

Jim felt a wave of relief sweep over him.

"Now, lad! Can you keep a secret?"

Jim assured him that he could.

"My father has been very ill for some months now and he wants me to take over his business for him. He has a big workshop in Gloucester, much bigger than mine, and I am moving there in the next few weeks. I have already had an offer for this place, workshop and all. The buyer seems a good enough man and has agreed to keep on the apprentices and see them through their term. Apart from you no one in the workshop knows yet. I'm telling you because if you want to leave now's the time to do it."

Mr King stood up from his chair. Jim stood up too and carefully placed the chair he had been sitting on in its original position under the table.

"Now we had better get back to work," said Mr King. "And not a word, mind, about what we have talked about, to the others. I shall have a word with them in my time."

Jim thanked him for his confidence. As they made their way back to the workshop Jim noticed that Mrs King was still fast asleep in the kitchen.

Back at his bench Jim felt elated. Everything seemed to be falling into place for him so easily. He had been worried about leaving his job with the complications of the apprenticeship but that hurdle had been overcome. It was, he thought, almost as if he were destined to become a sailor and God or an appointed Angel was steering him through the obstacles to clear a way for him. Of course, there was still the matter of his father's reaction but Jim thought that he could turn Mr King's sale of the workshop to good advantage.

The afternoon passed slowly for him although he busied himself with his work. He wondered what information Aunt Esther had been able to glean from Will Ranger's mother and was anxious to get home and find out.

At last it was time to clear up the workshop, a task that he tackled with great energy and speed. He was about to leave the workshop when Mr King called out to him.

"I'd like a word with you before you go, Jim!"

Bob Tanner gave Jim a solemn wink as he passed him, probably thinking that Jim was going to be admonished for some shortcoming. When Bob had left the workshop Mr King said "I won't keep you a moment, lad but I've been thinking over what we talked about earlier. You're obviously too young to join the Navy so you'll have to go in as a boy entrant. I suppose you realise that."

Jim nodded his head.

"My aunt is going to talk with someone she knows to find out more about it."

"Well, if you need anything from me to help you just let me know."

Jim thanked him again for his kindness. Mr King smiled and then jangling his bunch of keys told Jim to run along home as he was going to lock up and get home himself for his tea.

Jim hurried home anxious to discover what news Aunt Esther had for him. As he let himself in he could hear Aunt Esther's voice. She was obviously talking with someone in the kitchen. Having no wish to intrude, he was about to go upstairs to his room, when he heard the unmistakable sound of his father's deep voice.

"What's it all about, Esther?" his father was saying.

Fearful that his aunt might say something that would not bode too well for him Jim decided to go into the kitchen and confront his father. Jim could feel an empty sensation in his stomach that he knew was nothing to do with hunger.

His father was standing beside the kitchen table. The expression on his face when he saw Jim was a mixture of surprise and anger. He was holding in his hand the note Jim had left for him. Sternly he tapped a finger on the paper and said:

"What's the meaning of this?"

"I'm going to join the Navy, father." Jim announced. The voice seemed to come from someone else. He felt surprised that he had said it so calmly and factually.

"What fool notion is this?" his father asked at last, obviously quite taken aback by the reply. "What about your carpenter's apprenticeship? I suppose you had not thought of that!"

"Mr King is selling the workshop and going away. He told me so himself so that I could find myself other employment." Jim answered. It was not quite the truth but it seemed to fit the situation so well that he felt it was not incumbent upon him to go into too much detail.

His father was not prepared for this. Jim could see from the surprised look on his father's face.

"I see," he said, after a long pause. Jim noticed that Aunt Esther looked quite surprised too.

"Mr King told me that his father was ill and that's why he is selling the workshop," Jim explained. "He was ever so nice about it. I told him not to worry about me," Jim went on "as I would make a new career for myself in the Navy. He promised to help me in any way he could."

"I suppose he owes you that much," his father said touchily.

He pulled up a chair and sat down by the table. He looked troubled and Jim felt a little guilty. There was a long silence that was eventually broken by Aunt Esther.

"Would you like a cup of tea, Robert?" A cup of tea was always the immediate remedy for most problems with Aunt Esther!

"Thank you, yes." Jim's father told her. Then he faced Jim again.

"I wish that you had told me all this yesterday."

Jim did not answer. He could hardly say that he did not know himself yesterday.

"I expect he was too upset to tell you." Aunt Esther came to his rescue as she placed the kettle on the range. Jim fancied that she winked at him but thought that he must have been mistaken.

"Sit yourself down with your dad, Jim." she said. "I expect you can do with a cup of tea yourself!"

Jim sat down as invited opposite his father.

"Are you sure that you want a career in the Navy? It must have been a great shock to you when you learned that your job was coming to an end." Jim was more shocked to detect a note of concern in his father's voice. What was his father saying? It was as if there was a time warp. Jim felt as if everything had stopped. Even Aunt Esther had ceased rattling the cups and saucers. He pinched his hand to make sure that he was awake. Yes, he was awake all right.

"...and not just doing it because you thought you might be out of work?"

Jim was so preoccupied by the sensation of unreality that he had missed part of what his father was saying. Mistaking the reason for his son's silence his father sighed loudly.

"You don't have to go into the navy, boy. I daresay that we can get you fixed up in another apprenticeship somewhere."

"Oh, no!" Jim cried out. That was the last thing he wanted. He realised that things were starting to take a turn that might place all his hopes in jeopardy.

"He could do a lot worse than make a career in the navy." Once more Aunt Esther, like a guardian angel, came to Jim's rescue. "Funnily enough I was talking to a friend today. Her boy trained with the Marine Society as a lad. I believe he's doing very well for himself now and loves the life."

Jim's father looked up at Aunt Esther as she poured the tea from the brown earthenware teapot first into his cup, then Jim's and finally her own. She sat down at the table.

As they sipped the hot tea Jim watched his father closely. He wondered what effect his aunt's statement had made upon him. However, the look on his father's face betrayed nothing of the thoughts that he held. Once he took his handkerchief from his pocket and lightly wiped his moustache. When he had finished his tea he straightened his back and looked first at Jim then at Aunt Esther and then, finally, at Jim again.

"All right!" he announced, having made his decision. Jim was aware only of his heart hammering as he awaited his father's decision.

"All right!" his father repeated. "I suppose the boy could do worse. If that's what he wants, so be it. Just one thing, boy," he added, turning his full and undivided attention on Jim, "There will be no turning back on your decision. When you join the Navy, that is it—so you had better be sure that it's the life you want!"

Jim was so relieved that he set his cup down awkwardly on the saucer but just managed to steady it in time.

"Watch what you're doing, boy!" his father said sternly. Then turning to Aunt Esther, he said. "If he's as clumsy as that at the table I expect that you'll not be sorry to see the back of him."

Esther laughed. "Oh, he's not a bad lad," she said. "It has been quite nice having him here. I was glad of the company and he has helped me in many ways. He gets the coal in for me, sweeps the yard, cleans the shoes and generally makes himself useful ... don't you, Jim?"

Jim was too modest to answer her. The truth of the matter being that he was so fond of Aunt Esther, particularly at that moment, that he would gladly have done anything for her.

"Well, that's settled then," Jim's father said, returning to the other subject they had been discussing. "I'll get in touch with the

Marine Society straight away. The sooner things are arranged, the better."

Standing up he announced "I had better be on my way. Thank you for the tea, Esther. Do you want Jim to go with me or stay on with you?"

Aunt Esther stood up too.

"If you don't mind he might as well stay on here until things are sorted out. As I said earlier I am glad of his company."

And that was that. Jim felt relieved that it was over and even more relieved to find that he would not have to return to his father's home. He recalled that he had felt a certainty that he would not be returning there and was now aware how prophetic his inner pronouncement had been.

At dinner that evening, after Jim's father had left, Aunt Esther asked Jim whether Mr King was really selling up. When Jim assured her that he was, she remarked how fortunate it was that all things had worked out so well. She added that she hoped that they would continue so doing.

After dinner, when Jim was washing up and his aunt was gently drying the dinner plates and replacing them carefully in the cupboard, she told him all about her conversation with Mrs Ranger. Jim wanted to know every detail, which did not displease his aunt. For her part she was glad to have such an attentive audience.

When the evening chores were finished they sat together in the kitchen talking about the navy, the war, the shortages of some of the foods suffered since it all began, Mr King and the workshop and many other topics including his aunt's neighbours and their problems. After listening to that part of the conversation about which Jim had no real interest and frequently did his best to stifle yawns, Aunt Esther said that she guessed he was tired after such a day, especially following a late night and that he had better get himself up the wooden hill.

Jim slept well. He felt contented so even though his mind was engaged on the future, his thoughts were untroubled ones and he soon fell asleep.

The days that followed seemed to drag by for Jim. Although he put his hands to work at Mr King's his mind was elsewhere. The workbenches and the tools seemed to be already something of the past for him. He chatted to his workmates and to Mr King doing his best to listen to the things that interested them without steering the conversations round to the thing paramount in his mind. It was not too bad in the evenings with Aunt Esther as she would be willing enough to talk about the navy but Jim noticed that she appeared to be more thoughtful and a little sad as the days went by.

One morning when he joined his aunt in the kitchen he noticed an envelope and letters on the breakfast table. His aunt told him that she had received a letter from his father, which she gave Jim to read. Subject to a medical examination Jim read that he had been accepted by the Marine Society for training on board that Society's Ship Warspite from 17th May 1915!

Jim was too excited to eat breakfast. He thankfully gulped down a cup of tea however which Aunt Esther poured out for him.

"The seventeenth! That's less than a week's time Aunt Esther!"

"You will have to tell Mr King that you will be leaving at the end of this week, Jim," his aunt reminded him. He kissed her on the cheek and hurried off to the workshop.

Mr King received the news very calmly, Jim thought.

"Well, Jim," he said, when Jim had finished talking "It is obvious that you will find it difficult to settle down today in the workshop so you had better come along with me to Attleboro."

It seemed that Mr King had received a request from Bunwell Rectory to fit some new shelves in the kitchen and to repair one of the stalls in the Church. Jim helped Mr King load tools and timber in the green van, which bore the legend in gold letters: "Wm. J. King. Cabinet Maker, Carpenter and Joiner." With Mr King at the wheel and Jim beside him in the cab they set off. Not far out of Norwich and before entering Swardeston, Mr King asked Jim if he would like to have a go at the wheel. Jim was more than willing to do so. He had never driven anything other than his Cousin George's motorcycle but he had observed Mr King's gear changes and other actions and felt that it would present no difficulties. When the van had pulled up by the side of the road he exchanged places with his employer. Mr King explained the purpose and positions of the clutch, accelerator and brakes, which Jim thought obvious although

22

he did not say so. Jim felt quite confident behind the wheel of the van and apart from a slightly jerky pull away as he familiarised himself with the pressure needed on the pedals he drove the vehicle well. Mr King was so impressed by all this that he allowed Jim to drive through the villages of Swardeston, Mulberton, Bracon Ash, Toprow, Tacolneston, and Forncett End. Just before the approach to Bunwell Mr King asked Jim to stop the van and the two of them exchanged places again.

"You are a natural born driver, lad," Mr King announced, then added: "It took me much longer to master the steering let alone the controls and it seems to me that you can handle them as well if not better, than I can!"

Mr King obviously had his own reasons for not letting Jim drive the van right up to the Rectory.

A young woman, whom Jim judged to be about his own age, opened the door of the Rectory. Although he thought that she could have been older. She was a couple of inches shorter than him. She had an elegant figure, a very pretty face with bright blue eyes and really long eyelashes. Her hair was fair and curly. She looked first at Mr King and then at Jim who fancied that she took that little longer in studying him. He felt that by the look in her eyes it was a favourable appraisal.

Mr King announced who he was and what they had come to do and the young lady invited them into the hallway while she went off to fetch the Rector. Jim watched her as she crossed the hallway to one of the doorways in the front part of the house. He heard her say that there were two gentlemen who had called to do some work. He heard the Rector say: "Thank you, Dorothy."

Jim made a mental note of her name. He thought her most attractive and hoped that he would see her again and have the opportunity of talking to her. Apart from the girls at school who had flirted with him in his last year there he had, up to that morning, very little to do with the opposite sex. The young lady, Dorothy, had stirred feelings within him that he had not felt before.

The Rector, a man with a kindly and somewhat cherubic face and grey wispy hair above his clerical collar, shook hands with Mr King and Jim and then led them through to the kitchen at the back of the Rectory. He explained that he needed some extra shelves built into one of the corners of the room. Mr King left Jim to measure up for the shelving and then followed the Rector across to the Church to inspect the damaged stall. Jim was intent on his work and was startled to discover that he was no longer alone. The girl, Dorothy, had entered the kitchen. She proceeded to wash up some crockery at the sink by the window, stealing occasional glances at Jim of which he was acutely aware.

"Is the Rector your father?" he asked her.

She shook her head.

"I just come over to help," she said. Then, in her turn, asked him a question. "Is Mr King, *your* father?"

Jim laughed. "No! I am just helping him out."

She broke the brief lull in the conversation.

"Will you be here long?"

"It all depends on what Mr King needs to do in the Church," Jim answered. He inclined his head towards the corner where the shelves had to be fitted. "This job won't take all that long."

The two of them talked together for about fifteen minutes before Mr King returned alone. Although Jim had felt a little nervous at first when he had started talking, that had soon passed and he and Dorothy were quite at ease together. Jim thought that the way she spoke and some of her mannerisms reminded him of Vi. Perhaps it was this that made him feel that he had known Dorothy a long time.

Mr King looked at the girl and then at Jim.

"You two seem to be getting along well together!" he exclaimed, giving Jim a knowing wink. "I think that I had better leave you to get on with this job, Jim while I take care of the work in the Church."

Before leaving he went over the measurements Jim had recorded, then satisfied that everything was in order, said "There's plenty of good timber in the van. Help yourself to what you need. I'll pop in later to see how things are shaping up, Jim."

Jim worked conscientiously all morning, sometimes alone in the kitchen but quite often Dorothy would be in and out attending to various chores. The morning passed quickly. About a quarter to twelve, Mr King came back, "just to check progress." He was evidently satisfied.

"I think that I will drive back to Norwich for something to eat," he told Jim. "Do you want to come back with me?"

Jim told him that he had brought his own lunch along with him and had stowed it in the back of the van with the tools and wood. He explained that it would be quicker if he ate his sandwiches at the Rectory so that he could get straight back to the job in hand.

"Just as you like, Jim." Mr King looked around the kitchen to make sure the girl was not in the room. "I suppose that young lady will make you a cup of tea." He nudged Jim in the ribs with his elbow in a friendly way. "You'd better collect your lunch-box from the van."

"I brought it in earlier, Mr King."

Mr King chuckled and then left the room. Jim heard the van's engine start up and the even more unmistakable sound as Mr King engaged bottom gear and the van pulled away. No sooner had the sounds died away than Dorothy was back in the kitchen. The two of them eagerly resumed their conversation. As Mr King had prophesied Dorothy did make him a mug of tea. Jim accepted it gratefully. The tea helped to wash down the sandwiches Aunt Esther had prepared for him. Normally he ate lunch enthusiastically but trying to eat and talk at the same time had been difficult. As he drank the tea he told Dorothy that he would soon be leaving his job with Mr King to join the Navy. This seemed to impress her very much. She told him that she was nearly fifteen. She asked Jim if he had a girl friend and when he hastily assured her that he hadn't she asked him if he would write to her when he went away. He felt very pleased and the two promised to correspond regularly.

When Jim had finished his tea he returned to his work, which was progressing well. Dorothy seemed reluctant to leave the kitchen but he heard the Rector call out to her and she had to leave to attend to something for him which took her away for a time.

When Mr King returned after his meal, smelling of onions, he studied Jim's work.

"You've done well, lad," he said, obviously well pleased with what he saw. "I'd best be getting back over to the Church. I've still some more to do there but I reckon that we'll both be through here before the end of the day all right."

The afternoon passed by and about five o'clock Mr King came over to the kitchen once more and told Jim that he had finished the repairs in the Church and would help Jim "tidy up" as he put it. When the tools had been stowed away in the van Mr King went in to see the Rector and Jim waited for his employer in the hallway. He was hoping that Dorothy would put in an appearance before they had to leave.

He was not disappointed.

"That's my address," she told him, pressing a piece of paper into Jim's hand. "If you don't get a chance to see me before you join the navy then you can write to me like we agreed."

Jim folded the piece of paper she had given him and placed it carefully in his pocket.

"If possible I will do my very best to see you, Dorothy. Otherwise I will write to you. I am so glad that we have met." He spoke with such sincerity that Dorothy impulsively squeezed his hand.

"So am I," she whispered just as Mr King and the Rector came into the hall. Dorothy quickly made her way back to the kitchen.

Jim drove the van back to Norwich. Mr King had asked Jim to drive as soon as they had left the Rectory.

That evening, alone with Aunt Esther, they talked as usual. Jim told her that he had been working all day at Bunwell Rectory and that Mr King had allowed him to drive the van. When Aunt Esther began talking about the neighbours, Jim found himself going through the events of the day in his mind. He thought a lot about Dorothy and she continued to fill his thoughts when he was in bed that night, even making her appearance in his dreams.

The remainder of the week passed by uneventfully but on Friday afternoon, just before closing up the workshop, Mr King called the apprentices and carpenters together and made a short speech on behalf of them all wishing Jim every success in his new career. He then handed Jim his final wages with a bonus crisp new ten-shilling note and presented him with a black pocketbook that fastened. Jim felt he had a lump in his throat when he shook everyone's hand in turn. Even Mrs King came over to the workshop to say goodbye to him.

Instead of going to Diss over the weekend Jim decided that he would say his goodbyes to his few friends and relations in Norwich and the surrounding area. His cousin, George lived in Cowgate Street. George had bought himself a motorbike and sidecar some weeks before and Jim had helped him clean it up and make one or two adjustments to it. Jim liked tinkering about with mechanical things. George had let him try out the machine. He decided to visit George and ask him if he could borrow the bike for a few hours.

George, as it happened, had a heavy cold when Jim went to see him. He consented readily enough to Jim's request to borrow the motorbike.

"I suppose you want to get round to say goodbye to everyone," he said. Jim nodded.

"You'll need to get some petrol, the tank's nearly empty, Jim."

"That's no problem," said Jim.

"There's just one other thing ... there seems to be something wrong with the drive belt."

Jim inspected the bike. The leather belt-drive was extremely slack and it took him well over an hour to make the adjustments to his satisfaction. Aunt Mary, George's mother, allowed him to scrub his hands afterwards in the scullery but it took another fifteen minutes to remove the oil and grime from his hands and finger nails.

"I'll bring the bike back this evening, George."

"No hurry. I shan't be using it this weekend, that's sure." George blew his nose loudly as if to place emphasis on his words.

Jim decided to drive first to Old Lakenham to say farewell to Uncle Edward who lived in a railway cottage and with that done he thought that he had better see his Aunt Winifred who lived in Attelboro'. He had not seen her for years but the slip of paper in his pocket with Dorothy's address, also in Attelboro', had influenced his decision!

Aunt Winifred did not recognise him at first. She was hanging out some washing on the line when he arrived. Her dark straight hair was tied behind her head in a bun. She looked thinner than he had remembered her. When it dawned on her who Jim was, she exclaimed:

"I barely recognised you, Jim! What a fine young man you've grown up to be. Here! Let's get the rest of the things on the line and then we can go in and have a talk."

Once inside the cottage Jim told her that he was going to train to be a seaman and was to report to the Warspite in a few days. Apart from raising her black eyebrows a little Aunt Winifred gave no other hint of surprise. Jim recalled that she had never been a particularly demonstrative person. She listened while he brought her up to date with all the news of their kinsfolk in Norwich and Diss. Afterwards she told Jim that his cousin, Harry was in the army stationed in Fermay, County Cork. Uncle Charlie had moved to Walkden, Manchester.

"I'll find their addresses for you," she said.

Jim watched her rummage through a kitchen drawer. She found what she was looking for eventually and copied the addresses down for him on a slip of paper torn from a note-pad. Jim thanked her and declining her offer to prepare something for him to eat, bade her farewell. He felt that his leaving was hurried but while his aunt had been copying out the addresses for him he had glimpsed through the open window what was unmistakably Dorothy's fair hair!

He kick-started the motor bike and drove away in the direction Dorothy had taken. He rapidly caught her up some quarter of a mile past his aunt's cottage. She was just opening a wooden gate as he pulled the motorbike up beside her.

"Hallo!" he shouted above the noise of the engine.

She turned. He saw the mixture of surprise and pleasure on her face at seeing him. He felt reassured and switched off the engine.

"How about coming out for a drive with me?"

"That would be lovely," she replied. "I must see first if my mother will let me go."

Jim waited by the gate while Dorothy went into the house. It was a fine house, Jim thought. He was later to make a note in his address book, which read *"Some address!"*

Dorothy's mother came out to the gate with her daughter. Jim thought her to be a very beautiful lady and he had no doubt where Dorothy had inherited her own good looks. Dorothy introduced Jim to her mother. Jim was conscious of being scrutinised kindly but closely. Finally she said: "So you are the young man I heard so much about last evening who is off to join the Navy!" She looked then at the motorbike and sidecar and pointing her finger at it, asked: "Where are you two going on *that*?"

It was Dorothy who answered. "It's such a lovely day that Jim has agreed to take me over to Happisburgh (being a young Norfolk lady, of course, she actually said 'Haisbro') so that I can at last see the Church of St Mary and the lighthouse."

It appeared that Dorothy's mother idolised William Cowper, the poet and hymn writer who had spent part of his life in the Happisburgh area which he loved. Jim was familiar with William Cowper's work. His choir work had been his first introduction to the talent of the man but later, at school, he was taught more about him. Jim was able to discuss the poet's life and whether it had really been Happisburgh, and the views of the North Sea from there which had inspired him to write the famous lines, which Dorothy's mother began to recite, Jim joining in.

"God moves in a mysterious way
His wonders to perform,
He plants His footsteps in the Sea
And rides upon the storm."

They laughed together and consent for Dorothy to go with Jim was given without further ado. Jim thanked her mother politely promising to take good care of her and then Dorothy clambered into the side-car as Jim started the engine. Dorothy's mother stood beside the gate waving to them until they rounded a corner and were out of sight.

Their route took them through Norwich and out towards the Broads. They stopped once at Stalham for a short while for something to eat but shared an eagerness to reach their destination. The weather was really good and they were able to spend a very pleasant afternoon together.

First they made their way to the cliff near the lighthouse and looked out over the North Sea. It looked quite calm and peaceful that day but Jim knew from his talks with Uncle Jack that the North Sea could soon change her face from serenity to fury, lashing at boats and driving them aground. It was said that the Sea had also claimed villages and Whimpwell, once a thriving community, now lay submerged. The idea of a whole village being engulfed by the sea made Dorothy shudder.

"Let's go and look at the Church, Jim," she said.

They made their way to the Church of St Mary with its wonderful west tower and battlemented parapet. The original church was said to have been built in the time of the Norman Conquest but was demolished in the fourteenth century. They entered the church together, stopping to admire the octagonal font with its carved angelic figures holding musical instruments, and the Four Living Creatures representing the symbols of Revelation seen by St. John the Divine in his heavenly vision. At the base or stem beneath canopies they saw the Lions interspersed between Woodhouses (wild men of the woods) holding clubs. Jim examined the old woodwork in the choir and return stalls of the Chancel. Then they stood in some reverence studying the beauty of the stained glass window over the High Altar. Later, in the Churchyard they examined some of the gravestone inscriptions and the large green mound on the north side, which marked the grave of one hundred and nineteen members of the crew of HMS Invincible wrecked on the sands in the year 1801.

An elderly clergyman with white hair and stooped shoulders had been watching the young couple with interest and when they nodded to him and smiled he came across to them. He told them that the famous, or infamous, Jonathan Ball was buried in the Churchyard along with a Bible, a Plum Cake, a Poker and a pair of fire-tongs, all of which at his request had been placed beside him in his coffin. The elderly priest said that the man was supposed to have poisoned people by giving them drinks that he had laced with arsenic. They thanked the Priest for giving them such extra facts. He waved to them as they left the Churchyard.

They walked together down Church Lane listening to the sounds of the insects humming and watching the antics of two butterflies that kept close together almost as if joined by a fine thread.

Jim took Dorothy back to her home in the early evening. He stopped the motorbike outside on the verge next to the wooden gate.

"Thank you for a lovely afternoon, Jim."

She left him at the gate, leaning over it and kissing him lightly. Then she ran up the pathway, calling back over her shoulder that he was not to forget to write to her.

"I promise," he called after her.

After returning the motorbike to George and thanking him he shook hands with his cousin and aunt and walked back to Aunt Esther's.

Dorothy occupied his thoughts for some time but gradually gave way to the more immediate considerations and excitement of the new life on which he was about to embark.

The following week he said goodbye to Aunt Esther, telling her that he would miss her home cooking. Aunt Esther gave him a hug and as he set off he turned back once to wave to her and noticed that she hurriedly removed her handkerchief from her eyes and pretended to blow her nose.

That day began fifteen months of intensive and hard training on the Warspite to fit him for the career he had chosen. At times he was to doubt his choice and to think nostalgically of his aunt, Mr King and his workmates and the life he had given up. However, they were but fleeting moments of regret and his determination carried him through. His new companions were all lads of his own age. Many were orphans from Dr Barnado's homes. Most of them were used to a communal life but although it was a new experience for Jim he soon settled to it. His sense of humour, he quickly realised, was his key to acceptance.

He learned how to swim properly. He learned what every part of a ship was called, every knot he might ever have to tie. He learned Morse code and semaphore and academics, which included more advanced mathematics than he had ever tackled at the Church School.

Progress was monitored by tests and examinations both written and oral. Additionally there was time devoted to rigorous gymnastics and sport under the tuition of fit instructors. During that fifteen months Jim put on several pounds of muscle; his chest expanded three inches and he grew some four inches in height.

On 18th August 1916 he was among some of the lads who joined HMS Powerful under Captain C. Fox with the rating of "Boy 2nd Class". This further training was that of the Royal Navy itself but no less arduous. Specialised instruction was given to prepare them for every situation, condition and hazard they were likely to encounter at sea.

Jim found little time to write to his friends and family and the daily diary he had started to keep had to be written up when he had a precious few moments to himself and then, quite often, he would fall asleep before he had completed the entry.

In October 1916, however, he began to feel unwell. He noticed that his skin had turned yellowish and he decided that he would have to report sick. The Medical Officer gave him an examination and then made arrangements for Jim to be transferred to the Royal Naval Hospital at Stonehouse where Jim was admitted on 17th October 1916, suffering Catarrhal Jaundice and was very ill indeed. At times he thought that he was going to die and prayed harder than he had ever prayed in his life that he might recover and be given the chance to follow the career he had chosen. His early weeks in hospital were difficult for him to recall clearly and he learned afterwards that he had been delirious for most of the time. The excellent care he was given, coupled with his strong will power and zest for life, gradually brought him through the crisis. Christmas came and went and although he was by then able to walk about the ward he felt weak still. Determined to overcome the weakness he persisted in taking as much exercise as he could in the somewhat confined environment of the ward and on 19th January 1917 was declared fit to resume duty and reported back to HMS Powerful. On 2nd March 1917 he was told that his rating to Boy 1st Class had been awarded retrospectively to 18th August 1916. He felt elated and wrote in his diary that his training on Warspite had stood him in good stead. On 21st April 1917 he was given orders to join HMS Victory at Portsmouth to complete his training. He then spent more training aboard HMS Redoubtable and HMS Venerable. It was on the Redoubtable that he met with Harry Hanford again. The two had struck up a friendship in their earlier training. They embraced warmly when they saw each other.

"Jim, it's good to see you again!" Harry cried with delight. "What have you been up to?"

Jim filled him in with all the news, glossing over his own recent spell in hospital as lightly as he could. Harry, with arms folded across his chest, listened in silence.

"We heard that you were pretty ill, Jim," he said.

Jim shrugged his shoulders. "I'm here."

Harry was a month or two older than Jim but several inches shorter. He was quite sturdily built. His blue eyes were set well apart and he had a small but wide nose. His mouth turned down slightly at the corners giving those who did not know him too well the impression that he was regarding them disdainfully. Harry had a strong jaw and a cleft chin. An unusual face, thought Jim.

Harry was a good friend and a reliable companion. On a couple of days ashore together the pair of them decided to make a tour of the public houses in Portsmouth. It was the first time that Jim had ever had too much to drink. He only knew that he felt like singing and the two of them walked through Portsmouth, arms linked, singing together as they tried various bars around the harbour area.

Harry shared Jim's interest in photography. Both of them bought box cameras, a good supply of films and plates for their own developing and printing. There were no problems in finding places aboard ship for use as dark-rooms. They agreed that they would capture for all time their adventures at sea. Jim told Harry that he would keep his diaries up to date too and that one day he would write a book where the photographs would be useful illustrations.

The days passed by happily for Jim. It was good to have a friend like Harry who shared common interests. However, in June 1917, with his training completed, Jim received his first commission and was ordered to report to Greenock to join HMS Caradoc on 16th June.

He broke the news to Harry. Jim felt excited to be going to sea at last but at the same time was saddened at the thought of leaving his friend. HMS Caradoc was a light cruiser and part of the Grand Fleet, which would mean that she would be going into action against the Germans. At that time the war was raging on land and sea and casualties on both sides were heavy.

On 15th June Jim left Harry on the Redoubtable and as the two of them clasped their arms around one another Jim wondered whether they would ever meet again.

"Good luck, old son!" said Harry in an unusually gruff voice.

"And to you too, you *old* sea-dog!" The "old" was a jocular reference to the fact that Harry was over two months senior to Jim in age. The pair of them frequently referred to it in fun particularly if Jim was about to do something irresponsible. Harry would then play-act the role of maturity before joining in and the pair of them would laugh together at their antics.

"Mind what you get up to on your own!" called Harry as Jim left him on the Redoubtable. "Remember you won't have me to look after you!"

Jim left with a lump in his throat. What a pity that Harry hadn't been "told off" for the Caradoc too.

Chapter Three

On 16th June 1917 Jim arrived at Greenock and had his first sight of HMS Caradoc—his first commission! She was to become his home for the next three and a half years.

Jim studied her with interest and pride. In later years he was to remark that she was his first real love!

Having feasted his eyes on Caradoc's smooth and elegant lines he was keen to get aboard her. A Leading Seaman was the first person he encountered aboard. Encouraged by the man's affable nod and smiling face, Jim walked over to him and announced who he was.

"Welcome aboard, lad," the man said. "I'm Leading Seaman Frost."

The man was older than Jim by several years. Jim judged him to be in his early twenties. He had dark brown hair, brown eyes, stood about 5'10" in height and was well built. He looked strong and capable. His straight nose, dark eyebrows and well-shaped mouth, now turned up in a smile, made Jim think that the man was one of the most good-looking he had ever met.

Jim was anxious to learn all about Caradoc. Where did she get her name? What was her armament? How fast could she travel? When was she first commissioned? How long had Leading Seaman Frost been with her?

Leading Seaman Frost, a kindly man, seemed impressed by Jim's obvious enthusiasm.

"You'll gradually fill in all the answers you need," he told Jim. "But right now we had better get you along to Lieutenant Fisher. He's the Gunnery Officer on board."

"What's he like?" Jim asked.

"Oh, he's all right," answered Frost. "A good Officer. He came to Caradoc when she was first commissioned in 1914, as I did."

Jim duly reported to First Lieutenant Douglas Fisher, RN. The man was in his thirties, Jim judged. He held himself very erect and looked every inch an officer, Jim thought. He was about Jim's height, lean built and had a strong jaw. His alert grey eyes looked Jim over carefully as Jim stood to attention before him. He did not smile.

"You will be with the A-Gun crew," he told Jim, glancing down at some papers on the table. "You'll be with White Watch."

"Yes, sir!"

"I see this is your first commission."

"Yes, sir!"

"Well, you'll find it's a good one! Our Captain is Captain Munro Kerr and one of the best to serve under."

He spoke with pride and respect. He then went on to advise Jim to familiarise himself with the Caradoc.

"Get to know her better than your own mother." As Jim had never known his mother he thought to himself that that would not be difficult but he kept his thoughts to himself and listened to what the officer had to say.

"Get to know every inch of her so well that in pitch darkness you will be able to find your way about equally well as in broad day-light. Your life and the lives of your fellow men may depend on it." He went on to say that the officers and crew were justly proud of their ship and her team spirit and he hoped that Jim would quickly become a worthy member of the team.

As the days passed by he did as Lieutenant Fisher had advised him to do, exploring every section of Caradoc. Sometimes he would close his eyes as he moved around for a few moments to ensure that he had the ability to trust to his memory, or intuition, or whatever extra sense it was that he needed. Leading Seaman "Jack" Frost and the members of the A-Gun crew were always ready to offer him advice. All this Jim recorded in his "*Rough Log of HMS Caradoc*" which he set up and which he was to keep faithfully throughout his service with her. He had equipped himself with a very good book for this purpose and inevitably his first entry had to incorporate the information he had discovered. That night he wrote:

"Caradoc—her name came from the name of a British Chieftain in Roman time who was captured by the Romans and taken to Rome but later released by them because of his bravery. The first

Caradoc was launched at Blackwell on 13th July 1844 and did war service in the Sea of Azov and the Crimea. Her weight was 870 tons, engines 347 HP and she carried four guns. The new Caradoc was commissioned in 1914; weight 4,120 tons, Scott Engines of 41,200 HP, length 425 feet, breadth 42.9 feet, armed with five 6 inch guns, two 3 inch and four twin 21 inch torpedo tubes, she carried a complement of 350 to 380 officers and men and was capable of a maximum speed of 29.8 knots. She was part of the Sixth Light Cruiser Squadron comprising HMS Calypso, Ceres, Cassandra and their Flagship, HMS Cardiff."

When Jim had recorded the very first entry in his Log, he read it through to check that he had made no spelling mistakes. He carefully mounted a photograph of the Caradoc inside the front cover of the Log. He felt a thrill of pride that he had become one of her crew and wondered what adventures he would experience on board her.

The next fortnight all hands were busy getting in stores and ammunition. Steam trials and testing the guns were carried out on the River Clyde to make ready for joining the other ships of the Sixth Light Cruiser Squadron. The Flagship, HMS Cardiff was carrying Rear-Admiral Alexander Sinclair.

"With a name like yours perhaps you'll be a Rear-Admiral some day!" teased Wiggy Bennett, one of the Y-Gun crew.

A healthy rivalry existed between the gun crews. They were always ribbing one another. Jim had taken an instant liking to Wiggy Bennett even though he was a member of Y-Gun crew! Wiggy seemed to have reacted to Jim in the same way. Wiggy was older than Jim by three or four years; not that age seemed to make any difference as Jim had come to realise. He was about the same height as Jim but more heavily built. He had a plump face, a prominent nose, hazel eyes with a permanently quizzical expression accentuated by the left eyebrow being set slightly above the right one and sloping upwards. His mouth was upturned, good-humoured, Jim decided on their first meeting.

"Admiral, maybe," Jim laughed. "But you'd have to make *Rear*-Admiral with that back-side!"

Wiggy aimed a good-natured blow at Jim's chest.

On 1st August 1917 Caradoc steamed out of the Clyde on her way to join the Grand Fleet at Scapa Flow, arriving there two days later. Jim had never seen such an array of fighting ships. The next few days were spent in manoeuvres and firing practice with Caradoc having to attack some destroyers in harbour.

A week later, as part of the practice, Caradoc put out to sea torpedo and PV running. During this operation Jim injured himself crushing his feet in the Cable Holder with PV wire. He realised that he had been lucky to escape with his life. He resolved to be more careful in the future. The crew members were concerned but when they realised he had escaped without serious injury they called him "Lucky Jim" and other names like "Hoppy" and "Hobbler" as he limped painfully about his duties. He did not want to report sick and in spite of the pain tried to make light of his injury.

Three days after that incident the Sixth Light Cruiser Squadron of which Caradoc was part went out to sea on North Atlantic patrol. The weather was extremely rough. On their fourth day out an unidentified merchant ship was sighted and as she did not answer Caradoc's signals the Captain ordered the men to stand by and "told off" a boarding party. However, the merchantman was a Scandinavian ship bound home from Iceland and was unarmed so allowed to proceed on her way. Len McCarthy, a signaller, told the lads in the mess that evening that once a Dutch Steamer had been signalled to declare what cargo she was carrying and she had signalled back her answer:

"One perpendicular one horizontal to meet
Two semi circles for a circle complete
One perpendicular, two semi circles meet
A left-handed triangle standing on two feet
Two semi circles and a circle complete.
Tobacco!"

Len raised his right eyebrow as he related the verse, standing with his left hand on his hip. He looked quite comical with his wide mouth pulled downwards in an attempt to look serious although his green-blue eyes belied seriousness as they twinkled above his wide nose.

"Where did you hear that, Len?" asked Wiggy.

"I was the signaller," replied Len, bowing to the men.

"Bullshit!" the cry went up. Jim would normally have joined in the fun but was nursing his feet, which were extremely painful, although he did manage to force a grin.

On 15th August the Sixth LCS turned back for base, the weather conditions having deteriorated still further. The seas were so rough that Caradoc's bows dipped and were awash before she rose up to meet the next wave. Visibility became worse during that night and at 4.00 am Caradoc struck a rock at Fair Isle. It took six hours struggle to get off the rock. When she was eventually free they limped to Scapa Flow but when the divers had gone down to examine the damage their report indicated that it was severe so the Captain ordered the ship to proceed to Newcastle for repairs. Caradoc arrived at Newcastle on 18th August, docking in Scott's Yard.

Jim reported to the sick bay that same day. His feet were by then so painful that he could not walk. Trying to keep his balance in the rough seas had not helped. At times as he had been flung about he had nearly fainted with pain. The ship's doctor examined each of Jim's feet in turn then asked him how the accident had happened. When Jim explained the MO told him that he had had a lucky escape but that he was certainly not fit for duty, should have reported sick immediately following the accident, and ordered him to remain in sick bay and rest his feet as much as possible.

Wiggy Bennett, Frank Butler, John Murray, Don Lawrence and the other members of the Gun Crews came into the sick bay to see Jim. They told him that Caradoc was as crippled as he was and was likely to be in Dock for a month. They added that most of the crew were being sent on leave for three weeks, those that could walk that was! Sadly, they said, they would have to say their farewells! Jim being in no condition to walk at that time had no alternative but to remain in the sick bay to his disgust and annoyance.

The M.O examined Jim's feet daily and on 28th August said to Jim, as if doing him a great favour:

"The swellings have gone down a bit and I'm recommending you go on fourteen days shore leave. After that I'll recommend ten days light duty."

As Jim was the only member of the crew in sick bay it crossed his mind that the M.O probably wanted to get rid of him so that he could get away on leave himself. Jim got up and dressed himself but when he started to walk he did so painfully and he realised that he was still very lame. The M.O had gone by then, obviously having no intention of hanging around to see how well Jim could walk!

Jim was given his pay and a railway warrant and a leave pass covering him until 10th September. He had decided to spend the leave in Manchester with his Uncle and Aunt and hoped that they would be able to put him up. With his cousin in the army in Ireland he guessed that they would have a spare bed. He was glad to get aboard the train at Newcastle and selecting a third class compartment which was unoccupied he removed his shoes and stretched himself out across the seats thankfully being able to take the weight off his feet.

When he arrived at Manchester some hours later he realised that he was feeling hungry and thirsty so decided to get a sandwich and a glass of beer in the nearest pub he could find. He selected a seat at a table in the corner of the public bar and after putting his ditty bag on one of the chairs hobbled across to the barman and ordered his beer and sandwich. The bar was not crowded. He noticed that at one of the adjoining tables a young lady, dressed in the somewhat unbecoming uniform of a landgirl, was talking to two soldiers who were sitting one on each side of her. Jim thought that she was very attractive. She had dark hair and bold, almost black, eyes topped by long dark lashes. She had a naturally healthy complexion without the need for make-up. She was laughing at some remark made by one of her companions, her full lips parted and revealing even white teeth. The man sitting to her left was a lance-corporal of about thirty years of age with a thin face and small moustache. The other man was much younger, a private, with ginger hair and a freckled face. As Jim moved towards the table he had selected for himself, with his tankard of beer in one hand and a cheese sandwich in the other, he heard one of the soldiers remark:

"They must be making the matelots go on route marches these days!"

The two soldiers broke into loud laughter. They sounded as if they had had too much to drink.

"I've heard of sailors having to find their sea legs but that one must have lost his!"

Jim felt inclined to ignore them. Then the ginger haired soldier, not to be outdone by his companion, said loudly: "Perhaps all the standing about doing nothing gives the sailors bad feet!"

It was a tasteless remark and the landgirl told the man not to be so rude.

Jim felt a sudden wave of anger. He did not know whether he was influenced by the young woman's presence or whether his anger was because of the detrimental remarks about the Navy, *his* Service. He faced the young soldier.

"At least I've never yet met a sailor who couldn't hold his liquor!"

The soldier regarded him in amazement at first, and then his face reddened.

"Good for you, Jack," the girl said, looking at Jim with those bold black eyes. "He had that coming!"

The girl invited Jim to sit down in the vacant chair opposite her. The lance corporal and the ginger-haired private did not look too pleased.

"Come on now, there's a war on and there's no room for squabbling amongst ourselves. Let's be friends together."

Jim placed his beer and sandwich on the table and sat down opposite the girl and between the two men. The girl introduced herself and her companions.

"My name's Lillian—Lily." She pointed to the lance corporal. "This is Bob," and finally she pointed to the young man. "And this is Vic."

"I'm Jim!"

"What happened to you? Were you injured in action?"

Jim nodded.

"Got myself fouled up in the North Atlantic when we were firing torpedoes."

He tried to maintain a matter-of-fact tone to his voice, giving he hoped, the impression that such hazards were the accepted thing and likely to occur to anyone on board ship on active service.

The two soldiers stood up and crossed over to the bar to order more drinks. They did not ask either Jim or Lily if they wanted a drink.

While they were gone Lily told Jim that Bob and Vic were on the tail-end of their leave and were being sent to France. She said that she had known Bob for several months having met him at a dance in Derby and had come across the pair of them that morning by accident. Bob, it seemed, had insisted that she joined them for a few drinks for old time's sake and she, having nothing better to do, had accepted the invitation. She added that her home was in Ilkeston, Derbyshire but that she had been spending two or three days in Manchester with her grandparents.

Bob and Vic were standing at the bar. At least Bob was standing but Vic seemed to be experiencing some difficulty in doing so. Jim noticed that he was swaying about and the snatches of conversation between the two men that came across the room indicated that he was becoming more and more intoxicated. There was a sudden crash as Vic lost his balance altogether and there he was sprawled on the floor with beer pouring over the bar counter where his glass was laying on its side. Bob told him to get up. The barman was not looking amused and Jim heard him tell Bob that he had better drink up and get his mate outside. Bob helped Vic to his feet, supporting him with one arm while he lifted his glass to his own mouth with the free arm. The two of them returned, somewhat unsteadily, to the table where Jim and Lily were talking. They made no attempt to sit down. Bob looked at Lily.

"We're leaving here... are you coming?"

Lily shook her head.

"I don't think so. Not with Vic in that state."

There was a silence.

"Well, I guess that's it then," he said at last. He looked rather peeved.

Lily stood up and gave him a kiss on his cheek.

"Take care of yourself over there and come back safe," she said.

Vic was swaying about alarmingly and Bob was having some difficulty in holding his companion up and maintaining his own balance. The situation was made worse when Vic insisted on having a kiss too. Lily good naturedly gave Vic a quick kiss on his cheek but the young soldier tried to grab hold of her with his free arm, his other arm being drooped around Bob's neck.

"Pack it up, Vic," he said, angrily. "Leave her alone and let's get the hell out of here."

He turned to Lily. "I'll write to you, Lily."

She nodded her head with accentuated enthusiasm. "Yes, do that, Bob".

The two soldiers left the bar together. It was a relief to Jim when they had gone as he had been expecting trouble from them. An awkward silence followed the soldiers' departure, which was broken by Lily.

"I feel sorry for them going to the Front. So many of our soldiers have been killed or maimed over there." Jim felt sorry for them too at that moment and said so.

"How long leave are you on?" Lily asked.

"Fourteen days."

"Are you spending it in Manchester, Jim?"

Jim told her that he intended visiting his uncle and aunt and he hoped that they would be able to put him up.

"Don't they know you are here?" she asked.

"Not yet. My cousin is in the army in Ireland. I'm hoping to have his bed!"

She asked whereabouts in Manchester Jim's relations lived.

"In Walkden," he replied.

Lily told him that her grandparents had a house in Salford. The two of them stayed talking until the bar had emptied of customers. The barman was looking in their direction with an expression on his face conveying the unmistakable hint that he wanted them to go too. They looked at each other and laughed.

"I suppose we had better be leaving," said Lily.

Outside in the street Lily took hold of Jim's arm. It was pleasant having such an attractive woman by his side. They found a cafe near the pub, as it had started to rain, and decided they would have a pot of tea together. Jim sensed that Lily was not keen to part company with him.

Over their tea she told him that she would be staying with her grandparents a few more days but then had to return to Ilkeston where she lived and worked. They exchanged addresses and arranged to meet the following evening outside the Railway Station at six o'clock.

Jim stayed with his uncle and aunt! They were pleased to see him and were happy to offer him George's bed. They talked about their son a great deal and Jim listened politely. They were concerned about Jim's injuries and fussed over him a lot. Jim felt that he had become something of a substitute for his cousin in their affections. He did not mind this and was glad of the rest for they would not allow him to do anything and waited on him throughout his stay, his aunt even serving him breakfast in bed. He rested during the mornings but saw Lily several times during the afternoons and evenings of the first few days of his leave. As Jim was still having difficulty in walking properly they usually went to cafes or to pubs. Once she spent the evening with Jim at his Aunt and Uncle's home and once Jim visited her grandparents' home where they were invited to tea.

So far as the relationship between them was concerned it began as a friendship but the platonic kisses gradually gave way to more passionate embraces. Lily told Jim that she had fallen in love with him. He was flattered but apart from that he was unsure of his feelings for her. She was attractive, stirred passions in him, and was an amusing companion, but he doubted that he loved her. His thinking at times of Dorothy reinforced his doubt. He still felt some longing to see her again and told himself that he would hardly have been entertaining such thoughts if he truly loved Lily.

He saw Lily off at Manchester when her stay with her grandparents came to an end and she had to return to Ilkeston. They embraced passionately at the ticket barrier.

"God bless you, Jim," she whispered. "Please write to me. I shall write to you and I'll be thinking of you every moment."

He promised that he would write to her. The guard was blowing his whistle and Lily had to board the train. She waved to him until the train had moved out of sight. Jim turned and made his way out of the Station. He passed other servicemen and their sweethearts embracing one another.

With Lily gone Jim felt rather at a loss to know what to do with his time. The second week of his leave dragged and he was restless, anxious to get back. Although his leave pass covered him until 10th September he decided to return to Caradoc on the eighth.

Back aboard Caradoc he was assigned to the easy duty of aft-deck messenger and continued with this light duty for ten days, until the Medical Officer declared him fit to resume normal duties.

Caradoc, her repairs completed, came out of Dock on 13th September and the crew prepared to go to sea to rejoin the Squadron at Rosyth where they arrived two days later. The other cruisers were in harbour there but HMS Cassandra was missing. It seemed that she too had struck a rock and was severely damaged and still in dock. The rest of the Squadron proceeded to sea with the Grand Fleet patrolling around Jutland. Dark clouds had begun to gather in the sky. The strong breeze, which had been blowing when they left Scapa Flow, strengthened. The sea was rough and gradually worsened. They engaged no enemy ships in combat but caught sight of two German trawlers and opened fire on them but the trawlers were barely in range. The sea had become extremely choppy causing the ship to dip and roll and the weather had deteriorated making visibility poor. Heavy rain swept the decks and the wind increased in force. The Fleet returned to base.

On October 11th the Squadron was sent out to patrol the waters around Heligoland, Dogger Bank and Dunkirk. The weather was still very rough with gale force winds, heavy rain and poor visibility. The sea became more violent with huge waves lifting the ship and dropping her again. The decks were frequently awash as the bows dipped and rose up again from the sea. The violent pitching and rolling of the ship made it difficult to move about on the slippery surface of the deck and progress was painful and slow in performing the necessary daily work. It was even worse at night, being several degrees colder and seemingly wetter. The men swore aloud as they collided with obstacles, grazing their shins or bruising their knees.

The storm raged for four days and nights with what seemed no sign of abating. It seemed improbable that enemy ships were likely to be out in such conditions and the Squadron was ordered to return to base. Jim could sense the relief in the crew as the order to return to base came through. Morale had not been at its best during the storm. The men were tired and had lost something of their usual humour. The bantering had ceased even from Wiggy Bennett.

As the ships turned to head for base above the noise of the storm a sudden cry was heard and quickly taken up by the crew.

"Man overboard!"

Chapter Four

There was something eerie about the sounds of the mens' voices as the cry of man overboard echoed around the ship. It was as if each man became part of a note in an awful lament. Jim listened to it with shock and horror. *Who* had gone overboard?

He wanted to go up on deck and moved forward, his legs trembling, but Mo caught him by the arm.

"Hold fast, Jim! Where do you think you are going?"

He did not shout. His words were spoken in a soft voice but they stopped Jim in his tracks. Mo was looking at him and the man's hold on Jim's arm had tightened.

Although the ship was still being pitched and tossed by the waves, Jim was aware that her engines were pounding and she was still moving.

"Why are we still under steam?" he shouted. "Why hasn't the ship stopped if there's someone overboard?"

The others, Frank, Little John, Don, were reacting in the same way.

"Let's get up on deck," Frank Butler cried.

"Why hasn't the Captain ordered the ship to turn about?" Don had directed his question at Mo.

"The Captain knew that there was no chance of seeing anything in such conditions," Mo answered. "It's not a bit of use going up on deck. If those up there couldn't do anything, what do you think that you could do?"

Mo was right, of course. The heavy black seas made it impossible to see anything. Even in daylight the chances of sighting a man in those rough waves were remote but at night, impossible. The Captain had no alternative but to continue on course abandoning any idea of searching for the man in those conditions.

Jim learned later that the man who had fallen overboard was Leading Seaman 'Jack' Frost. Jim took the news very badly as evidently the other crew members did too. Jack Frost had been well liked, always kind and gentle in his manner with a cheery word for all. The emotions, which the loss of a comrade aroused in him, were new to Jim. He felt a heavy sadness mixed with guilt. The guilt arose from the sense of relief that it was not he out there. The older hands had known the loss of shipmates before, many had been through the awful "Man overboard" situation too and experienced the frustration and utter helplessness of it. Mo, seeing the distress on the faces of Jim and the others, said:

"There was more chance of finding a needle in a haystack than of finding Jack in those seas."

The Sixth LCS remained in base for a week. The loss of Leading Seaman Frost had been communicated to all the ships' crews. Captain Munro Kerr called the Caradoc's officers and men together on deck and prayers were said for their lost comrade.

Shortly afterwards the Captain ordered Caradoc to sea. This time she went out on coastal patrol alone. Mo told Jim that the Captain was probably doing the best thing to keep the crew's minds and hands busy. Mo looked so serious, his dark curly hair matted and his thick lips held more tightly together than usual. He was an untidy looking man and tended to stoop forward as he moved, making him appear even more slovenly. Jim knew enough of the man to realise that in spite of his appearance he was an efficient sailor and the best gunner in the A-Gun crew.

Three days later Caradoc rejoined the rest of the Squadron to escort a convoy to Norway. The return trip took four days and was executed in appalling weather conditions. There had been no sign of any enemy ships or submarines. Their escort duties over, the Squadron were joined by twelve destroyers and ordered to proceed to sea again immediately. When the ships steamed into the Skaggerak Jim felt excited and nervous. He noticed that there was a slight tremble in his hands. His intuition told him that there was going to be some action.

They passed the Kattergat Light at 4.00 am on 31st October and proceeded into the Kattergat. Two days later enemy ships were sighted and the gun crews ordered to action stations. They had come upon a small fleet of armed trawlers and Raiders. The cry "open fire!" had barely died away when the gun crews went into action. The noise was terrific and the acrid smell of the guns filled the air. The German Raiders were equipped with four 5.9inch guns but apart from loosing off a few rounds ineffectually seemed more intent on escaping from the British ships. The destroyers and the cruisers between them sank nine of the armed trawlers and one of the raiders, the Kronprinz.

Fifty-six survivors from the trawlers and the raider were picked up from the water with Caradoc assisting in the rescue operation. Interrogation of the survivors taken aboard enabled the Captain to identify four of the trawlers sunk—the Frankfurt, Leischfurt, the Triscka and Markelle.

With their prisoners on board the Squadron returned to Rosyth. There had been no casualties aboard any of the British ships. "All safe" as Jim wrote in his Log that night.

The keeping of the Log was not maintained without ribald remarks from the other gun-crew members. As Jim picked up his pen there would be the usual comments from Wiggy, Frank, Little John and Don.

"Hush! The scribe doth write!"

"Now cease your cackle, you swabs! Give the man the silence he needs to record the facts for posterity."

"Who or what is posterity? I'm just a humble AB please tell me!"

"Isn't education a wonderful thing? Wish they had had it in *our* schooldays!"

Jim took it all in good humour. However, one night after coming off duty he could not find the Log. He guessed that his mates had hidden it for a joke. He tackled them one by one but all of them affected complete innocence.

"I haven't seen Jim's Log, Don, have you?"

"Not me!"

"Have you seen it, Frank?"

Jim eventually recovered it from Lieutenant Fisher to whom it had been handed in by one of the gun crew jokers. The man had told Fisher that he had found it and that it looked to be an important and official document that ought not to be left lying around but placed in safe keeping. The lieutenant, realising that it was a leg-pull merely gave the Log back to Jim, solemnly. Jim was relieved to get the book back. Realising that it would be senseless attempting to hide it from his shipmates and, seeing the funny side of the practical joke that had been played on him, he continued to record his daily entries. He composed a little rhyme, which he wrote on a card and placed on top of the Log:

> *"My book is number one,*
> *My boot is number two.*
> *He that stealeth number one*
> *Shall feel my number two!"*

The Log was never removed again but frequently his mates added little notes of their own to his entries. Jim did not mind this quite so much. In fact, he encouraged it on several occasions. Eventually the Log was accepted and regarded almost with pride by them all Poems, amusing anecdotes all found their place in the book. One such entry was entitled "A Day's Work in the Navy":

Reveille!
> *All hands! Again that dismal cry.*
> *Turn out! In your Warm blankets you no longer may lie.*
> *Lash that bedroom nice and taut and stow it neat away!*
> *Hands to wash and tie at the dawning of the day.*

Scrub decks! 5.30
> *Scrub, scrub, scrub! Fore and aft and back again!*
> *Grime around the ash-last and oil around the gun.*
> *Rub it up! Scrub it up! You'll soon be black and brown again.*
> *You will have plenty of this before your 12 years is done.*

Breakfast. 8.00am
> *Sing "Key" for the festive bloater*
> *And the chanty chanting cheese*
> *And sausage brown from Canning Town*
> *And egg that grows on trees!*
> *In hazard of digestion—*
> *In peril of your lives,*
> *You've 30 mins to stow it in and shift in number fives!*

Divisions 9.00 am (officer goes rounds)
> *Your jumper isn't uniform*

Your pockets fixed with pins
You'll master bag at dinner-time
To answer for your sins!

Work & Exercise 9.30 am. Hands told off for work:

Now some go to drill and instructions
And some go performing with paint.
And "The Bloke", he's annoyed
If we ain't all employed
But, no! Hell, some of us ain't.
Some go to fairy gymnastics
Bending, extending the bones
Which some of us loves,
which the rest disapproves
With deep but inaudible groans.

Dinner. Seven Bells (11.3O)

Grog.
Oh! The roast beef of old England is very good stuff
But "a cut off the horns" is eternally tough
And the cook went to sleep and cindered the duff.
The murphies are scattered and nubbly
But be not dismayed, there is joy to be found
When the Matelots line up at the trumpeter's sound—
So fill your basins and pass it around
And drown all your sorrows in bubbly!

Pipe down. Eight Bells 12.00 Noon.

Hands make and mend clothes—Sometimes!

Tea. Seven Bells (3.30 pm)

Jam, jam, jam! Dainty bread and jam!
Scorn the false allurements of the sardines, ham!
Oh! Happy we shall be
With a kettle of Bokee
And a Passer's loaf and Passer's tin of jam, jam, jam!

Rounds - 9.00

Rounds!!! 'Ware the rounds! Number One is going his rounds.
He's diving down the flats, and scaring up the rats.
What an awful thing is rounds, rounds, rounds!

Pipe Down, 10.00 pm

Now the day is over
Stars begin to peep,
Rats begin to scamper,
Matelots go to sleep
... But, Oh! The mad Caradoc!
She's ploughing 'cross the Deep!

* * *

On 12th November after several days on coastal patrol an enemy Light Cruiser was sighted but fled before Caradoc could get within range. Three days later the Squadron proceeded to sea with the destroyers and HMS Courageous and Glorious— their destination, Heligoland. The ships reached the Bite on 17th November and sighted the German Light Cruiser again. HMS Courageous opened fire on it first followed by the ships of the 6th LCS and the destroyers. Half an hour later the 1st LCS came up and joined in the firing. The enemy cruiser must have signalled for help when she first came under fire as a much larger enemy craft was sighted simultaneously with the arrival of the British ships of the 1st LCS. The devastating gunfire from the new arrival blew away the bridge of HMS Cardiff, killing her bugler and six ratings. HMS Calypso's bridge was also carried away killing her Captain, Navigator and thirteen of her hands. With two of the 6th LCS hit Captain Munro Kerr brought Caradoc well to the fore, where HMS Repulse of the 1st LCS joined her. Both ships steamed towards the enemy and as they drew closer positioned themselves for firing, unloading salvo after salvo. They could see that there were several German Warships gathered. This time it was the turn of the British ships to score. They hit and set ablaze two German cruisers and sank an armed trawler.

The Germans had had enough and began running. Only five survivors were picked up from the sea; a German Lieutenant and four seamen. HMS Courageous turned back for base with the prisoners on board but HMS Repulse and the Caradoc pursued the enemy ships for two hours until they ran into minefields so bad that they had no alternative but to turn back.

That evening Jim and Frank Butler discussed the action in which they had taken part. Both were in jubilant spirits. Jim brought his Log up to date while Frank sat with a pencil and writing paper. Jim thought that Frank was writing a letter home. Frank's fair hair, blue eyes and boyish face coupled with his small stature and height made him seem to Jim like a schoolboy intent on writing an essay. Suddenly Frank put down his pen.

"How's this, Jim?" he queried, reading aloud from his paper:

"The Caradoc is a smart Cruiser
And a little bit of a bruiser!
She caused the end of a German Cruiser."

Jim could not stop himself from laughing. Frank's face reddened and he looked so embarrassed and comical that Jim had to steady himself as he fell about laughing uncontrollably.

"Is that all you can come up with, after all that writing?"

"Well, I've never written poetry before," Frank said, sheepishly.

This set Jim off laughing again. However, when he had managed to control his mirth he made one or two suggestions for expanding the verse. The two of them sat down together and after several attempts put together:

"The Caradoc is a very smart Cruiser
And a little bit of a bruiser!
When in the Bite
She took place in a fight
Which caused the end of a German Cruiser."

They each put their initials beneath the verse.

"Not exactly a masterpiece," declared Jim. "We need more practice until we can produce some verse."

The other members of the Gun Crews seemed to like the verse and Mo, being musically inclined, put it to music and the crew sang it together. The novelty of composing verse caught on and Bert Featherstone became quite adept at the art. Bert was a handsome looking man with slightly wavy brown hair parted on the right side. He had very fine features and looked every bit the poet, Jim decided.

Bert came up with his own verse:

"To see a British Bulldog quake
would cause the Huns huge delight.
But, lo! That Bulldog still can take
A nibble in the Bite!"

"That's good!" said Jim. "Here sign it and I'll put it in the Log."

Bert signed it, obviously pleased.

Later, Frank Butler came over with another verse.

"Old times were good,
New times are pleasant,
For wishing you well
No time's like the present!"

"Now that's better!" Bert Featherstone exclaimed. "Are you sure *you* wrote it, Frank?"

Frank was not prepared to answer. Whether or not he was the author, the verse was faithfully recorded in the Log with his initials beneath the entry.

This new game kept the gun crews occupied during their free time. It amused Jim to see them competing with one another. With great affection he wrote once more, Oh, The mad Caradoc!

At 8.30 pm on the evening following the engagement with the German ships, the dead were buried at sea and the British ships returned to base.

Throughout the remainder of that month and the whole of December the 6th LCS was assigned to escort duties taking convoys to Norway and home again. These escort duties were necessary as the most active part of the German Navy at that time was its Submarine Service. The U-Boats preyed on British Merchantmen making the Atlantic and North Sea crossings.

Christmas Day was spent on escort duties. The crew celebrated as best they could but the sea was rough and the lookouts had to keep alert for U-Boats. New Year's Eve was celebrated at Scapa Flow with the Grand Fleet, the signallers keeping busy for a time relaying good wishes for a *Peaceful Year* from one ship to another.

The Caradoc put to sea again on lone patrol. She was away a week and ran into appalling weather with blizzards and rough seas making the navigation hazardous. Immediately on return to Scapa Flow she was ordered to sea again with the 6th LCS screening a large convoy. The seas were still rough and the blizzards worse than before. Morale was not at its peak and the crew were impatient to get back to base. The German U-Boats were still very active and were releasing mines along the routes the convoys travelled. This further hazard had to be reckoned with and allowed no time for any relaxation of vigil. The 6th LCS, reinforced by many other ships from the Fleet, carried out mine sweeping and convoy escorting throughout January and February. The Caradoc's part in the operations only came to an end when she developed engine trouble and had to proceed to Rosyth where she was taken into Dry Dock on 15th February. The heavy seas and the arduous and long periods at sea had finally taken toll.

Jim and his mates were given a week's shore leave. The extent of the problem with the turbine was assessed as involving at least two week's work.

Jim decided to spend the leave in Norfolk. The long awaited mail had reached them at Rosyth and Jim had received several letters from Aunt Esther and other relatives and no less than half a dozen more from Dorothy, who now signed herself 'Dolly', the nickname Jim had used when he first wrote to her from the Redoubtable. So much had happened since those days. His mind flitted back to Harry Hanford and he wondered where Harry was serving. Jim smiled to himself as he recalled the verse Harry had written when Jim had told him about Dolly.

"Dolly is her name
Single is her station
Happy is the man
Who makes the alteration!"

Jim had copied the verse and incorporated it in a letter he had sent to Dolly.

Her letters to him were always beautifully written and catching the mode of communicating in verse she wrote poems of her own frequently which became bolder with each letter. Jim found himself caught up in the exchange of loving thoughts and particularly so when at sea. His imagination was then given free reign, spurred on by the longing for female companionship.

Dolly had written:

"Amidst the strife of battle
Wherever you may roam
Remember you are in the heart
Of those you left at home."

Yes, he decided, he would definitely spend his leave in Norfolk, but not with Aunt Esther. He felt a little guilty not having written to her more often, and a little guilty too that he would not be going to stay with her in Norwich. He dashed off letters to his relatives spending extra time on the one to Aunt Esther.

His Aunt Winifred was surprised to see him later that day when he arrived at her door. He told her that he had a few days leave while his ship was in dock and, as he had hoped, she invited him to stay with her. His uncle by marriage was a somewhat taciturn man and uncommunicative. He worked on a farm and generally spent his spare time playing dominoes at the local. Jim was quite prepared to suffer his uncle's bad humour if it meant having a base near Dolly.

He called to see her the next day. Her mother answered the door and, recognising Jim immediately, invited him in. She called out to her daughter that there was a sailor calling to see her. Dolly came out from one of the doorways leading from the small hallway. She was surprised and happy to see Jim.

"What a handsome young sailor you have become!" her mother said to Jim then, addressing Dorothy, asked: "Don't you think so, Dorothy?"

Dolly blushed but managed to smile at Jim.

He received invitations to tea there throughout the week. Dorothy's father was serving with the Army, an officer in the Norfolk's, Jim learned. The couple managed to get some moments alone together. Even though the weather was cold they were disinclined to stay indoors with Dorothy's mother all the time. They had so much to talk about. They walked hand in hand along the lanes and when they were sure no one was likely to interrupt them eagerly embraced each other and exchanged passionate kisses.

Then, his leave at an end, Jim said goodbye to Dorothy's mother. Afterwards Dorothy left the house with him and they walked along the lanes for the last time together.

Jim reported back to Rosyth on February 22nd only to discover that Caradoc was still in dry dock. His shipmates were very talkative exchanging details of how their seven days leave had been spent. One of the crew, George, said that he and his young lady had decided to get married on his next leave. The rest of the crew teased him about taking better precautions. George took it all in good part, even managing a laugh himself. Jim had befriended George soon after joining the Caradoc as the pair of them had been "new boys" aboard and George had a sense of humour that was very similar to Jim's own. Not that all their conversations together were humorous. Banter was dropped in favour of gravity when the subject happened to be the opposite sex. Jim had often talked to him about Dorothy, mainly because George had a steady girl friend of his own in London of whom he was fond and could enter into serious and frank conversation about his feelings towards her. As Jim was a little unsure about his own feelings towards Dorothy, he found the discussions helped him to sort out things a bit. He knew that he was not ready for marriage, as George appeared to be. George told Jim that he had decided on a Register Office wedding and asked Jim if he would be best man. Jim promised that he would. He had never been to a wedding as a best man and the idea was something that appealed to him.

"That's settled then," said George, giving Jim's hand a shake. "The next leave we get I'm definitely getting married. With your sense of humour, Jim, I know that you'll make a very good best man."

The crew were put on various duties on board but Jim thought it was all a waste of time. Most of the crew felt the same way and grumbled that they could have been given a few more days shore leave. The grumbling must have reached the ears of the Captain who decided to have a talk with the foreman in charge of the repair work. After his discussion he announced that Caradoc's repairs were likely to take another two to three weeks and in the circumstances extra leave would be given the crew. He allowed half of each Watch to have seven days leave, promising the other half that they would be granted seven days too when the others had returned. He added that it was up to each Watch to draw lots for who went first. Jim was pleased to find that he was lucky in the draw and was amongst the first batch from White Watch.

Wiggy, Frank, Little John, George and several of Jim's friends were lucky too. The men decided that as Jim and George would be going to London it would be a bit of fun for them to spend the bonus leave in London as well and have a really good time in the big city. They felt that it might be the last time they would get any leave for months so they might just as well make the most of it. The idea appealed to Jim and he put aside any thoughts of going to Norfolk to see Dolly or anyone else there. The wedding would be a bit of fun and the days and nights with the other members of the gun crews even more so.

It proved to be a week of riotous living too! Drinking together in pubs, going to dances to find girls, and generally "letting off steam" as they put it. Most of the time they kept together as a group, linking arms and singing doubtful shanties in the streets when the pubs closed. Frequently they had to break and run when military and naval police patrols were seen. At one of the dances Jim and Frank Butler met two very attractive French girls who were amused at the antics of the two sailors. The girls worked at the French Embassy and told Jim and Frank that their names were Veronique and Odette. The girls were in their early twenties and were vivacious partners. They frequently spoke together in French and laughed when Jim and Frank asked them what they were saying. Frank and Odette were about the same height so it was natural that they paired off, leaving Jim and Veronique together. Veronique reminded Jim of Lily. She had dark hair and brown eyes and a delicately shaped face but unlike Lily used lipstick and powder. The French girls had a small apartment that they shared and to which Jim and Frank were invited. Veronique called Jim "Jacques" which he found amusing.

George's wedding was arranged for a date towards the end of the leave. The lads took him out on a stag night doing their best to get him drunk but he was far too wily for that. He asked Jim not to drink so much that he should oversleep the following morning.

The wedding held in the Register Office was quite a simple ceremony. George and Jim wore their uniforms. The reception was held at George's father-in-law's home and was attended by a few relatives of the couple. There was not much drink there and George's father-in-law was not a very light-hearted person. Jim's sense of humour amused some of the guests but the stolid faces of the others made Jim wish that he had the support of the rest of his shipmates who had not been invited to the wedding. Jim doubted that they would have made it on time anyway as the ceremony had been arranged for 9.30 am! Jim kissed the bride, shook hands with everyone, wished George all the best and excused himself from the reception as soon as he had the opportunity, explaining that he had a date with a young lady.

He had told Frank that he would meet him at the girls' apartment as soon as the wedding festivities were over so his excuse for getting away wasn't a complete fabrication.

When their leave was up and the two sailors had to say their farewells to the girls, Veronique gave Jim her home address and invited him to go over there when the war eventually came to an end. She handed him a photograph of her father's house, which looked very grand, Jim thought. It was in Neuilly Plaisance, Avenue du Marechal Foch.

The men returned to Rosyth on March 8th to allow the other halves of the Watches to go on leave. For their own part they were given the tedious jobs of painting and cleaning the ship for the week, which was quite sobering after their high living in London! The men talked together as they worked, sharing some of the experiences, reliving them. George talked about the wedding and his life, coming in for the usual fun-poking by those who were working alongside him. Although Jim joined in the fun he felt disinclined to relate his own experiences with Veronique. He was unable to stop his thoughts, however, and found himself at times in reverie savouring the exquisite perfume and warmth of Veronique's young body.

The work on Caradoc was eventually completed and she put to sea for turbine trials before rejoining the rest of the Squadron, sixteen destroyers, HMS Caledon and two mine layers, the Princess Margaret and the Angora. Their mission was to lay mines in the Kattergat and to seek out enemy ships and attack them. HMS Caledon had been assigned to the 6th LCS to replace the Calypso who was still in dry dock. The weather conditions were not good although visibility was moderate. The lookout on Caradoc sighted an enemy minelayer and Captain Munro Kerr ordered the Caradoc to break away from the other ships to engage her. As Caradoc steamed towards the enemy minelayer it turned and sped away under full steam. The Captain ordered pursuit and under full steam too Caradoc chased after the German ship. The pursuit continued for what seemed several hours by which time a mist had come up and gradually began to thicken. They lost the minelayer and the Captain reluctantly decided to call off the search for her and rejoin the Squadron as quickly as the weather conditions would permit. It was in the forenoon that someone shouted:

"Mine to port!"

The cry of alarm had barely died away when it was echoed from the starboard side.

"Mine to starboard!"

Chapter Five

Miraculously Caradoc had passed between two German floating mines with only feet to spare on either side of the ship. The ship had had a very narrow escape indeed.

The mist had become so dense that Wiggy described it as being worse than a London fog, although admitting that it was a better colour and smell! The crew were laughing at Wiggy's remarks when, again, cries went up that further mines had been sighted.

As Caradoc nosed her way through the fog floating mines could be seen to port and starboard. She had run into a minefield and the weather conditions could hardly have been worse. The tension on board could be felt. Jim wondered what the Captain was thinking. He guessed that the man would be faced with the agonising decision of whether to proceed on the course being taken or attempt to turn back. That they had been very lucky to have avoided colliding with one of the mines so far, Jim had no doubt, but would their luck hold out? There was nothing that could be done but grit one's teeth and pray.

The Captain maintained their course. It had no doubt been a difficult decision for him but evidently he had judged the risks of turning about more dangerous than keeping on a straight course.

Although visibility in the mist was bad and progress necessarily slow it was still daylight. If they did not get out of the minefield before darkness fell the risk would be considerably increased. At least with some visibility there was a chance. The thought of being in that situation at night was too horrible to contemplate.

The mist showed no sign of lifting and how far they had travelled at that pace Jim had no idea. The crew were silent - unusually so, helpless, waiting.

After another hour had passed the word went round that no further mines had been sighted for well over fifteen minutes and it seemed that Caradoc was safe. The crew slowly began to talk again, nervously at first.

"The Captain made the right choice," Frank Butler said, in a hoarse voice.

"What a choice to have to make," Little John commented.

"Thank God that he did!" Jim cried.

"Aye! Something must have been guiding us," Mo said.

The Caradoc, on the course she had maintained, must have been travelling in a lane that passed through the minefield. It was nothing short of a miracle. That it was by the Grace of God Jim had no doubt and gave thanks that Caradoc had emerged from the minefield unscathed and all aboard her were alive and safe.

* * *

Darkness fell and the fog persisted. It was quite eerie on deck and oppressively silent. The Captain decided to sit things out until the morning in the hope that by then visibility might have improved sufficiently to find the rest of the Squadron. When the night had passed, however, and the fog had still not lifted, the Captain, probably fearing that a U-boat might see them and take advantage of such a stationary target were it to come across them by chance, decided to proceed. So the Caradoc made her way slowly, cautiously in the general direction towards where she had broken away from the other ships. It was two days before they found the 6th LCS when the fog eventually dispersed. It had been an extremely hazardous trip for the Caradoc's crew and Jim felt a great sense of relief when they were reunited with the Squadron. He again offered prayers of thanksgiving to God.

Later that day they were joined by the 1st BCS and the 5th BCS. This considerable force searched for enemy ships together for two days but Jim had to record in his Log "Nothing doing in the scrap line," as the ships set out for base.

On 7th April the 6th LCS were ordered to return to the Kattergat to complete their mine-laying operations but once more ran into heavy sea mists and the operation had to be abandoned. At first watch on 12th April the ships returned to Scapa Flow and joined the Grand Fleet's manoeuvres. The weather conditions were deplorable and Jim wrote in the Log:

"The weather was far too rough for the Stonewallers (Battleships) so they returned to base, but the poor little ships had to patrol."

A week later the 6th were again ordered to the Kattergat to finish minelaying! Twenty destroyers, themselves capable of minelaying, joined them. At 4.00am on 15th April a large pack of armed enemy trawlers were sighted travelling in convoy. The British ships caught up with them that time and in the ensuing engagement sank no less than thirteen of them. One hundred and eleven survivors were picked up from the sea. The mine laying was resumed and completed in the forenoon and the Squadron returned to base.

How the lads celebrated that night! Every man joined in the fun. The hornpipe was danced and the grog and beer flowed. Even Mo was seen to smile and once someone thought that he might even have laughed a little! The Gun crews, of course, were in jubilant spirits. There was no completing his Log that night for Jim except for a few words scribbled on the back of one of the photographs of the Gun crews—*Oh, The Mad Caradoc!*

At first light on 21st April the 6th LCS joined by the 1st Battle Cruisers Renown and Repulse were sent on operations around Dogger Bank and North Heligoland. The remainder of the Grand Fleet joined them there two days later. This mighty fleet carried out extensive searches for the enemy but not one was sighted. The fleet returned to base three days later when the weather deteriorated.

"Do you get the impression, lads," chirped Frank Butler. "That the Hun is laying low?"

"I'm not surprised," Wiggy said. "With the whole Grand Fleet out in force. We've done better when we've been out alone seeking them."

"At least," said Jim, philosophically. "I can spend my birthday in the peace of Scapa Flow!"

He regretted saying it when Wiggy triumphantly shouted:

"Hear that, lads! It's Jim's *birthday*!"

The crew, spurred on by Wiggy, carried Jim up on deck and amidst curses from Jim proceeded to give him seventeen resounding bumps! Jim took it in good part as he massaged his tender rear. After all, he thought, he had joined the crew few weeks earlier administering similar birthday treatment to Wiggy.

Two days later, almost as if Command had heeded Wiggy Bennett's words, Caradoc with only two destroyers was sent out on forty-eight hours North Sea patrol to search for U-Boats or other enemy ships. Their patrol was without success, warranting only an "all quiet" in the Log.

May was a month of assorted missions of patrols, mine-laying and convoy screening which terminated with Caradoc going into dry dock at Rosyth because of under water defects. There was no leave for the lads on that occasion as the work on her was completed in less than three days and Caradoc rejoined the rest of the Squadron in the Firth of Forth.

Patrols continued, interspersed by convoy screening and mine laying operations. On one of the latter around Dogger Bank several enemy ships were sighted to the sou'west. The 6th set out towards them but once again the German ships immediately steamed away. Although the Squadron pursued them, the enemy ships were out of range and continued to maintain that healthy distance away. Caradoc was ordered to link up with a convoy leaving Sweden and escort it back to Cromarty. On the way the 6th BS "Yankee" joined them. The mission was completed without incident.

A week later, while escorting another convoy, two German U-Boats were reported and Caradoc and the destroyers began searching for them around the Skaggerack off the coast of Sweden and into the Kattergat but without success. In the Kattergat several enemy patrol vessels were sighted but managed to get clear before the British ships could engage them. On the return trip the Renown, the Repulse and the ships of the 1st LCS joined the 6th LCS. Further patrols brought no actions with enemy ships and Caradoc and two of the destroyers were placed on stand-by, dropping anchor in Largo Bay. It was becoming increasingly clear that the German ships were intent on avoiding any confrontation. Their tactics were to steam away at full speed whenever they came within sight of British armed vessels. Caradoc was ordered to patrol the following day but she ran into very rough weather in the North Sea and was forced to return three days later.

On 29th July Calypso rejoined Caradoc, out of dry dock at last, and the two light cruisers screened a convoy bound for Norway.

Apart from rough seas there were no other hazards and when the convoy had returned safely to harbour Caradoc put into Rosyth Basin for repairs to Y-Gun.

Y-Gun crew came in for the usual comments from the A-Gun crew.

"Obviously they haven't been cleaning the gun properly," said Frank, ducking out of the way as Wiggy aimed an oily rag at his head.

"You have to load the gun with the shells this way on," yelled Don, drawing an imaginary shell in the air with his hands and going through a pantomime of gunloading.

"All right, you clever buggers! Could be that Y-Gun has had more action!"

"With the amount of action any of us has had lately," Mo suggested, "It could be rust!" Both crews applauded this droll contribution.

When Y-Gun had been repaired Caradoc slipped the buoy to which she had been moored and proceeded to sea at first Dog Watch with the other ships of the 6th, several destroyers and the Glorious and Furious. Their mission was to take them right into enemy waters raiding Cuxhaven. The raid lasted some six hours. Similar raids were carried out two days later.

On 24th August Caradoc on lone patrol ran into the fiercest winds Jim had so far experienced. Mo thought that they were hurricane force. The seas were really heavy. Huge waves crashed on deck and one of the Whalers was smashed to pieces, also the first Cutter and the Battery doors were damaged, so the Captain ordered return to base.

When the weather conditions improved Caradoc resumed patrol and sighted five enemy ships. Caradoc's guns opened fire but the enemy were barely within range and immediately began running. They were faster ships than Caradoc and outran her.

September gave way to October with further convoy screening, mine laying and patrols but the situation showed no real change. Enemy ships were sighted and pursued on many occasions but seldom engaged in battle. On 24th October the 6th LCS was joined by the 1st LCS and then by the 1st Battle Cruiser

Squadron and by a flotilla of destroyers. The weather conditions were rough and the seas heavy. Several of the Caradoc's crew had reported sick with fever and had been taken into sickbay. All that day further members of the crew fell ill and had to leave their posts. The diagnosis was that a virulent form of influenza was rampant.

The weather worsened with wind and rain lashing the decks. The wind had increased in violence when, in a position off West Heligoland, the British ships ran into a large force of enemy ships. Both sides were taken by surprise by the unexpected encounter. It was evident that the Germans had thought it safe to shift their positions in such appalling weather. A sea battle then began in the confusion of the storm.

By this time no less than seventy-four of Caradoc's crew were too ill for duty and were in sick bay with fever. The Gun crews were so depleted that the Captain had no alternative but to report the desperate situation to their Flagship, HMS Cardiff and was given orders to disengage from the action and turn back for base. HMS Calypso was ordered to provide an escort for Caradoc and to stand by to render any assistance that might prove necessary. As Caradoc turned, shells from the enemy ships were ploughing up the sea all around her. The sounds of the guns from the British and German ships added to the noise of the crashing of waves cascading over the decks. It was chaos, like all hell let loose. Jim stayed by his post but he felt hot and his throat hurt and with every movement he made he was overcome by giddiness.

"You don't look too good, Jim." Mo was evidently concerned about him.

"I feel bloody rough," Jim croaked.

And then the Caradoc's bridge was carried away. Lieutenant Brent was injured. Captain Munro Kerr ordered full steam and Caradoc pulled away heading for base.

She reached Scotland on 26th October and by that time eighty-six members of her crew had become victims of the influenza virus, including Jim. The sick men and the injured Lieutenant Brent were transferred to City Hospital, Edinburgh. Huts were allocated to accommodate the influenza victims.

Jim felt so ill that he was not even aware who was in the bed next to his. He knew that he was running a high temperature and that it had become difficult to swallow the saliva in his mouth. For several days he lay there, feeling so ill that he wondered if he would die. The nursing staff, working under severe pressure with the sudden influx of patients, did their best and remained kind and caring. One of the nurses was very concerned about Jim and after taking his temperature and checking his pulse insisted that one of the doctors should examine him immediately. He was vaguely aware of a doctor bending over him and examining him and then of being transferred from the bed to a stretcher and then away from the hut where some of his mates were. A nurse told him that he was being taken to the main hospital building. In a half delirious state he was later aware of people around his bed and heard someone say:

"This man has contracted diphtheria."

Chapter Six

Jim was to learn later that he had been stricken by not only Influenza but also by Laryngeal Diphtheria. The vigilance of Nurse Leggett had fortunately enabled the doctor to diagnose the diphtheria in its early stages and administer 36,000 units of Antitoxin intravenously. Jim had been transferred to Ward 16 of the main hospital wing for both the purposes of medical care and of isolation from the other sailors; it seemed isolation was necessary because of the very nature of the disease. A doctor and nurse together administered Mechanical suction, through a laryngoscope. It was not very comfortable at the time but afterwards Jim felt a lot easier.

His bed had no pillows and he was told that he must lie flat like that for a week. He was given only fluids for three days and then sloppy foods, "semi-fluids" as the nurses described them, for another week before he was allowed normal foods. A nurse supported Jim whenever he was given a drink or fed. His arms and legs were massaged daily by the nurses, a treatment which Jim did not mind at all! The doctor examined him regularly and took swabs of his throat.

Although Jim was glad to be out of the war for a while, he also felt rather bored. He was not permitted to read or to write and had nothing to occupy his time except his thoughts. Lying there, flat on his back, he thought of the many months he had spent in action on board Caradoc. He thought too of the lucky escapes he and his comrades had had from death and wondered whether God had appointed a Guardian Angel to look after the ship and her crew.

He thought of Wiggy, Mo, Bert and the rest of his shipmates; he thought about Aunt Esther and he thought about the earlier years of his life, his boyhood, and he thought a great deal about his sister.

The nurses who attended him in the isolation ward wore white linen masks covering their noses and mouths. Some of the nurses were slim and had attractive figures, others were more plump and matronly, and one was very thin and bony. Most of them were kind and gentle and talked to him as much as their duties would permit. Although Jim could not see their faces he could tell them apart by their eyes and their build.

One day, about the time that he was given the first semi-fluids, the nurses were clearly excited about something. They came into Jim's room and told him the good news—*the war was over*. One of the nurses said:

"The Germans agreed an armistice today!"

"What day is it?" Jim asked, having lost track of time.

"It's November 11th!"

So, the war was over at last, thought Jim. His mind filled with thoughts of his shipmates. He imagined how they must have been reacting to the news. There would be grog and beer flowing and perhaps even the officers would be "splicing the mainbrace" with the crew. Jim felt a sudden pang of regret that he could not be with them. It was so frustrating having to remain in a hospital bed at such a time. He was filled with impatience at his sickness and willed his body to get fit again.

At the end of the week he was allowed a pillow. It felt good to have his head slightly raised. Jim thought that the doctor seemed pleased with his progress. He explained to Jim as he took more throat swabs that they were necessary to monitor progress. He added that Jim would need to remain in isolation until the swabs revealed negative results for three consecutive days. Jim asked the doctor how much longer he was likely to be in hospital.

"About a month. Are you getting bored?"

Jim told him that he was *very* bored.

"I see no reason now why he shouldn't be given newspapers and books to read," the doctor told the nurse who was on duty.

Jim was pleased to have the newspapers and books that the nurse brought to him later. He asked the nurse whether any of his shipmates were still in hospital.

The nurse's bright blue eyes twinkled above her mask. She told Jim that she had been looking after them in the huts but had returned to duties in the Hospital that morning as the last of them had been discharged the previous day.

"What about Lieutenant Brett, the officer who was injured?" Jim asked.

"I think that he's recovering well but he's still in the hospital."

"What's your name, nurse?" Jim asked her. He felt that he already knew the answer but had to ask.

"Mary Leggett."

"I thought so!" Jim said, excitedly. "I think that I owe you a lot. You are the nurse who first realised that I had something wrong with me besides influenza. If it hadn't been for you I might have died."

Her eyes were shining. He knew that his remarks had pleased her. She placed a hand on his head and tousled his hair.

"Well, it's good to see that you are still very much alive and growing stronger by the hour!"

She spoke in a husky voice and with a strong Scottish accent which Jim thought pleasant and amusing. He asked her when she was going to massage his arms and legs as the other nurses had done.

"Och! Get away with you! You sailors are all alike!"

They both laughed.

The next day she brought him several letters all but one of which had be directed to the hospital from the Squadron. One, however, was addressed to him at the hospital and he recognised Wiggy's scrawl. There was a long letter from Dolly, one from Lily, two from Aunt Esther and even one from Aunt Winifred. He read every one of them several times over so that he almost knew them by heart. Dolly had included a little four-lined verse with her letter, which was written in tiny letters:

Someone is thinking of someone
Far over the wide ocean blue
I am that someone who's thinking
And that someone I think of is you.

She added that she loved him and was looking forward to seeing him again.

Lily had not written any poems. Her style was totally different from Dolly's. She brought Jim up to date with news of her own activities, and told him that Bob, the Lance-Corporal, had been slightly wounded in action in France and was on his way home to

Blighty. She ended her letter by saying that she missed Jim very much and hoped that he would soon get leave so that they could be together. Aunt Winifred's letter was mainly about his cousin who was still in Ireland. Aunt Esther's letters, or rather the later one, brought some exciting news She had enclosed a postcard from his sister, Vi, post-marked 'Tunbridge Wells'. Vi had not given any address but the post-mark was unmistakably 'Tunbridge Wells, Kent'. The postcard contained a few lines to say that she had changed her job and that she was well and she hoped one day to be able to have a holiday in Norwich. Aunt Esther said in her letter that she could not understand why Violet had not put an address on the card. Jim pondered on this for a long time. It was the first communication that he had received, albeit second-hand, from Violet since she had been taken into service when he was a boy. It was all a mystery but one he was determined to solve one day.

The letter from Wiggy and his other shipmates was full of their good wishes; they told him to make the most of his rest in hospital. The letter had been signed by every one of the members of the gun crews. A postscript from Wiggy informed Jim that the Log was safe and that the lads had decided to keep their own record of Caradoc's movements so that Jim's Log could be brought up to date on his return. Wiggy assured Jim that no one had written in the Log itself although Frank had wanted to but had been warned off by the rest of the lads!

Three weeks after being admitted to the hospital Jim was allowed to get out of bed and take a little exercise walking slowly round the ward under the watchful eyes of the nurses. The doctor explained to Jim that the throat swabs had proved negative for the past three days and consequently there was no longer any need for him to be kept in isolation.

The exercise regimen was gradually increased and Jim was allowed to walk about the ward and corridors, eventually being permitted to dress in warm clothes and go outside under the care of Nurse Leggett. Without the mask, which had covered the lower half of her face, she was quite an attractive young woman with her high cheekbones, full lips, dark bobbed hair and her bright blue eyes.

Finally on 16th December Jim was given a sealed envelope to hand to his Captain and was discharged from Hospital. He reported to Rosyth the following day but as Caradoc was at sea he went aboard the Calypso, which was the only ship of the Squadron docked there. After examining the report from the hospital, in consultation with the ship's doctor, the Captain told Jim to go to the Mess and get himself something to eat and drink and in the meanwhile arrangements would be made for him to proceed on leave until the Caradoc's return.

An hour later Jim had left HMS Calypso with a leave pass covering his absence until 13th January, a railway warrant, a considerable amount of money representing arrears of pay due to him since October and an advance of pay for his leave. Jim had not had so much money in his life and felt himself a very rich man!

He had decided to go first to London to spend a few days with Veronique, afterwards to travel to Tunbridge Wells to see if he could locate Vi, and finally to go to Norfolk. However, in the late evening, after calling at the apartment the two French girls had occupied, he was disappointed to learn that they had returned to France the previous day. As he knew no one else in London and had nowhere to stay he decided to put forward his plans for visiting Tunbridge Wells. He caught a tram and eventually arrived at Victoria Station only to be told that the last train had left a few minutes before his arrival and there would be no trains to Tunbridge Wells until early the next morning. Not having anywhere to go he decided to 'doss down' in the waiting room until the morning.

It was in the waiting room that he met Julia. She was a woman many years older than Jim. She was smartly dressed in the fashion of the time and was sitting in the waiting room, her hands folded in her lap, looking very sad, Jim thought. He noticed that she was wearing black clothing and he guessed that she was in mourning for someone. There were several other occupants in the waiting room but there were numerous places to sit down. He chose a place next to the woman. She glanced at Jim as he sat down beside her so he spoke to her.

"I've missed the last train tonight," he said. "It means waiting here until the first one is due to leave tomorrow."

72

She seemed pleased to have someone to talk to and told Jim that she had missed her train too.

She had dark brown hair cut in a fringe across her forehead, hazel eyes, a well-shaped mouth and an olive skin giving her an almost Latin appearance. Jim judged her to be about thirty.

He was aware that she was studying him with interest. She seemed to find some comfort in the fact that he was in naval uniform, that he could be trusted. She told him that she lived and worked in Woolwich but had been staying in Bristol with her father following the death of her mother. Jim noticed that her eyes filled with tears as she spoke and that she was doing her best to fight them back. Jim listened sympathetically as she told him about her mother's short illness and her death. When she had talked through what was evidently her immediate distress, she said:

"Well, here I am talking about my problems and I don't even know you!"

"My name's Jim. I'm on leave from the Caradoc."

She told him that her husband had been in the Navy. It was the emphasis that she placed on the past tense that alerted Jim.

"What happened?" he asked her.

"He lost his life when the Vanguard went down two years ago." She sighed deeply. "We had been married just under three years when the war started."

Jim said how sorry he was. He remembered the Vanguard blowing up in 1917 with heavy loss of lives. It was said that the explosion was the result of sabotage. On board Caradoc with his Log was a photograph of some of the survivors who had been picked up. However, he did not tell her that.

By the time the first signs of day-light appeared through the grimy waiting-room windows Jim had, at her request, told her all about himself. They had talked together right through the night!

"It seems to me that some folk have to face a lot of misfortune in their lives, while others have all the luck." She shook her head sadly.

"You seem to have had more than your fair share, Jim."

Jim had never looked at his life in that way. He regarded life as a day-to-day adventure, taking things as they came. The words from the good book "sufficient unto the day" just about summed it up for him!

There were unmistakable sounds of activity in the station and the other occupants of the waiting room were beginning to make a move.

"Look, Jim," Julia told him. "If you would like to come back to my place for some breakfast and a wash and shave before you set out to find your sister, you are most welcome to do so."

Jim hesitated. Julia had obviously taken a liking to him and he had to admit to himself that he liked her too. He had no idea where he would find Vi, if at all. Had he not, he persuaded himself, a full months leave that he had intended spending time with Veronique anyway. so he would not be losing anything by accepting the invitation? One day was not likely to make much difference. He ran his hand across his chin; he could feel the stubble. Yes, he could do with a shave.

Seeing that he hesitated she added:

"It won't take us long to get to Woolwich from here."

There was something appealing in her voice so Jim accepted.

It was three days later when he left Julia's home and then she had been reluctant for him to go. She told him that he was the first man who had stirred any feelings within her since her husband's death. He knew that she spoke the truth.

"You have been a real comfort, Jim," she said as he gently disengaged himself from her embrace. "I hope you find your sister. You know where I live and you're welcome here any time."

Although the time with Julia had been an experience it was with some sense of relief that he boarded the train back to London.

The journey to Tunbridge Wells Station did not take as long as he had imagined it would. He had a third class compartment to himself and gazed out at the countryside as the train steamed on its way. It looked very pleasant with the fields and the occasional farms nestling in the hills. The train stopped at Tonbridge and Jim wondered whether he should get out there. The guard on the platform told him that Tunbridge Wells was the next stop.

The station was near the Pantiles and he walked through that unusual place with interest. He called in at the Swan Hotel for a beer, making enquiries of the barman where he might find somewhere inexpensive to stay during his leave.

The barman, scratching his bald head, said, "Might be difficult this time of the year, particularly this end of the town. You could try the Camden Road area."

He gave Jim directions and Jim finished his beer and left the hotel. He continued along the Pantiles, stopping to investigate the Church of King Charles the Martyr, and turned into Chapel Place as the barman had directed. He carried on along the High Street but at the far end of it became a little confused. He asked a passer-by where Camden Road was and was directed "...up Mount Pleasant, past the Great Hall to Monson Road, just by the Opera House turn into Monson Road, that leads you right into Camden Road." At the corner of Camden Road was the Camden Hotel. He decided to have another beer and perhaps be given some advice in his search for somewhere to stay. He ordered the beer and stood by the bar counter and engaged the barman in conversation.

"I know that it's getting near Christmas," Jim said "but I'm hoping to find some digs somewhere in the town for a couple of weeks."

The barman told him that he did not think Christmas made much difference and there were usually plenty of places off Camden Road that took people for bed and breakfast or full board. Jim thanked the man and left.

He was intrigued by the many public houses he passed in Camden Road. He found a house in Garden Road where he could stay, the terms being well within his budget. The landlady, a short woman in her late fifties with dyed red hair and garish make-up, seemed pleased to have him. His room was somewhat sparsely furnished but it had the essentials and was reasonably clean so he thought that it would suit him nicely for the two weeks he would be staying there.

During the daylight hours of the following fortnight he spent his time walking around the town in the hope of seeing his sister. He had bought a map of the town and began his search in the Mount Ephraim area. He reasoned that if Vi were working in Tunbridge Wells she would probably have a living-in job and that it would be in the more affluent part of town. There were so many affluent sectors of the town that was the problem! He had no recent photographs of Vi but hoped that he would recognise her in spite of the years that had passed. He ticked off on his map the roads he had covered in his search—Mount Ephraim, Royal Chase, Boyne Park, Molyneux Park, Bishops Down. He trusted to a sort of providence that if Vi were near she would be working in the front of one of the large houses and he would see her. As he walked he peered at the houses. He saw plenty of housemaids shaking dusters out of windows, cleaning steps or polishing brass door-handles, but none of them resembled his sister. Sometimes, the girls, seeing Jim staring at them, would smile at him or wave to him. Others would turn away, obviously embarrassed. He waved back to those who waved to him and then proceeded on his way. As the days passed he realised that his task was hopeless. Discouraged, he spent Christmas Eve touring the pubs instead. He knew that he would not find Vi in them so he could relax a bit. He drank quite a lot of beer and sometimes would get caught up in groups of people bent on having a good time. Of course, the Navy's part in the war had not been forgotten and his uniform brought him a certain amount of popularity and numerous free drinks. The Camden Road area was a working class district and the pubs a social focal point. For the most part they were cheerful places and there were plenty of customers day and night. The atmosphere was generally friendly but occasionally arguments started when the beer had been flowing heavily and on a couple of occasions fights broke out. Jim was not involved in any of them regarding that sort of outcome of drinking to be at the wrong end of the scale that measured a good time.

As a complete contrast to the pubs he also attended several Church services in the hope that he might see Vi among the congregation, possibly with her employers, perhaps alone. It all proved fruitless and the time arrived when he decided he had better leave Tunbridge Wells and make his way up to Norfolk where he planned to spend the last week of his leave before returning to the Caradoc.

The journey alone gave him the opportunity to think. He realised that it had been an outside chance finding his sister in Tunbridge Wells. After two weeks or so paying for digs and drinking heavily he had gone through quite a large part of his money, and what had he gained by it? He knew that he had developed a taste for alcohol and was already looking forward to finding a pub and having a drink or two. He thought of Tunbridge Wells and what a strange town of contrasts it was with its mixture of wealthy residential areas and working class ones. It was quite different from the towns in Norfolk where he had grown up. He told himself that he would enjoy being back in Norfolk but pictures of Tunbridge Wells reappeared in his mind vividly and he could not rid himself of the premonition that he would be returning there some day.

He stayed with Aunt Esther in Norwich for three days and then went over to Aunt Winifred's and stayed with her for the remainder of his leave, seeing Dolly as he had done on his last leave there. She seemed to Jim to be unworldly, almost child-like in her innocence. He knew that he was fond of her but began to doubt that there was any future in their relationship. She, for her part, seemed to sense the change in him and remarked on it several times during their walks together in the lanes. Jim shrugged his shoulders and told her that it was probably her imagination.

On 13ᵗʰ January he returned to Portsmouth as instructed, his leave over. Caradoc and her crew were back. He could hardly wait to get aboard her and get back to his mates.

They were just the same—full of fun and good humour and glad to see him too. After their initial warm welcome it was almost as if he had never been separated from them by the episode in hospital. Wiggy threw his arms round Jim while others tried to slap him on the back or shake his hand. Even Mo shook his hand warmly.

"You've lost a bit of weight, Jim lad," he said.

"What have you been doing with yourself while we've been at sea?" Frank Butler asked.

Jim gave them an up-date on what had happened since the hospital admission. The gun crews had all gathered round him—Wiggy, Frank, Little John, Don, Goodie, Hemma, Nobby, Scottie and the rest of them. Wiggy handed Jim some sheets of paper.

"What's that?" Jim asked.

"We've kept the Log up to date for you, Jim," explained Wiggy. "You'll find all of Caradoc's movements written down there. So, tonight you'd better bring your own Log up to date... that should keep you out of mischief for a time!"

Just as Wiggy had said, the crew between them had faithfully recorded all the movements of the Squadron since that day in late October when Lieutenant Brent was injured and so many of the Caradoc's crew were sick.

"Mind you, Jim," Wiggy said. "You missed something with the surrender of the German Navy. It really was a sight for sore eyes!"

Mo had kept back a little from the excited group but suddenly pushed his way forward. He was clutching a book in his hand.

"This is for you, Jim," he said, offering the book to Jim. "I got an extra copy for you when I bought mine."

The book was entitled *The Graphic Souvenir of the German Navy's Surrender* and contained thirty-two pages of photographs of the historic surrender including HMS Cardiff, their own Flagship, leading the line of German ships in. Jim flicked through the pages. He was really grateful for Mo's thoughtfulness in procuring a copy of the book for him.

"That's really kind of you, Mo. Thank you!"

Mo shifted his weight from one foot to the other. Then, to cover his embarrassment, he said:

"You can pay me the one and sixpence for it whenever you like!"

Everyone joined in the laughter as Jim counted out from the loose change in his pocket fourteen pennies, six ha'pennies and four farthings and solemnly handed them to Mo.

Jim faithfully copied into his Log everything that had been written in the notes his friends had given him. He was tempted to correct the spellings but decided that he would prefer to write *exactly* what was said in the notes, spelling errors and all. He chuckled to himself as he wrote.

The notes were headed "*Esay* of the Movements of Caradoc and Squadron in the Surrendering of the German-High-Sea Fleet", and went on to say:

"Caradoc with most of her crew back aboard after the *inflewenza epidemmic* joined the rest of the 6th LCS and ten crack destroyers and proceeded out from Rosyth and brought the German Light

Cruiser, Konigberg into *Inch Keith* with German Admiral where we layed all night, all hands closed up at Night Defence Stations. The following day we escorted her to Scapa Flow.

On November 20th HMS Cardiff proceeded to sea alone at 5.00 am to meet German Fleet, the 6th LCS and 1st LCS following at 7.00 am, sighting them at Noon, Cardiff directing *there coarse*. The first line was the Battle Cruiser Von-Der-Tann, Moltke, *Hindinberg*, Derflinger and *Seydlitz*. Then came the Battleships König, Kaiser, Kaiserin, Bayern and Kronprinz. The German Admiral Meurer leading the Friederick-der-Grosse. Then the Phaeton *come* leading the German Light Cruisers and forty-nine destroyers. All enemy ships passing down through the Grand Fleet. We then proceeded to Scapa. The 6th LCS ordered to return to Rosyth and was told off for the Baltic Squadron.

On November 27th the 6th LCS and eight destroyers provisioned— got in sheepskin coats, extra blankets, extra *amunition*, rifles, bayonets and .303 *amunition* then proceeded for Copenhagen, Denmark and then on to Riga, North Russia, bombarding at different times at Helsinfor and other places. At Helsinfor Calypso, Caradoc and two of the destroyers captured two Bolshevik destroyers, *Spartack* and *Aftroil*. HMS Cassandra was sunk when she hit a mine on the way to Riga near Dago Island. Calypso ran over some rocks and had to return to Rosyth for *prepairs* to her propellers.

January 9th the 6th LCS and destroyers returned home, arriving at Portsmouth on 12th January; Cardiff and Caradoc docking and refitting at Portsmouth, Ceres at Devonport and Calypso at Chatham."

Someone had copied "The Great Surrender" out too. It looked like Frank's handwriting.

"The surrender of 150 German submarines at Harwich, beginning on 20th November, and of 74 surface warships in the Firth of Forth on 21st November will be remembered for all time as the most striking symbol of Germany's utter failure to attain that World Power for which she really undertook the Great War in August, 1914.

The British Fleet was the one force that stood between Germany and world domination, and in order to achieve Weltmacht she designed her own Fleet and started the war; but her ideas were those of a land power, and Sea Power destroyed her. Not only did the British Fleet prevent food getting in to Germany, but it prevented the Germans from getting into this Country, and formed a great screen behind which we could raise a huge land force to meet her on her own element. A Navy works slowly, like an acid, and the action of our fleet ate away the last resistance of Germany, for while her landsmen kept on fighting to the last, even when they knew they were fighting a losing game, the seamen became keenly conscious of the utter inequality of any contest at sea and openly mutinied in October. Their collapse involved the destruction of the whole programme on land; hence the Great Surrender.

The failure of Germany consists, however, less in the disgrace of declining to fight at sea than in the loss of national reputation involved by the atrocious methods adopted by her unrestricted submarine campaign. These were so outrageous that they arrayed the whole World against her, and will brand her for all time with a mark of the beast. That is the Price of Piracy.

The surrender of the German Fleet has secured the freedom of the seas for such as pass thereon upon their lawful occasions, and is a testimony to the value of sea power, which the people of the British Empire will forget at their peril.

Admiral David Beatty".

Jim read through the book Mo had procured for him. It did not take him long as most of it comprised photographs of German ships and submarines, British ships of the Grand Fleet, Admiral Beatty, His Majesty King George V and other members of the Royal Family. He pondered for some time on the Admiral's remarks about the value of Sea Power. Jim felt glad that he had enlisted in the Royal Navy himself. It was true that he had gone through some grim experiences but at least the war was over and the hazardous North Atlantic and North Sea patrols. He was pleased that he had kept the Log and other records and thought that one day he might show them to Uncle Jack if ever he could bring himself to return to Diss.

The crew had a fair amount of time on shore while Caradoc was laying in number thirteen dock at Portsmouth refitting. Much of the time was spent in drinking and going to dances. On board, the crew sometimes played cards during their off-duty periods, or wrote letters home or to their girl friends. Most of the time Jim enjoyed the company of his shipmates but sometimes he liked to be alone. Such times for him were essential so that, alone with his own thoughts, he could reflect on his experiences and try to see where he fitted into the Great Divine Plan. His early life had been unusual having no mother and losing his sister's companionship. He often thought about Vi, what she was doing, where she was, what she looked like. Although his earlier ideas on religion were going through some form of change he believed in God. Often when ashore he would slip into a church and in its peace and silence attempt to recapture something of the impact and reverence relating to his earlier experiences at St.Mary's. On one such occasion he sat down in a church beneath a stained glass window and when the wintry sun emerged from behind the clouds its rays shone through the stained glass onto him. The pale golden light touched him delicately, almost like he was being given a gentle baptism of his own. He wrote in his notes: "Peace is silver; silence is Golden".

Rumours about a return to action against the Bolsheviks were circulating on board. There was an air of excitement into which Jim found himself caught up. He wondered about himself and his reactions. He asked himself how it was that at times he could be at peace with himself and his Maker, and at other times be swept along enthusiastically in the excitement of a return to sea, action, and the guns.

Chapter Seven

It was not until March 4th that Caradoc with her full crew aboard pulled out of dry dock and tied up to the slip jetty. Four days later she left Portsmouth for engine trials after which she anchored at Spithead. She was joined by HMS Cardiff on March 10th and the two ships moved out into the English Channel en route for Malta.

Little John was singing a little ditty aloud to the tune of the National Anthem, which made Jim smile.

"We're on the move again
Soon we'll be nearing Spain.
We're on the move!"

The winds were strong and heavy swells were encountered in the Channel, which became worse as they entered the Bay of Biscay. John was still singing, making up the words as they carried on through the Bay.

"It's bloody rough today,
We've really earned our pay.
At least it's not raining o'er us!
We're on the move!"

"Pipe down! You've got a voice like a bloodshot foghorn!" shouted Don.

On March 13th they passed Cape St. Vincent at 9.00 am and at 7.00 pm that evening were passing Gibraltar.

"There she is!" Mo said. "The rock itself. Solid as ever."

Jim thought that Mo was not unlike the rock. Steady and reliable, perhaps at times, pretty solid!

Later they sailed past Algiers. A few French warships were anchored there. The weather had become very much warmer and the ship moved across calm seas. It was pleasant to feel the sun's warmth and the crew were in high spirits.

At 2.00pm the following day HMS Centaur joined them. The

three ships were travelling in column, HMS Cardiff in the lead with Caradoc behind and HMS Centaur bringing up the rear.

Although the weather remained warm and sunny the ships encountered heavy swells in the early hours of March 15th as they passed the island of Sardinia. However, by the afternoon the sea became calmer. The rest of the journey was uneventful and at 8.15 am on March 16th they arrived at Malta.

Whilst laying at Malta in beautiful warm sunshine they received orders to provide a firing party to take part in the burial of the late Admiral Lyons, RN; consignments of men would be taken from all of the ships. That meant a lot of activity cleaning up their uniforms, blancoing webbing, and general spit-and-polish for a smart turnout. Jim was selected to be one of the firing party. The funeral procession of the late Admiral on 18th March comprised two hundred and fifty seamen who made up the firing party and some two thousand mourners. The procession moved at slow march following the Admiral's coffin that was mounted on a gun carriage. The sun shone down with intense heat on the procession and Jim could feel the perspiration running down his face.

On 23rd March HM Destroyer, Steadfast arrived at Malta with General Allenby. The General was transferred to HMS Caradoc, which was ordered to take the General to Alexandria, Egypt. With such an important passenger the discipline was tightened and there was very little merriment aboard for the two days of the trip. Jim felt a sense of relief when, at 11.30am on 25th March, General Allenby left the ship at Alexandria. Caradoc was then ordered to proceed to Constantinople, Turkey.

They put in at Mudros at 9.00 am the next day but remained there for only a half hour entering the Dardanelles at 10.30am and arriving at Constantinople at 4.00pm.

They remained there exactly a week but it gave Jim the opportunity of buying some postcards and taking a few photographs. He had obtained an enormous album to house his growing collection of postcards, and photographs of the ships and the crew. Caradoc now had two pet cats, which the crew had named Tom and Mia. Tom and Mia came in for a lot of fuss and frequently followed the crew members into the Mess where they were treated to tit-bits from the men's plates. The two cats were white and tabby in about equal amounts of these shades, their fur was thick and quite long. At one time it was thought that they would make good ratters and they did, in fact, help to keep the rat population down but they rapidly rose from the rank of ratters to that of the ship's mascots. As Jim was mounting some photographs in the album, Doug Braun joined him. Doug ran his fingers through his brown hair combing it back over his head and out of his small widely spaced eyes. Doug had a prominent almost Semitic nose and a wide mouth, which broke into a broad grin as he leaned forward to see what Jim was doing.

"Remember that day, Jim?" he asked, pointing to a snapshot of a group of the lads, including Jim, holding a placard indicating them as the winners of the Whaler competition in the Squadron Regatta, 1918.

"Don't I just!" answered Jim. "The lads certainly gave us a toasting afterwards."

"I guess so. They had backed a fair bit of their pay on you winning!"

"Well, I didn't see any of it," Jim said. "Still, we had a lot of fun and the exercise did us good!"

"Some said that the Captain was cheering louder than some of the crew when you came in first. He's quite a good sport, the Captain."

The two men went through the album together enjoying the memories brought back by the photographs and postcards.

Caradoc left Constantinople on April 2nd bound for Odessa. As she crossed the Black Sea the weather became colder. She arrived at Odessa the following day. There was great consternation there as rumours were circulating that the Bolshevik army was advancing rapidly and would be at the outskirts of the town within the next twenty-four hours. Large concentrations of refugees gathered at the harbour, hoping to get aboard the ships to escape the invading army. The men on Caradoc could hear the sound of gunfire as the Bolshevik army reached the outskirts of Odessa. The gunfire increased in volume and intensity; the enemy had entered the town and were advancing rapidly towards the harbour area. The ships began taking the refugees aboard as rapidly as possible.

The following day the harbour itself came under fire. The scene that Jim witnessed was one of chaos and fear. Men were jumping into the harbour and swimming out to the boats. Those who evidently could not swim rushed about in all directions trying to find anything that could float in their attempt to escape. As shells began exploding in the harbour the French Admiral aboard his Flagship ordered all ships to get clear of the harbour immediately. Jim watched the Russian refugees leaving in a variety of boats. The British and French ships moved out of the range of the Bolshevik guns and dropped anchor. Caradoc remained there until April 9th giving protection to the escaping refugee boats that were setting sail for Constantinople and Corsia, South Russia, where the Bolshevik army had not penetrated. Caradoc was ordered to proceed to Yalta where she arrived the following day. She anchored there until 16th April and the scene was similar to Odessa—the Bolsheviks entered the outskirts of the town on 13th April and the following day red flags were hoisted all over the town. Again Caradoc weighed anchor and left, that time heading for Novorossijk where she arrived at 6.30 in the evening of 16th April.

Novorossiijk was still occupied by the Volunteer Army so the refugees Caradoc had taken aboard were disembarked there.

"Poor devils!" Wiggy Bennett said with emotion. The crew were glad of a couple of days break from the misery that they had witnessed at Odessa and Yalta. Caradoc was ordered to proceed to Feodosia at 4.00am on 18th April and arrived there at nine o'clock in the evening. The Bolsheviks had already reached the outskirts of the town by then so Caradoc shifted anchorage to Kaffa Bay. The signal came through "Stand by, ready for action". The town of Vladislovska was under occupation by the Bolsheviks and a heavy concentration of troops and guns were centred there. The enemy had at that time been placing shore batteries in position. Captain Munro Kerr waited until 22nd April before he ordered Caradoc's gunners to open fire. The gun crews loosed fifty rounds that day. The bombardment continued the next day and the crews were kept on twenty-four hour alert. On 23rd April the gun crews were ordered to commence bombardment at 4.30 am and fired one hundred rounds "for breakfast!"

The early morning shelling was resumed later in the morning and was continued throughout the rest of the day and well into the evening.

On 24th April a large white flag was hoisted in the harbour and a Bolshevik delegation set out in a small boat, also carrying a white flag, towards the Caradoc. As their boat came alongside several Bolshevik officers asked to be taken aboard to discuss peace terms with the Captain. The crew of the Caradoc began relieving them of their revolvers and other arms as they came aboard.

One of the Russians spoke passable English and acted as interpreter for the others. There was some sort of heated discussion between them and the interpreter explained that the officers wished to retain their revolvers and were prepared to give their assurance to the Captain that the guns would be kept holstered throughout their discussions with him.

"Tell them that they either hand the guns over this minute," snapped Lieutenant Fisher, "or they can get back in their boat and push off back to the harbour!"

The interpreter translated the lieutenant's message to his comrades.

There was another discussion between the Russian officers and then one by one they disarmed and placed their guns on the Caradoc's deck.

The interpreter spoke to Lieutenant Fisher again.

"May we please have your assurance that our arms will be released when our discussions with your Captain have been concluded?"

Lieutenant Fisher gave the assurance. The Russians were then escorted to the Captain's cabin where the interpreter and two of the Senior Russians were admitted while the remaining three were asked to wait outside in the company of several of HMS Caradoc's Dreadnoughts.

Dreadnought Morris was a friend of Jim's and told him later that the peace terms were totally unacceptable to Captain Munro Kerr. Morris said that he heard voices raised in anger coming from the Captain's cabin and he heard the Captain say "Nothing doing!" Shortly after that the Russians left the Captain's cabin and by the look on their faces they were most displeased. They were escorted back to the point where they had come aboard and were directed to get back in their boat. One of the Russians made a move to pick up his revolver from the deck but found himself looking down the barrel of a rifle in the firm grip of one of the Dreadnoughts.

Again angry discussions broke out amongst the Russians who were pointing their fingers towards their revolvers and obviously were demanding the return of their weapons.

Captain Munro Kerr had by then joined Lieutenant Fisher and several other officers.

The interpreter spoke to the Captain.

"We were given an assurance that our guns would be released!"

The Captain turned to Lieutenant Fisher.

"Is that so, Lieutenant?"

"Yes, sir!"

"Did you actually say *released* or returned, Lieutenant?"

"I said released, sir."

The Captain kept a straight face. He then turned to some of the crew who were standing near by. Jim was one of them.

"Give me a hand with these!" he ordered them as he picked up one of the revolvers and proceeded to carry it to the side whereupon he released his hold of the weapon and it splashed into the sea. The crew readily followed his example.

The Russians in a filthy mood were helped on their way as they scampered over the side to return to their boat. As it moved away the Caradoc's crew enjoyed a good laugh together.

To give him his due, the Captain allowed the Russian boat to get safely back to harbour before he ordered his gun crews to recommence firing. They continued the bombardment all that day and the following day too. On 26th April HMS Iron Duke arrived and fired a few salvoes from her 15inch guns to assist Caradoc in the bombardment. She remained with assisting Caradoc until the forenoon of 27th April. After she had gone Caradoc still carried on firing.

Jim was rated as Ordinary Seaman on his eighteenth birthday on 28th April. As the gun crews were occupied throughout the day in their bombardment Jim was spared the eighteen bumps he would otherwise have received from his shipmates.

On 29th April HMS Centaur joined the Caradoc and commenced firing on the Bolshevik positions. Jim wondered what it must have been like on the receiving end of the combined bombardment from the two ships. The next day HMS Emperor of India arrived to join in and she was equipped with 13.5 inch and 6 inch guns. Lieutenant Douglas Fisher, Caradoc's Gunnery Officer directed the firing of all three ships throughout the days and nights of 30th April, 1st May, 2nd May and 3rd May when Caradoc's ammunition ran out. Whereupon Lieutenant Fisher handed over to HMS Centaur's Gunnery Officer and Caradoc left Kaffa Bay for Malta to reprovision.

Caradoc arrived at Constantinople on 5th May and proceeded to Malta where she anchored two days later, in the Grand Harbour. She went alongside Dockyard jetty for refit on 9th May and the crew were given a forty-eight hour leave ashore. As Jim's birthday had been spent in action he decided to have a celebration ashore with the other members of the crew. They thoroughly enjoyed themselves looking around for bars and other entertainment. They discovered a photographic studio and everyone decided to have their photographs taken much to the photographer's delight. Jim also found a tattoo shop and as he had by then knocked back quite a few drinks had some tattoos done on his forearms. Several of his friends thought it a good idea and several even had some done on their backs and torsos.

They showed each other the tattooist's artwork.

"You haven't had Dolly's name put on your arm," observed Wiggy.

Jim smiled to himself. Unlike several of his shipmates he had confined his tattoos to an anchor on each arm. In spite of the booze he was not so irrational as to brand himself with any female's name. He had no intention of ever doing so especially at eighteen!

In one of the bars they met some soldiers from the Island's Garrison. They were a lively crowd too. One of the men photographed the Caradoc coming into Malta Harbour and Jim persuaded him to part with the photograph in exchange for a double whisky, the soldier being Scottish!

They all went to a dance that first evening ashore. Sitting at one of the tables on one side of the dance floor was a Maltese woman with jet-black hair, dark eyes and a most attractive face. She sat alone and Jim went over to her and asked her if she would dance with him. She was two or three inches shorter than him, Jim noticed, as the young woman stood up and permitted him to lead her onto the dance floor.

She had a very attractive figure too which was accentuated by the white dress she was wearing. As they danced Jim was aware of the faint but unmistakable aroma of the perfume she was wearing; it reminded him of the scent of roses on a summer's evening. As they danced together she told him that her name was Beaty.

They danced several more times together and between dances sat at the table and talked. He introduced her to Wiggy, Frank, Bert and his other friends. Wiggy sat with them for a little while but seeing that Jim wanted to be alone with the girl he took the hint and moved off to join the others.

"See you later, Jim!" he called out as he walked away from the table. "Enjoy your birthday!"

"Is it your birthday, Jim?" she asked. "Is that why you and your friends are celebrating?"

He confessed that it was not his birthday *that* day but as his ship had been in action in the Black Sea on 28th April he was having a somewhat belated celebration.

After the dance was over he escorted her home and arranged to call to see her the next day.

The following morning Jim called for her as arranged. Beaty's parents were a couple in their fifties. Her father was short, of medium build and his hair was receding. Her mother was of stockier build than Beaty and her hair was greying but the shape of her face and the set and colour of her eyes were very similar to Beaty's. The couple seemed to accept Jim as if he were an old friend of the family and he found them easy to talk to and felt very relaxed in their company. He spent the morning and afternoon with Beaty going shopping and sight-seeing. He liked Malta very much, he decided, the weather was excellent, the people friendly and there were so many interesting things to see and do on the island. He procured for himself a seaman's trunk in one of the shops near the Harbour. It was exactly what he needed to house all his souvenirs and other personal things. The trunk had a fitting so that it could be secured by a padlock but as the padlock was missing he and Beaty hunted around the shops until they found a shop that sold knives, scissors and an assortment of other things and he was able to buy a padlock with two keys. He had left the trunk at the shop, arranging to pick it up later as it was bulky and heavy even when empty.

Beaty was a delightful companion and when it was time for him to leave her to rejoin Caradoc he felt that they had established a sort of understanding, that she was his girl friend and he, her boy friend. He collected the trunk and rejoined the ship. His shipmates were returning to the ship in groups. When they saw Jim climbing aboard with the trunk balanced on one shoulder he was greeted with cries of "Yo,ho,ho" and "Pieces of eight" and other such remarks. One sailor asked him if he was bringing his girl friend aboard in the trunk. Jim took all of it in good humour. He was by then, of course, well initiated into the Caradoc's brand of humour.

Caradoc remained alongside the Dockyard refitting and provisioning another fortnight during which time the crew were employed in painting the ship and generally preparing her for sea. On May 16th Jim and ninety-nine others of the ship's crew were selected to form a firing party at the funeral of the late Commander Tinsley, RN. The day was extremely hot, identical to that day two months earlier when the late Admiral Lyons had been buried.

With all preparations completed with the exception of ammunitioning, Caradoc left the jetty at 7.15 am on May 25th and tied up to a Buoy in the Grand Harbour and hauled the ammunition Lighters alongside. The ammunition was loaded on board the following day and as it was Queen Mary's birthday the ship was dressed overall and a 21-gun salute was fired. At 7.00am the next day Caradoc left Malta for Constantinople passing through the Dardenelles. She arrived at Constantinople at 5.00 pm on May 29th, remaining there for five days during which time the ship was dressed overall and 21-gun salutes were fired to salute the commemoration of Italian Independence day on June 1st and His Majesty King George V's birthday on June 3rd. Major General Holman and

Captain Freemantle, RN, were taken aboard ship on June 4th and the mail for the Black Sea fleet was loaded aboard too. Caradoc left Constantinople for Novorossiijk where Major General Holman and Captain Freemantle disembarked. Having transferred the Black Sea mail to HMS Destroyer Tumult, Caradoc was ordered to return to Constantinople. When the Caradoc anchored at Constantinople there was a heavy swell and the ship nearly swung onto HMS Iron Duke's bows. The Captain ordered the crew to shift anchorage.

The reason for Caradoc's return to Constantinople was made clear to the crew; she was to have an engine fitted for a Kite Balloon before proceeding on action duties in the Black Sea. Caradoc went up the Golden Horn stern to wall, a somewhat difficult and hazardous manoeuvre for her crew. In the early afternoon of June 7th fire broke out in the After Engine Room and the crew were ordered to Fire Stations. Jim and the gun crews were ordered to douse the Aft Magazines, an unenviable job as the Magazines were fully loaded and could easily have exploded from the heat. Eventually the engine room fire was brought under control but not before both it and the Aft Magazine had been flooded. Jim and his shipmates were forced to stand waist deep in water working with hand pumps for an hour and a half before submergible pumps were fitted up and a further eight hours, until mid-night working with those.

Cold, wet and exhausted the men climbed into their hammocks.

The following morning and afternoon was occupied in removing the defective ammunition and the careful checking of the containers that were above water level to ensure that they were all right. Two days were then spent ashore drilling with small arms!

All hands were called at 3.30am on June 11th and Caradoc left the dockyard an hour later, destination Feodosia. Jim was glad to be back at sea. The return to Constantinople had been one of those times when it seemed as if a jinx had been on the Caradoc, he reflected. First there had been the near collision with HMS Iron Duke, then the hazardous stern to wall trip up the Golden Horn, followed by the fire.

A thunderstorm broke out as the Caradoc reached Kaffa Bay. HMS Marlborough's Kite Balloon was struck by lightning, caught fire and came down in the sea. When the storm had finally abated a few rounds were fired at some Bolshevik garrisons and later HM Sloop, Dianthus arrived with a new Kite Balloon for the Marlborough and some bottles of gas for the Caradoc's own balloon. On June 19th all hands were called at 3.10am and the gun crews went to action stations at 3.30am. The Volunteer Army was mounting a counter offensive against the Bolsheviks on the entire front and all ships, north and south, were ordered to give the Volunteer Army support. Caradoc shelled Bolshevik positions at Koi-Asan in the south while Calypso tackled similar positions to the north. HMS Marlborough was assigned to shelling Bolshevik trenches from Koi-Asan to Zarkof and having wrought some havoc with these weighed anchor and steamed two miles westward, where a heavy concentration of Bolsheviks had taken up position, shelling the moving troops the whole two miles of her route. Anchoring off the village of Kot she let fire with both high explosive and shrapnel shells. The Russian Cruiser Kagoul landed troops of the Volunteer Army to the south of Feodosia under the support of HM Destroyer Seraph. A further party of troops, supported by Calypso and HM Destroyer Montrose, were landed on the shores of the Sea of Azov. Russian motor launches were physically hauled across the sands and refloated in the Sar-Hai. The Volunteer Army advanced some ten to fifteen miles during that day, reaching their objectives with their new lines running roughly north to south and consolidated about six miles west of Vladislavoka, which was reported to be on fire with two other villages nearby.

Caradoc continued her bombardment throughout the day and the night. By the afternoon of the second day she was running low in ammunition. Arrangements were made for ammunition to be taken aboard from other ships and she was then ordered to patrol the coast and shell any Bolshevik troop movements in the hills. The Volunteer Army had held the line gained and were preparing for further advances along the whole front. A huge pall of smoke hung above Vladislavoka where fires were still raging and continued to burn for days. HMS Marlborough had been ordered to withdraw and Caradoc went alongside her to take her Kite Balloon and spare parts. During this operation Calypso appeared in sight having come round from the Sea of Azov and was cheered loudly by Caradoc's crew. The Store Ship Dago went alongside the Caradoc and then the Calypso, with oil and provisions. The crew of Caradoc were busily engaged in familiarising themselves with the Kite Balloons—and "had a lovely time" as Jim put it in his Log.

Apart from carrying Russian Officers from one area of activity to another and occasionally opening fire on Bolsheviks lurking in the hills there was no major action for the Caradoc. The Captain even allowed small groups to go ashore in the small boats for recreation. On June 23rd the British ships held a sailing regatta but the boats had to be called in when a heavy thunderstorm broke out. Things were very quiet on the battlefront and the Captain told the crew that they could pack up keeping watches at the guns.

On June 29th the Captain called the crew together and read over a message from Rear Admiral Sinclair congratulating the 6th LCS on its gunnery efficiency and thanking all the men and ships taking part in the operations against Bolshevism. The Captain announced that news of peace being signed had been received and with that announcement he ended by saying "Splice the Mainbrace!"

That was one order the crew needed no second briefing to execute!

Caradoc moved into harbour. The weather was extremely hot and the crews of the ships held swimming races, water polo matches and sailing regattas. It was all good fun, more like a holiday than a war as Frank Butler put it!

On July 3rd the Emperor of India and HMS Heliotrope arrived, the latter going alongside Caradoc and landing supplies. The Caradoc had received orders to proceed to Yalta. She got under weigh at 3.00pm arriving at Yalta four hours later. For the first time in four months the crew were given shore leave in turn but had to report back by 9.00pm each night. Those whose turn it was to remain aboard carried out General drill—"out stream anchor, and away all boats' crews" or helped unload stores from store ships which came alongside. Sometimes those operations could be extremely tricky whenever there were heavy swells. Jim went on shore leave with his mates but there was not much to do ashore except wander around the town and he had no taste for vodka. He preferred spending time on deck watching the arrival and departure of ships and taking photographs of them. HMS Montrose arrived and Spear left. A French sloop came alongside for oil. Small Russian ships, many of them under sail, scurried about the harbour. He had been on deck so much in the hot sun that he had quite a tan, he noticed.

On July 17th Caradoc left harbour and went alongside a tanker to take on oil. HM Destroyer Seraph joined them. The two ships had received orders to proceed to Sevastopal. At Sevastopal the Russian fleet was in harbour, if "fleet" was the correct term to describe the motley assortment of ships loyal to the Volunteer cause. HM Destroyer Montrose was in harbour but left the following day when HMS Engadine arrived.

"Hey!" Mo called out to the gun crews, "Look at her! She's an aeroplane ship."

On 20th July all the Seamen were landed ashore at 4.30am for rifle drill.

"Might as well have joined the bloody army," Wiggy complained.

The drill continued daily much to the dismay of the crew.

"All this has got to have a reason," Bert Featherstone told Jim.

On 23rd July it became clear what the reason was. HM Destroyer Spear arrived with a Russian General aboard who wished an interview with Captain Munro Kerr. The General was welcomed aboard Caradoc by the officers while the Crew presented arms. The General was then taken to the Captain's cabin for discussions. HM Destroyer Montrose with Monitor 22 in tow, HM Destroyer Sportive with Monitor 18 in tow, a French Sloop, a French Destroyer, HM Sloop Dianthus and HMS Emperor of India with a Destroyer escort all arrived in harbour. The Dianthus had arrived with yet another Kite Balloon for the Caradoc but it was defective and was refused. HMS Emperor of India was filled with Russian soldiers who had been repatriated from German Prisoner of War Camps.

The Russian General on board Caradoc turned out to be the Commander-in-Chief of the Crimean Volunteer Army. The Captain gave orders for Caradoc to get under weigh for Tendra Bay where she anchored off Ockachov at 7.30pm on 25th July. HMS Engadine was laying at anchor across the Bay. In the late afternoon Caradoc was ordered to proceed to Sevastopal but on the way she encountered a Russian Yacht and boarded her to check her out but she was not carrying any Bolsheviks. The Caradoc arrived at Sevastopal at 7.30am with HMS Engadine and HM Destroyer Sportive towing Monitor 18, following them in. Shortly afterwards HM Destroyers Seraph and Swallow arrived. Sevastopol was not their ultimate destination, however, and the ships got underweigh for Yalta.

At Yalta the Russian Commander-in-Chief presented the men of the gun crews with medals, decorations of high honour, for the invaluable services rendered to the Volunteer Army. A concert, given by a Russian Party from shore to the men on board the Caradoc was followed by Liberty leave being extended to 10.00pm! The Russian General transferred to HM Destroyer Spear, which then left Yalta Harbour.

On 2nd August word was received that Russian ships were lying further up near Tendra Bay and that the Bolsheviks were preparing to launch new attacks. On the way to Tendra Bay Caradoc came under fire from Bolshevik shore batteries. Splinters from shrapnel shells hit the after-deck. Caradoc's gunners returned the fire sending over two hundred rounds. The batteries became silent. HMS Engadine with an escort of destroyers arrived shortly afterwards. Seaplanes from the Engadine went up and began scouting over the enemy positions on shore. HMS Swallow with Monitor 22 arrived during the afternoon and fired a few rounds from its six-inch guns.

The ships continued spasmodic bombardment of the shore positions, the seaplanes from Engadine giving locations and range for accurate shelling of the batteries and heavier troop concentrations. These operations continued until the evening of August 4th when Caradoc was ordered to proceed to Sevastopal and Yalta.

Jim wrote in his Log "August 4th—it is now five years ago since we went to war with Germany ... and we're still at it!"

The stop at Sevastopal was purely for the purposes of oiling and provisioning the ship and when that had been completed Caradoc had to proceed to Yalta where she patrolled with HM Destroyer Montrose for a week. On 12th August at 4.00am there was a sudden call out and Caradoc was ordered to Tendra Bay. The Bolshevik batteries had secured breach-blocks for their six-inch guns and were recommencing bombardments. Caradoc's orders were to destroy them. Steaming down the coastline the ship suddenly ran into heavy fire from shore batteries and returned the fire putting one of the enemy guns out of action and hitting an ammunition dump.

"Like Guy Fawkes night!" John Murray shouted trying to make his voice heard above the sound of the guns.

Then the remaining Bolshevik guns all opened fire at once having calculated the range accurately. Up to then shells had been screaming overhead but with the range set the next three shells struck Caradoc, one carrying away the top of the sounding boom, another going clean through the After Funnel and the third hitting the midship Gun Platform. Miraculously no one was injured and Caradoc steamed out of range maintaining her own fire from her six-inch guns until the early hours of the morning. A Russian ship carrying the flag of the Bolsheviks nosed around to see what success the shore batteries had accomplished and Caradoc opened fire on her whereupon she steamed away.

HM Destroyer Montrose and the Engadine arrived in the afternoon and seaplanes again went out to scout and report on the positions of the shore batteries.

A supply ship carrying ammunition for Caradoc arrived the next day as she was again running low having kept up day and night bombardments of the shore batteries. HM Destroyers Tumult and Seraph arrived, the latter had brought not only stores but also the long awaited mail. However, there was no time to sort it out and read it because a fleet of Russian Lighters with ammunition for the Volunteer army had to be given cover until they had moved up river far enough to be out of range of the Bolshevik guns. HM Destroyer Montrose fouled her propellers with stern wire and the Caradoc's divers were sent down to clear it. More Lighters arrived and Caradoc gave them covering fire too until they had safely passed the Batteries.

On August 18th Caradoc proceeded to Sevastopal and received a request from an Italian Destroyer for oil. The Captain signalled for her to come alongside, having agreed to assist her. HM Destroyer Montrose signalled that she was proceeding to Constantinople. The Captain having helped the Italian Destroyer out of her difficulties, was concerned about Caradoc's own reserves of oil so was relieved when the tanker, Rapidol joined them. She came alongside Caradoc and reserves were replenished. The Destroyer Stuart and HM Sloop Heliotrope arrived too. The Destroyer carried orders for the Caradoc to proceed immediately to Odessa where trouble was brewing. On their way there other ships, also ordered to Odessa, joined Caradoc—HM Destroyers Stuart, Tumult, Seraph, HMS Engadine and the Empress both carrying seaplanes, and the Russian Cruiser, Kagoul. Off Cape Fontana the gun crews were ordered to action stations. Seaplanes went up from the two carriers to scout, and transport ships arrived carrying two thousand soldiers of the Volunteer Army.

One of the seaplanes developed an engine fault and dropped about two miles inland where the Bolsheviks were heavily concentrated. Jim wondered whether the pilot had survived the forced landing and if so what his fate had been at the hands of the Bolsheviks who were notorious for their atrocities.

A new Captain with a background of Gunnery experience was put aboard the Caradoc at Odessa, Captain Colvin from the Admiralty. The crew were dismayed to learn that Captain Munro Kerr had been relieved of his command. They had served under him so long and they loved and respected him. The fact that he had been appointed Consulate General and Naval Attaché to South Russia, a feather in his cap, helped the crew to accept their loss but still left them in something of a state of shock.

Captain Munro Kerr introduced his replacement to the officers and men of the Caradoc and remained aboard Caradoc with him for a further three days. The crew were occupied in battle with the Bolsheviks throughout that time but it was good to see their former captain about ship.

The Volunteer army moved on Odessa with the British ships giving them cover, shelling the Bolshevik shore batteries and troop concentrations. Some leading Bolsheviks tried to escape in sailing ships but HM Destroyer Tumult captured them. Caradoc opened fire on the railway lines that were being used to take ammunition and supplies to the Bolshevik troops. Her fire was so effective that the tracks were destroyed beyond any hope of repair. A signal was taken on Caradoc "Good Firing! Fall of Odessa to Volunteer Army imminent."

On 24th August at 5.00am Caradoc recommenced bombardment,. concentrating her firepower on further sections of the railway, leaving the Russian Cruiser to deal with the shore batteries. An ammunition train had stopped further back along the line and the Bolsheviks were attempting to unload it and shift the desperately needed ammunition by road transport. While HM Destroyer Tumult fetched in two more Bolshevik sailing ships, Caradoc succeeded in hitting the ammunition train. The next day HM Destroyer Seraph left at 5.00am. The Volunteer army was on the outskirts of Odessa. Caradoc shifted anchorage nearer the harbour and the Destroyers went into the harbour itself when the reports came through that Odessa had been taken and the Bolsheviks, badly cut up, were retreating fast. Caradoc received orders to open fire on an armoured train, which was transporting the Bolsheviks away from Odessa, scoring another hit. With the whole town in the hands of the Volunteer Army Captain Munro Kerr left HMS Caradoc to take up his appointment.

"Many a tear were shed unashamedly as he went," Jim said.

"Amen!" said Mo, wiping the back of his hand across his own eyes.

Some of the ships were transporting the wounded from the harbour. One of the Destroyers had sick and wounded Ratings aboard and left for Constantinople. Caradoc had escaped any casualties and had been lucky.

On 28th August groups of men from the British ships were allowed ashore to witness the atrocities committed by the Bolsheviks. Jim described the scenes as sheer barbarity. Caradoc weighed anchor and proceeded to Sevastopal where she joined HM Destroyer Sikh and the Carrier, Ark Royal in the harbour. A boat was lowered and stores were picked up from the Princess Ena. Caradoc returned to Odessa and went inside harbour, her stern being secured to the harbour wall. General Shilling of the Volunteer Army came aboard and decorated the officers and Gun crew ratings with the Order of St. George.

"If we go on like this, Jim," Wiggy said "we'll need that damned trunk of yours just to keep the medals and decorations in!"

Jim smiled. He pulled Wiggy over to the trunk and unlocked the padlock, lifted the lid of the trunk and proceeded to remove some of the contents. In the bottom of the trunk lay a revolver displaying just above its butt the hammer and sickle.

Chapter Eight

Jim removed the revolver from the trunk so that Wiggy could examine it more closely. It was nearly new, of bluish-black colour and was heavy to hold. Beneath the hammer and sickle was the year 1919 in similar engraving.

"Where the hell did you get it?" Wiggy asked him, taking hold of the revolver that Jim held out to him.

"Do you remember when that Bolshevik delegation came aboard and we dumped their guns over the side?" Jim asked his friend.

"Yes, I do. You were one of the crew who assisted the Captain in that little operation."

"Well this particular souvenir somehow got caught up in my tunic," Jim explained. Wiggy's mouth had dropped open in surprise.

"I don't know how you managed it, Jim," he said at last. "But I've got to admire your nerve, you crafty blighter!"

"Keep this to yourself, Wiggy," Jim told him. "The fewer people who know about it, the better."

Wiggy assured him. that his secret was safe but he was still shaking his head in disbelief and repeated "I just don't know how you did it!"

He handed the revolver back to Jim who replaced it in the bottom of the trunk, covering it carefully with a cloth and replacing the other souvenirs, photographic equipment, books and other papers on top. Jim then closed the trunk and padlocked it.

The following day HM Sloop Hibiscus and HM Destroyer Stuart left and a Russian Destroyer came alongside for oil. The Russian crew waved and shouted greetings to Caradoc's crew. None of them knew any English but they were obviously very friendly and the Caradoc's crew waved back and gave thumbs up signs.

The Russian Destroyer left the next day when a Russian Cruiser arrived in harbour. She had received orders to join other ships in action further up the coast. Shortly after her departure the Store Ship Astoria came alongside Caradoc to take aboard empty cordite cases and Jim had to help carry the cases. Caradoc remained in the harbour for two more days and Jim watched HM Destroyer Sikh arrive and depart, followed by HM Destroyer Montrose bound for Malta. Strong winds had blown up and extra stern wires were needed. On September 4th they let go stern wires and got underweigh, anchoring outside the harbour at 5.30 am. HMS Emperor of India brought stores for the Caradoc. The crew were told to put all clocks on one hour. At 11.00am the next day HMS Tumult arrived carrying Rear Admiral Seymour, RN, who was piped aboard Caradoc. The Rear Admiral was to be taken to Nickoliev. Caradoc up-anchored and left at 12.30, reaching the River Bug at 3.30 that afternoon where she had the misfortune to run over a submerged wreck, losing her P.V chains in the process. She anchored off Nickoliev at 4.00pm, where the Rear Admiral left her. His negotiations in Nickoliev were expected to last several hours and arrangements had been made for HMS Emperor of India to pick him up the next day. Caradoc was ordered to return to Odessa and passed over the submerged wreck cautiously. HM Destroyer Steadfast came up, and learning that the Caradoc had been fouled by the wreck, offered to send her divers down to examine the screws. The divers reported that no damage had been done.

On September 7th HMS Emperor of India left with the Rear-Admiral aboard. Caradoc was experiencing some difficulty in maintaining a proper course so the Captain ordered her own divers to go down to carry out a thorough examination. A length of rusty chain that the Caradoc's divers were able to remove had fouled the rudder.

Lieutenant Douglas Fisher, the Gunnery Officer was delegated by Captain Colvin to make an address on his behalf to the crew. Evidently, the new Captain selected the lieutenant because of his long service with the Caradoc, preferring to keep a low profile himself.

"Captain Colvin has asked me to convey the commendations of Rear-Admiral Seymour to all the officers and men of HMS Caradoc for the exceptional smartness and cleanliness of the ship and her men. Well done, and thank you all!"

The next few days were spent in painting the ship to maintain its smart appearance. The crew did not seem to mind so much knowing that the ship had impressed the Rear-Admiral! As they worked, they saw HM Destroyer Stuart come alongside for oil and then depart in company with the Russian Cruiser. HM Sloop Heliotrope came alongside with stores and the Russian Destroyer arrived, its crew lining the deck and waving to the Caradoc's crew again. The Oiler Rapidol came alongside and White Watch "coaled 11 tonnes of oil". As the Oiler left, HM Sloop Dianthus came alongside with more stores for Caradoc.

On September 14th the Ship's company mustered by the ledger and Captain Colvin made his maiden speech. It was short and to the point.

"As your new Captain I would like to say that I have taken over a smart ship and a clean one and I am impressed by the smartness and cleanliness of you, her crew." He paused, then added "Let's keep it that way!"

Later, when the gun crews met together, they discussed the new Captain's speech. The consensus of opinion was that the Captain had come to them from the Admiralty and was a disciplinarian. It remained to be seen what he would be like in action. He would, most of them thought, be hard pressed to come up to the standard Captain Munro Kerr had attained in the eyes of the crew.

The following day brought general drill—"out Bower Anchor!" "Weigh by hand!" "Away all boats' crews!" "Cutters to boat drill by signal!"

News was received of an Independent Army advancing into the town, looting and massacring as they advanced. That army was fighting against both the Bolsheviks and the Volunteer Army to set up their own government for South Russia. HM Destroyers Tumult and Stuart were sent for to deal with the new threat. The two destroyers arrived the following day with the Chilkat. Chilkat came alongside and that time it was Blue Watch who coaled the ship with 11 tonnes of oil.

Meanwhile general drill continued aboard Caradoc. "Prepare to tow aft!" "Out collision mat, away all boats' crews!"

HM Sloop Dianthus arrived and left with ratings for Hospital.

The crew watched their shipmates leave. Sub Lieutenant Reice left with them.

"Hey, Jim," Don called. "Did you see that? Sub Lieutenant Reice has gone."

"Aye! Thank God!"

Shortly after the departure of the Dianthus, HMS Marlborough arrived and ten of Caradoc's ratings were invited aboard to attend her cinema. Wiggy Bennett was the only one of the gun crews who went, having won with the selection of the highest card drawn from the pack—the Ace of Clubs.

Back to drill the next day. "Small arms companies to drill on board!" "Blue Watch out stream-anchor!" General Shilling of the Volunteer Army came aboard during the afternoon. He was no doubt impressed by all the feverish activity!

"White Watch out Stream-anchor!" "General quarters!" During the afternoon whilst holding a sailing regatta, HM Destroyer Senator arrived with General Keyes and General Heyer aboard. The two generals were subsequently transferred to HM Destroyer Stuart and left the harbour. Jim, who concluded that something was up, duly noted all this activity. The Sloop Heliotrope brought additional supplies for the Caradoc. On September 20th HM Destroyer Stuart returned with a Russian General who went aboard Caradoc and later presented a cup to the ship's Captain. The cup was on behalf of the Volunteer Army and the free people of Russia to HMS Caradoc and her crew for their invaluable services rendered in the Black Sea.

It was, of course, a great honour but the crew felt that Captain Munro Kerr should have been there accepting the honour on behalf of them all.

After the presentation Caradoc was ordered to proceed immediately to Yalta where she arrived at 9.30am on September 21st in company with HM Sloop Heliotrope and HM Monitors M 22 and M 29 in tow. Caradoc tied up to a Buoy astern and the crew were assigned to painting the ship's side for the next two days. The ship's divers were sent down to reeve the P.V. chains. Able Seamen Nicklen was reported missing.

On September 24th it was back to General Drill! "Out kedge and stream anchor!" "Out collision!"

The Boys and Torpedo men had a race in the cutters, the Boys winning by fifteen seconds. A strong wind was beginning to blow and intensified during the afternoon so the Bower anchor was dropped and the stream anchor was laid out off starboard quarter to assist the buoy.

The Heliotrope with Monitors M.22 and M.29 had left for Constantinople but the Oiler Montreal arrived with additional stores. The Gunnery ratings and Torpedo ratings had a race in the cutters, the Gunnery ratings winning by eight strokes. White Watch was assigned the job of getting in the stores from the Montreal. HMS Emperor of India arrived. A big dinner party was held aft with people from shore attending.

Jim and the others of White Watch had to finish the taking on of the stores the following day; their labours had been postponed because of the celebrations on board. It was while the stores were being taken aboard that Jim noticed a body floating in the water. Several of the crew helped in getting it aboard—it was the body of the late Able Seaman Nicklen who had been missing three days. The sight of a body that had been in the water all that time was horrific. The remains were stitched up in a canvas bag and arrangements put in hand for proper burial at sea early the following day.

The service was attended not only by all the crew but also by officers of the Volunteer Army. The Volunteer Army band and HMS Emperor of India's band attended too. Shortly after the burial Caradoc slipped anchor and left for Odessa, anchoring outside the harbour early the next morning.

An Italian destroyer and HM Destroyer Stuart were already at anchor there. Were the crew of Caradoc going into action at last? Jim asked himself. It seemed so long ago yet it was only a month previous that the Caradoc's Gunners were bombarding the Bolshevik batteries.

He told himself that he ought to be grateful for the break but he could not still the restlessness he felt within himself. Surely the constant drills were in preparation for something?

"Control parties to drill!" "Gun crews to loader drill!" Jim worked with the other gun crew party getting up the sub-calibres for the six-inch guns, furling all awnings, preparing for sub-calibre firing and torpedo running. The Italian and British Destroyers left, their place being taken by a French Destroyer. Caradoc got underweigh to run torpedoes and fire the sub-calibres. These exercises lasted several days. During that time the French Destroyer left and another Italian one arrived.

"What the hell is going on?" Wiggy asked when the men were ordered to clean all equipment, polish brasses and drill on the decks with rifles.

On October 5th Caradoc reported to Sevastopal where she tied up to a buoy. The Russian fleet was in harbour. The next day a Russian Yacht arrived under the escort of HM Destroyers Shark and Senator; she was carrying General Deniken aboard. The Caradoc fired a nineteen-gun salute. The General went aboard one of the Russian submarines to watch another submarine doing diving tactics. He then came aboard Caradoc and gave his personal thanks to the assembled ship's Company for the fine work done in assisting the Volunteer Army to destroy Bolshevism. General Shilling and his guards were also taken aboard and Caradoc proceeded to Odessa.

At Odessa the Generals with their guards and a special guard of honour of fifty picked men from Caradoc, one of whom was Jim, went ashore. Paraded there were special contingents of Russian, French, Italian as well as the British to form a multi-national Guard of Honour to represent all who had taken part in the war against Bolshevism. General Deniken inspected them and then took the salute as they marched past. When Jim and the rest of the men who had formed the British contingent had returned to the ship Captain Colvin came to thank them personally.

"I would just like to thank you," he said. "You were the smartest Guard of Honour there today and you are a credit to our Service, our King and our Country. You men are also a credit to your ship and to yourselves and today I was glad to be one of you!"

The Captain spoke with such intensity and emotion that Jim was touched by his sincerity. Perhaps their new Captain was not so bad after all! Jim accepted that he was a disciplinarian. The question that was still unanswered, however and one that not only he but all his shipmates still needed to find an answer to was *what would he be like in action?*

The Russian cruiser departed on October 10th with General Kormilov aboard her. Rumour had it that further Bolshevik troops were massing and a flare-up of hostilities was imminent. Caradoc was ordered back to Sevastopal and arrived there on October 12th. The next day some of the crew members were put ashore in the morning for small arms firing practice. Compasses were swung in the afternoon and Caradoc was ordered to proceed at full speed to Berdyansk, Sea of Azov, to assist HM Destroyer Shark in dealing with a thirty thousand strong contingent of the Green Army who were advancing on Maripol and Tangamoy, General Deniken's Headquarters. Caradoc passed through the Kerch Straits and entered the Sea of Azov where she ran into heavy fog. HM Destroyer Shark was running low in ammunition and needed urgent relief. The fog was so thick that it hampered Caradoc's progress and she was unable to relieve the Destroyer until late morning of October 15th.

Lieutenant Fisher informed the Captain that the fog made it impossible to commence bombardment of the enemy positions with any hope of success. At 8.00 am the following day the fog lifted and Caradoc positioned just off Maripol, where she commenced bombardment on the approaches to Yalta and Urgriev, and continued it for twenty-four hours before going once more to the assistance of HM Destroyer Shark. A Destroyer was sighted on October 18, which turned out to be a Russian, the Pospeichny who was extremely low in oil. The Captain allowed her to come alongside to take on some of the Caradoc's oil.

HM Destroyer Shark also came alongside during the afternoon so that her officers could come aboard for a discussion with Captain Colvin. The Shark had been bombarding the enemy troops for several days and had been forced to ask for assistance when her ammunition ran out. The Russian Destroyer Pospeichny had come to her assistance but had run low on oil, although it seemed that she had plenty of ammunition.

Having sorted things out as best he could, the Captain ordered his ship to get underweigh for Feodosia where she anchored the following day, she was running extremely low in supplies.

At the invitation of the Volunteer Army, the Captain allowed a small shore party to land, Jim included. The town had suffered in the exchanges of fire between the Bolshevik and Volunteer Armies. Most of the men in the shore party had picked up a few Russian phrases and were thus able to exchange greetings with the soldiers and civilians they encountered. Everyone was friendly and greeted the British sailors warmly. The civilian population was quite used to seeing uniformed men about, having been under occupation from troops, Bolshevik or Volunteer, for months. One of the Russian officers spoke some English and French and explained that there had been considerable looting by the Bolsheviks during their occupation and perhaps, even more so, during their withdrawal. He told the sailors that the Bolsheviks had pillaged and raped when they occupied the town and had also slaughtered many of the civilians whom they suspected of being sympathisers to the Volunteer cause. It seemed that there had been no proper interrogations and whole families had been slaughtered on mere suspicion that they might have been sympathetic to the Volunteers. Any family who had someone who had joined the Volunteer Army had no chance. He said that some of his own men had lost families and were very embittered when they had discovered the bodies of their loved ones shot or hacked in half. The retreating Bolsheviks had set many of the houses on fire. The Officer was stationed in an area on the outskirts of the town and he introduced the British sailors to his fellow officers and men. The sailors were once again warmly received because of the part that the ships had played in support of the Volunteer Army's cause. It was evidently appreciated and the sailors were popular guests.

The troops were engaged with some civilian helpers in clearing up the aftermath of the Bolshevik retreat. They had already properly buried the dead people whose bodies had been found but there were dead animals about whose carcasses were decomposing and these had to be disposed of, an unenviable job Jim thought.

The sailors had noticed some young lambs running around. The Officer, seeing their interest in the lambs, said:

"There are many animals loose. The farms to which they belonged have been destroyed by the Bolsheviks and the people who occupied them have been killed."

Pointing to the lambs, the Russian continued, saying "Take some of the lambs back with you if you need fresh meat aboard!"

The sailors, with the help of some of the soldiers, managed to catch two of the lambs. Jim and one of the sailors held the lambs in their arms and the shore party started on its way back to the harbour. The Officer was smiling, obviously pleased that he had been able to do something for the British sailors. He escorted them back to the harbour where their small boat was tied up with two of the crew looking after it. The others climbed in and waving farewell to the Russian, rowed back to the Caradoc.

The other sailors made a lot of fuss of the two lambs and Jim took a photograph of their "captures" with Tom and Mia who had sniffed the new arrivals suspiciously. The lambs were not needed for food as HM Sloop Dianthus arrived at the time with their urgently needed supplies.

HM Destroyer Seraph also came into the harbour with a batch of deserters from the Bolshevik army who were being taken to Sevastopal for interrogation by the Volunteer Army there. Caradoc proceeded with the Seraph but had to stop as her progress seemed to be hampered in some way. The Captain ordered the men to drop anchor and then instructed the ship's divers to go down and investigate.

When they reported that the ship was really fouled up and would take several hours to get clear the Seraph was advised and she proceeded on her way alone.

The divers worked for two days before they had finally cleared the under water fittings. During that time HM Sloop Hibiscus and the Oiler Montreal came alongside with more stores and oil for the Caradoc. The divers ceased work while the Caradoc took on the oil that she needed. The Captain was obviously glad to have the oil, having run the ship's reserves low in helping out the Russian Destroyer. As soon as the stores and oil had been taken aboard and the Sloop and Oiler had pulled away, the divers returned to work.

The weather conditions were good and the sea reasonably calm so the divers were able to work unhampered. Jim thought that they had an unenviable task and not one that he would have relished.

"What was it like ashore, Jim?" Mo asked him.

"The town's been knocked around a bit, Mo," Jim replied. "In war that sort of thing is bound to happen. It was the Bolshevik atrocities that bothered me. Some whole families had been murdered by them."

Mo sadly shook his head, disturbed by what Jim had to tell him.

"Have you ever thought about what it must be like to have your home destroyed and your family slaughtered, Mo?"

Mo shook his head again.

"I guess that being English we have no real idea what it's like," he replied. "We haven't had our country invaded since the Norman conquest. We've come close to it a few times, mind you!"

"Yes, but the Navy has always been there between England and her enemies. Look what happened to the Spanish Armada!"

"You are right of course, Jim. You are pretty proud of being a sailor, aren't you?"

"It is something I wanted to do when I was a boy—my ambition!" They began talking about the problem with the underwater fittings that the ship had encountered, and which their divers were still working on.

"There must be a lot of submerged wrecks around the Azov and the Kerch Straits," Mo told Jim. "Some of them, most probably, go back to the time when the first Caradoc was here in the eighteen-forties."

Jim remembered the information in his Log about the first Caradoc. She too had been engaged in war service in the Sea of Azov and the Crimea just like their ship who bore the same name.

"I wonder how many of them the first Caradoc was responsible for," Little John said. "What a coincidence that the second Caradoc should be scrapping in the same seas!"

"Perhaps boats and ships *reincarnate*," Don chipped in. "Some reckon people do! Maybe we've all been here before on the first Caradoc and returned to the scenes of our crimes!"

"Not all of us," Mo answered him. "She carried a much smaller crew than us. Anyway, I for one don't believe in that reincarnation stuff."

"I didn't say that I did!" retorted Don, pulling a face at Mo. "You're always so damned literal."

"Do you mean literate?" Little John asked.

"I mean literal, like I said!"

The divers had finished their work but Caradoc remained at anchor. The Captain had no doubt received orders not to proceed for some reason or other. The following day a Russian Destroyer arrived with a fifty strong band aboard to entertain the officers and crew of HMS Caradoc. The cutter was used to transport the band to the Caradoc and back to their Destroyer later. It was a good band and played some popular English music as well as Russian. When they had gone the Caradoc remained at anchor.

"Something else must be in the wind," Wiggy said to Jim. "It's unlikely we stayed here just to be entertained."

He proved to be right, for HM Destroyer Seraph came alongside the next day and General Briggs was put aboard Caradoc for passage to Odessa. On arrival at Odessa the ship's Company was invited ashore to a concert.

Caradoc got underweigh for Sevastopal on October 29th but a strong wind blew up and became worse, the seas being very heavy. The second Cutter lifted clean out of her crutches and then dropped back on them at an angle, cutting two gaping holes in the keel. Sevastopal harbour was too rough to enter and anchors were dropped, and anchor watches maintained. HMS Blenheim arrived, escorting a Russian Battleship, the Alexiev, with a British Crew aboard her. The weather eased up a bit and Caradoc up-anchored and went into the harbour, followed by the Blenheim and the Alexiev ... and HM Sloop Dianthus with Caradoc's long awaited mail!

Jim had several letters to answer from his relatives and girl friends, including Beaty. It was exciting reading the letters but quite a business replying to them all!

The month of November was spent mainly in transporting Russian officers from one area to another with no more action for the Gun crew.

"We're becoming but a P and O liner!" Jim wrote in his Log that month.

There was some excitement aboard on November the fifth when a Russian Destroyer broke adrift in the strong winds and bore down on Caradoc. The general alert on board was relaxed when a tug managed to tow the Destroyer clear. Naval Chaplain Goodman joined Caradoc on November 7th and conducted a service aboard on November 11th on the upper deck, all work was stopped and the entire crew faced the Ensign aft with their caps off. The last post was sounded and then followed a minute's silence in honour of the glorious dead, it being the first anniversary of the end of the war. Lieutenant Fisher told the gun crews later that the silence had been carried out at the request of King George V. After the service an American Destroyer, the USS Dupont arrived and the crew waved to the Caradoc.

On November 21st HMS Concord, the Caradoc's relief ship arrived. The Caradoc's crew arranged a Concert Party on shore for the sailors and Russian guests. It went off well, giving the gun crews the opportunity to air their wit at a much larger audience! Some of them dressed in drag, Jim was one of them. They performed sketches, sung songs and generally enjoyed themselves.

On their way across the Black Sea they encountered some very rough weather with heavy swells, the sea boat's gripes being carried away. At Constantinople four prisoners with their escort were taken aboard for landing at Malta. Caradoc arrived at Malta at 3.30 pm with the ship's bands playing on the quarter-deck. HMS Ajax and Canada were in the Grand Harbour. The sun was shining and Jim felt good basking in its warmth. On 1st December after dressing ship for Queen Alexandra's birthday, Jim was given 48 hours shore leave and his pay! He could hardly wait to get ashore to see Beaty again.

Forty-eight hours! They passed too quickly for both Jim and Beaty. She had written to him, of course, but letters were not like being together. They drank and danced, walked and romanced. Jim summarised it in his Log as being " a *very* enjoyable time".

Leave over, the Caradoc got underweigh for Gibraltar where she arrived on December 9th and where Jim was rated "A.B" from Ordinary Seaman. The ship had been ordered to Gibraltar for extensive repairs and servicing. A and Y Guns were lifted and placed on the jetty, the other guns being lifted three days later. On 18th December the ship was taken into dry dock and all hands were employed scraping and scrubbing the ship's bottom. A few days later the Dockyard men stripped Caradoc's propeller shafts.

The crew were assigned to various work— "rigging party to lengthen Stump-mast", "party to scrape ship's bottom", "party to scrape ship's side", and then as work progressed on her and her propellers were replaced, the Dockyard men refitted the Bows and repaired the damage that the Bolshevik batteries had caused. On Christmas Day the Captain took his wife round the ship. On Boxing Day the crew put on another Concert for their shipmates and guests from Gibraltar. The Officers had a Banyan Party aboard on December 27th. After Christmas the starboard propeller was repaired and put back in position. The scraping, red leading continued, Jim being assigned to work on fixing up the Port-boom and working on the top-mast. Fumigation of the sleeping quarters and each mess was carried out, the refugees taken aboard had left a few lice behind them when they went! Then painting began—the sides, the mast, funnels, upper structures. The mainmast was refitted and wireless aerials put up. Members of the Crew who were not working on the ship were sent in turn to the rifle ranges for practice. Finally, the ship was provisioned and ammunitioned and dropped anchor in the sea after completing her steam trials.

On Saturday, 27th January Caradoc's football team played the Centaur team beating them 4 - 0, a brilliant goal being scored by one of the Caradoc's team kicking the ball backwards over his head straight into the net. The Caradoc's gun crews had equipped themselves with Rattles and Squeakers, A-Gun crew getting the rattles and Y-Gun crew the squeakers. The rivalry between the two crews seldom, if ever, ceased and they were able to compete with one another in making the most noise at the end of the match. Thereafter, the A-Gun crew earned themselves the nickname of "The Rattlers" and Y-Gun that of "The Squeakers". Oh! The mad Caradoc!

On January 31st Caradoc called at Malta to collect the Black Sea Fleet's mail but there was no shore leave for the crew and the ship proceeded to Constantinople. As Caradoc passed the Greek Archipelagos the weather was rough and when they reached Constantinople the crew were treated to snow storms! Jim was put on patrol in the town and it snowed the whole time. When he returned to the ship it took him awhile to thaw out!

Twenty hands were 'told off' for making canvas bags to put guncotton in ready for use in blowing up captured Bolshevik guns at Batoum. They made such a good job of them that the Captain went round to thank the Hands personally. Jim made a note of the other ships which arrived at Constantinople during the time he was there—HMS Cardiff, their own Flagship, HM Destroyers Stuart and Hibiscus, the Iron Duke, a Greek Battleship, an American Battleship and an American Cruiser, HMS Ceres, HMS Ajax, HM Destroyer Steadfast, the Russian Destroyer Pospeichny, the French Battleships Waldech-Rousseau and Lorraine and two French Destroyers. What a concentration of ships, he thought to himself, obviously things were hotting up again in the Black Sea.

Targets for firing practice were brought alongside and Caradoc got underweigh. Unfortunately the Port-Derrick went on the run and stove in the whaler but by the Grace of God no one was hurt. The sub-calibre firing was well on target and four torpedoes were fired and picked up later. The practice lasted three days in all and was extremely accurate.

"We haven't lost our touch," Don said. "Let's hope we are as good when we are back in action."

A French troopship, the Danube, came slowly into view. She had struck a mine in the Black Sea. Her boats had been lowered as she had been holed just on the waterline and was obviously in real trouble. Caradoc's Captain offered to tow her in and the troopship was taken into shallow water.

Instead of proceeding to action against the Bolsheviks the Caradoc received a signal to turn about and head at full speed to the Gulf of Ismid to render assistance to General Croker commanding the British Military Authority. The Turkish Military were causing trouble. All guns, including the Caradoc's Lewis guns were ready for action. HMS Cardiff, HM Destroyer Seraphis and the 1st Battle Squadron arrived too. The disturbance, which the General had anticipated, came to nothing. Jim wondered whether the sight of so many heavily armed ships had acted as a deterrent to the Turks. The Caradoc was ordered to take on board General Mills and his staff and then proceed to Batoum. HMS Calypso and HM Destroyer Spear were there when the Caradoc tied up to the jetty at Batoum. General Mills and his Staff were put ashore, the 56th Punjab regiment providing him with a Guard of Honour.

The Captain fell ill that day. The Navigator and some of the crew went out in the whaler to find the exact location of a wreck that had been something of a hazard to one of the British ships but was uncharted. Meanwhile the Caradoc's football team played the Royal Engineers team beating them 4 - 0, the Rattlers and the Squeakers having their own bit of fun!

Jim went ashore to Church on February 29th, leaving some of the gun crew in the Royal Engineer's Mess for drinks. Later he joined them for a beer or two. There was plenty of good-natured banter over the football match.

The following day a Russian ship carrying one hundred tons of explosives suffered an explosion aboard which carried away her steerage gear. The cause was a bomb exploding aft and sabotage had not been ruled out. The Russian ship was towed away from the harbour. Caradoc landed a party to dismantle guns on shore and the operation took several days to complete. Jim was assigned to Prisoner Sentry duties. The prisoners were a surly lot and had attempted to escape on two occasions. They murmured together in Russian and Jim watched them very carefully; he knew that any relaxation of vigil on his part would be taken advantage of immediately. A bearded man with a very evil countenance called out something insulting hoping to intimidate him but Jim looked him straight in the eye without flinching and eventually the man turned his head away.

During March 1920 Caradoc remained at Batoum. Friendships were struck up with the British troops there and also with the crews of American ships on duty in the Black Sea. Caradoc arranged one of its Concert Parties for the troops and the crew were invited to a dance at the YMCA the next night.

Cutter races took place between the Caradoc's crew and the crew of the USS Tatnall and for once the Caradoc "got lashed up to a wet!"

HM Destroyer Tobago brought in the long awaited mail much to the joy of the Caradoc's crew. The Captain had recovered from his sickness and general drills began again. The crews of the American ships, the USS Smith-Thomson and the USS Bridle, cheered when they watched the drills. Jim and the rest of the lads took it in good part.

"Wait until the next dance ashore," Bert Featherstone said. "Then we can get our own back on those Yanks. We'll cut them up on the dance floor!"

The drills continued: "Evolution out Bower anchor"; "all boats' crews pull round the fleet!" The second cutter did it *too* well so had the pleasure of pulling round the fleet for a week! The Marines from Caradoc came in for their share too, being sent ashore for drill and route marches.

Jim went to a dance on one occasion and returned to Caradoc at well past midnight. Three of the soldiers who had teamed up with the Caradoc's gun crews in the R.E's Mess were unloading army stores from the SS Katova.

"Hey, Jim!" they called out to him. "Don't board your ship yet—give us a hand with this lot!"

Jim, having had a little too much to drink, mucked in. The job was not completed until 8.30!

"Thanks, mate!" the soldiers shouted. "There'll be plenty of *Freeman's* for you next time you come over to the Mess."

Jim waved to them and went aboard Caradoc, assured that his next drinking session with them would cost him nothing. He was feeling quite sober but extremely tired when he went aboard—only to find that he was assigned to the party from Caradoc who were to load the ship's stores from the jetty, a job that took several hours!

A 17-gun salute was fired on March 26th when a French Battleship arrived with the French High Commissioner who was landed ashore to take up his position there. During General drill on March 29th things went wrong—"Weigh Bower Anchor by hand!"—when somehow the after-bulkheads and Jim's cabin started walking forward. "Away all Boats' crews!"

On April 2nd there was trouble at Poti and Caradoc and an American Destroyer went to assist the Volunteer Army there, but the situation was under control so Caradoc returned to Batoum where she took a Georgian General on board and was given orders to proceed with him back to Poti. Lieutenant Critchley and several of the crew escorted the General ashore and the Lieutenant was invited to join the Russian officers for a few vodkas. The Hands brought him back later in a semi-inebriated state clutching in his arms a church bell, which he had taken as a souvenir!

Caradoc returned to Batoum to pick up military officers to reinforce the Poti command. HM Destroyer Tobago and an Italian Destroyer followed Caradoc back to Poti. The Captain offered to prepare the Marines for landing but the offer of help was not required. Russian and American destroyers also nosed around but as the situation was well under control Caradoc returned once more to Batoum where a working party was detailed to assist in loading a Russian ship with flour for the Volunteer Army.

"What is the Navy doing?" Wiggy said when he returned exhausted from the working party.

"Sweating off some of your weight!" Don called out, dodging away before the tired Wiggy could get hold of him.

On April 13th the combined company of the men of the Caradoc, HMS Revenge, and Ramillies landed for a victory march in Russia where Russian officers decorated Jim and some of the others of the crew. Jim entered in the Log "Another medal!"

Four days later, after the Caradoc's Captain attended a "top brass" meeting with the Admiral and some Russian Generals, Caradoc was sent to Socka as the Bolshevik army was fighting fiercely in the area and making some advances on the Volunteer Army between Socka and Glogoski. HM Destroyer Steadfast and the Russian Destroyer Derski accompanied Caradoc. All guns were prepared for action, with high explosive and shrapnel shells ready. The largest Bolshevik troop concentrations were at Glogoski where they had captured intact the bridges crossing the river. The Bolsheviks were attempting to move their artillery across. The ships opened fire on the bridges, blowing up the largest of them and severely damaging the other two. Caradoc then returned to Socka where she anchored, watches being kept on the town all night. The following morning Steadfast reported that she was under fire from Bolshevik batteries and that she judged the batteries' guns to be 5 or 6 inch. Caradoc returned to Glogoski and opened fire on the Bolsheviks, sending over one hundred and fifty shells until 8.00 pm when the Captain ordered cease fire. At 3.00 am the following morning Caradoc's gunners opened fire again. The Bolsheviks retaliated with shrapnel shells but missed the Caradoc, which had moved out of range of the shells and recommenced her own bombardment from twelve thousand yards. HMS Ajax and the Carrier Ark Royal joined Caradoc and Steadfast shortly before noon and soon afterwards HM Destroyer Vesper arrived too. HMS Ajax fired about fifty rounds to give the Caradoc's gunners a rest. Caradoc then returned to action, firing some two hundred or so more rounds.

"Where's Ajax gone?" Little John asked. There was no sign of either the Carrier Ark Royal or HMS Ajax.

"She pushed off with the Carrier just after we recommenced firing," Mo answered. Then added, "She'll probably report that she saved us!"

The gun crews laughed at Mo's dry humour.

First Lieutenant Fisher, their Gunnery Officer, joined them a few minutes later when the bombardment had recommenced.

"It's a pity that the Ark Royal has moved off," he said to Jim and the gun crew when there was a short lull in the noises of the guns. "We've sent over quite a bit of metal and it would have been useful to know what damage we have done."

After the order had been received to cease firing, the Captain ordered the Caradoc to move in closer to the shore. As she moved in, the shore batteries opened up with shrapnel shelling. Fortunately no one was injured and no damage suffered but Caradoc had to move away from the shore again out of range.

Lieutenant Fisher was thoughtful. "We need to check the *exact* location of those guns," he said aloud. He was studying the shoreline, then suddenly he turned, his head and shoulders erect and walked away.

"There's something on his mind all right," Mo remarked.

They were to learn later what it was. Lieutenant Fisher had asked the Captain for permission to take a small boat out during the night with the object of landing him ashore to scout around. Some of the deck hands overheard the Lieutenant's conversation with the Captain and excitedly passed on the news to the gun crews.

"What was the Captain's reaction?" Jim asked.

"He didn't go much on the idea at first," Harry Mitchell answered. "But after Fisher had told him that it was the only way to pin-point the position of the Bolshie guns and to find out just how many men and guns there were, he agreed. He still wasn't keen on the lieutenant going ashore but Fisher can be pretty persuasive when he sets his mind on something! He told the Captain that with his experience in charge of the guns he was "the obvious person to go.""

Mitchell and the other deck hands hurried away as Lieutenant Fisher came back. He spoke to Jim.

"Round up the rest of the men who were with you in the cutter races!" he ordered. "I'm going ashore to locate the number and position of those guns and need a good team of oarsmen."

"Aye, sir!"

Jim soon collected the men together. There was an air of excitement that became infectious. Under cover of darkness Caradoc moved in quietly towards the shore. The boat was lowered and the crew took their places at the oars while the Lieutenant sat checking his revolver. With clean strokes it did not take the men long to pull for the shore. The Lieutenant leaped agilely onto the sand.

"Wait here for me," he whispered.

"Permission to accompany you, sir!" The men were all of the same mind.

"Permission refused!" The Lieutenant, sensing the disappointment, added "But thanks anyway, lads! If I'm not back here in two hours push off without me. Is that clear?"

"Aye, aye, sir!"

Then the Lieutenant hurried off into the night.

"He's got a lot of nerve, that one," Jim heard one of the men say.

"Wish he'd taken one or two of us along," another man said.

"There's probably more chance pulling it off alone."

They whispered together as the minutes slowly ticked by. Jim strained his ears, listening for any sounds that might have indicated whether the Lieutenant had been discovered or not. All was silent, however. So they waited in the boat, *willing* the officer to return. It seemed hours to Jim but suddenly the silence was broken by the sound of footfalls scuffing in the sand and Lieutenant Fisher was back with them.

"All-right, lads," he said. "Push off and row like hell back to the ship."

When they were approaching the Caradoc Jim could contain his curiosity no longer.

"How did it go, sir?"

"Pretty good." The officer was not disposed to go into details so Jim did not press for any further information.

Safely aboard Caradoc the Lieutenant hurried away to find the Captain. During the cover of the night Caradoc weighed anchor and proceeded along the coastline in the direction of Socka. She dropped anchor, however, after moving about a quarter of a mile or so.

Before breakfast the gun crews opened fire from the Caradoc's new position aiming between two hills with the range adjustments their officer gave them. The bombardment continued until the weather and sea conditions became unfavourable, when the Captain ordered "Proceed to Socka".

HMS Ajax was there and Caradoc took in ammunition from her, after which she pushed off for Batoum, en route for Constantinople.

"She's had enough, poor little thing!" Mo said.

With the weather conditions improving and more ammunition aboard, the Caradoc got underweigh and returned to Glogoski and taking up her former position fired another fifty rounds. There was no answering fire from the Bolshevik guns. Whether they were out of action, or whether the Bolsheviks had decided to lay low, there was no way of telling. Caradoc was ordered to return to Socka to take aboard a Russian Admiral.

With the Admiral aboard, the Caradoc once more made her way back to Glogoski. The Carrier Ark Royal joined them later and sent up seaplanes for scouting and then bombing of the Bolshevik troops and guns. Caradoc's gunner crews opened fire at 11.30am on April 22nd. The Bolsheviks returned the fire, once again using shrapnel shell but no damage was caused and none of the crew was hurt. The Russian Admiral asked to be put ashore at Loa, behind the

Cossack's lines. Having carried out the Admiral's request, Caradoc proceeded to Socka where she anchored overnight.

She got underweigh at 5.30am and proceeded to Glogoski, opening fire at 6.15am for an hour and three-quarters, after which she patrolled the coastline resuming firing at 1.30pm for two hours. Once more the Bolsheviks returned the fire but missed Caradoc completely. Caradoc's gunners had loosed two hundred rounds but the Bolsheviks were still firing back!

The next day was very foggy and unsuitable for there being any attempt at further bombardment. HM Tobago pulled alongside with stores and mail for Caradoc. Later a Russian Destroyer transferred an interpreter to the Caradoc.

Bombardment of the Bolsheviks was resumed at 7.30am on April 25th and continued during the morning. News was received that the Bolsheviks had been bringing in reinforcements for days, including artillery. It seemed likely that any knocked out batteries had been replaced, which accounted for the fact that shelling of Caradoc had resumed. The Volunteer Army had suffered heavy casualties. Mines had been sighted near the coast and it was rumoured that the Bolsheviks had been laying the mines, in the lanes normally used by the British and Allied ships, from a steamer.

A steamer was sighted during the afternoon and Caradoc pursued her. The interpreter at the Captain's side, hailed the Russian steamer and told her Captain to stand by to receive a boarding party. It turned out that she was carrying troops of the Volunteer Army and was allowed to proceed. Caradoc returned to continue bombardment off Glogoski until ordered to make speed to Socki to assist in the evacuation of wounded soldiers and refugees.

The fall of Socki to the Bolshevik army was imminent and refugees carrying stretchers with their wounded were all round the harbour. All boats from Caradoc and the Ark Royal were employed in rescue operations conveying first the wounded, then the refugees, from the jetty to the Ark Royal. The weather conditions deteriorated and the sea chopped around the boats making the rescue work difficult. The evacuation continued for two days. When the Ark Royal had no more room aboard and left for Yalta, a Russian Steamer, St. Nicholia took her place and the Caradoc's boats continued transporting refugees to her. HM Destroyer Tobago provided excellent covering fire throughout the whole evacuation, pinning down the Bolsheviks and preventing them from interfering.

Jim's birthday on April 28th was free of any "bumps" from his shipmates. Everyone was far too busy. When the evacuation had been finally completed Caradoc was ordered to Lu, a small village captured by the Bolsheviks, and bombardment there carried on for several hours.

"How do you spell Lu?" Jim asked. "I shall have to write it down in the Log later."

"How the hell should I know?" Little John shouted, trying to make himself heard above the noise of the gun.

"I don't know how to spell it but I know what it means," Mo told Jim. "Just about describes it too!"

At 3.00pm Caradoc proceeded to Adler, about twenty miles further down the coast. Blue Watch were assigned to getting up the empty cordite cases in preparation for unloading. Jim wrote in the Log—A very happy birthday? No!!!

The next day Caradoc steamed to Batoum, passing HM Destroyer Torch on the way. Caradoc tied up alongside the jetty. Blue Watch and the first part of White Watch went on liberty leave from 9.00am to 5.00pm while Red Watch and the second part of White Watch (Jim's Watch) did a little graft ammunitioning the ship, coaling her and taking on supplies. Jim, having missed his birthday celebrations, tanked up with booze to "uphold the birthday tradition" anyway. When he later consulted the Log a scrap of paper had been slipped inside which was in Frank Butler's scrawling handwriting. It alluded to Jim's semi-inebriated condition and that of most of the second part of White Watch who had joined him in his celebrations. Using Jim's favourite phrase it said: Regarding your insertion for April 29th Red Watch did the best part of that little graft so speak the truth and shame the devil, from an Observer!

An Italian Battle Training Ship, the Etna arrived the following day and was given the usual routine of welcome by Caradoc's crew!

May 1st was the anniversary of the Russian Revolution, which brought some clashes in Batoum between rival factions. No liberty leave was granted any of the crew as the Captain did not want his men involved in any brawls. HM Destroyer Tobago arrived and her crew were given warm greetings by the Caradoc's crew who were mindful of the great help she had given in the evacuation of Socki. HM Destroyer Swallow arrived with Caradoc's mail. Caradoc was then ordered to proceed full steam to Adler to assist in the evacuation there. She arrived at 7.30 am to find a similar situation to that at Socki. All boats were lowered to evacuate men, women and children, Cossacks and Volunteer Army soldiers. HMS Cardiff and Caradoc took the refugees aboard as they were the only ships available that day. Evacuation continued all that day and the next when HM Destroyer Torch and HMS Marlborough arrived about mid-day of the second day to assist. Marlborough had the space and facilities to accommodate refugees so Caradoc went alongside her and transferred the refugees she had picked up and then proceeded in shore and started all over again. The process was repeated until Marlborough was filled and then Caradoc took a further 1,100 refugees aboard herself. Marlborough had by then left. Caradoc proceeded out to sea where she was to wait for a Russian Steamer who would take the refugees from her. The evacuation had been completed successfully but the refugees aboard were in a filthy condition.

"We took aboard more than just the refugees," Mo said, as he scratched himself vigorously.

The refugees were transferred to the Russian ship the next morning. The crew were glad to see them go—not because they had acted badly in any way, on the contrary they had been most friendly and grateful for their rescue, but because of their lice. The crew mucked in with cleaning and fumigating the ship with a will. There were no grumbles at those chores!

The crew were given liberty leave ashore at Gragri further to the South where the Bolsheviks had not penetrated the Volunteer Army defences. The weather was quite warm and the lads sunbathed and swam. They joked about getting a nice tan ready for their next *real* leave. HMS Marlborough and HMS Cardiff, having disembarked the refugees, arrived. HMS Cardiff turned over her ammunition to Caradoc as she had been ordered to proceed to Constantinople.

The Carrier Ark Royal also put in during the early evening. HMS Marlborough had been equipped with a cinema and an invitation was extended to Caradoc's crew to go aboard to see Charlie Chaplin. The cinema fans thought it quite a treat and fancied they were back home, only sorry that they had no "skirt" with them!

On May 9th Caradoc proceeded to Batoum, tying up alongside the Oiler, Apple Leaf. HMS Cardiff and HMS Royal Sovereign were already anchored there. Liberty leave was granted to the Watches in turn. The Captain addressed the crew, delivering a message of thanks to the officers and men from the Commander-in-Chief of the Mediterranean for the great number of Russian lives they had saved and for their good work in the bombardments of the Bolshevik positions.

"Another Medal!" Jim whispered to his friends.

While the Captain was addressing the crew, the Sloop Rose-Marie arrived carrying General Mills aboard. HM Destroyer Swallow followed her in.

On May 12th Bolshevik prisoners were put aboard Caradoc and Jim was given the unenviable job of guarding them. They were a surly lot and Jim guarded them closely. Caradoc put out to sea for Constantinople where she arrived two days later. There the Bolshevik prisoners were handed over to the Army. Caradoc took on fresh ammunition and supplies but remained at Constantinople for four days for inspection by a series of high-ranking officers, the "frock-coated brigade" as the lads called them! The Navigator left the ship at Constantinople and his replacement was taken aboard. HMS Resolution, HMS Revenge, the Iron Duke and the USS Cole put in for a while. The Resolution had lost one of her Leading Seamen overboard. The USS Cole left with her "Paying-off Pennant" flying. Caradoc was ordered to return to Batoum!

On the way to Batoum Caradoc turned sixteen degrees off course to investigate a mine which had been reported but which turned out to be nothing more than an empty beer barrel! Caradoc anchored at Batoum early on the morning of May 20th. HMS Cardiff, HMS Marlborough and HMS Royal Sovereign were already at anchor there.

On Saturday May 21st HMS Cardiff challenged the Caradoc to a race in the whalers. Although the whaler boys were out of practice they beat the challengers by five lengths. The gauntlet was then thrown down for a water polo match that ended in a draw. Finally, a football match was arranged which Caradoc won to the accompaniment of the Rattlers and Squeakers who had a hey-day!

The crew were ecstatic having given the Flagship a good licking.

The Marlborough's crew had watched all that and on Sunday threw out challenges to Caradoc for a whaler's race and water polo. Caradoc won the whaler's race by a good ship's length and held the Marlborough's team to a draw at water polo. The lads on Caradoc were in jubilant spirits and chanted "Not a bad week-end for a Light-Cruiser!"

The Admiral's inspection took place the next day. Jim described it as "Follow the leader Brigade". At the conclusion of his inspection the Admiral gave a speech in which he praised the Ship's Company for the cleanliness of the ship, the efficiency of the crew, the fine performance of the Band, and concluded by praising the whaler's crew for their splendid performances over the weekend, which he had seen with his own eyes!

Caradoc received challenges from other ships in the whaler racing, all of them hoping to wrest away her reputation. HMS Resolution's best whaler crew competed against the Caradoc crew on June 1st but were beaten by twelve lengths. During the month of June the weather was very hot and most of Caradoc's crew had healthy tans and were looking forward to getting to Malta for a bit of fun. Caradoc was assigned to patrols along the coast— Sukhamkale to Poti and Batoum. Little John's birthday was celebrated aboard on June 7th off Sukhamkale. Although the ship was close in to the shore there was no firing from Bolshevik batteries.

Remarking on this to the rest of the Gun crews Jim was told by Little John that he had swallowed enough fire himself having drunk a great quantity of grog. Jim described him as "one drunken sailor!" but added, "why not?" After all, it *was* his birthday.

HMS Ajax and HMS Marlborough engaged in some action on June 16th and Caradoc went to action stations the following day but was ordered to proceed to Constantinople. Rumours were circulating that the ship was on its way to Malta and that it would not be returning to Black Sea action.

At Constantinople an English General, an Italian General, a French General and a dozen Turkish Peace Delegates were taken aboard and the Caradoc received orders to take them to Taranto, Italy. The ship stopped at Chenac to pick up naval ratings for passage to Malta and arrived at Taranto at 11.30 am on June 27th. The delegates and their luggage were taken ashore and the Caradoc immediately proceeded to sea for Malta, where she arrived the following day. HMS Cardiff and the Europa were already in harbour there.

"Well, that's it!" Wiggy said to Jim, "The end of Black Sea operations for us. See how the sun is shining, Jim? A good omen."

Jim nodded his head. He was very thoughtful. At times in the Black Sea operations he had dreamed about being in peaceful surroundings but he had also experienced a growing affection for the Russian people.

That evening the gun crews looked through the many photographs, post-cards and souvenirs of the Black Sea. Besides the revolver, Jim had acquired a fine Cossack sword, a dagger with brass and mother of pearl handle and a Russian bayonet. He had also a collection of Russian newspapers, which none of them could read but the Interpreter on board had kindly translated for them. Jim read the translation to Wiggy and the others. They listened attentively and he watched the pride on their faces. The translation read as follows:

EXTRACT FROM RUSSIAN NEWSPAPER—THE "CARADOC" LEAVING SEVASTOPOL

"CARADOC" IS LEAVING US

"Caradoc", dear to the heart of every citizen of Sevastopol and of other towns formerly under the yoke of the Bolsheviks, leaves us today to proceed to Malta, where her crew will be given some well-deserved rest. For seven weary months this light cruiser has carried out her arduous and difficult duties in the Black Sea and Sea of Azov. From the "AK-MANIA" positions up to the last moment, she has fought with us against the Bolsheviks. By her gallant deeds and powerful assistance she has rendered invaluable help to the Volunteer

Army, especially at the capture of Feodosia, Perekop, Vladislavoka, Ochakov and lastly at Odessa. At Ochakov, regardless of heavy fire from the coast batteries and being struck several times, "Caradoc", under her brave Captain did not flinch, and replied with great effect from her own guns, dismounting and disabling several of the guns of the batteries, and eventually silencing their fire.

In this action "Caradoc" lost her forward funnel and suffered serious damage to her hull, happily there were no casualties to her officers and men.

"Caradoc" has been mentioned several times in the Volunteer Army reports and some of her officers and men have been decorated with the Cross of the Order of St. George for gallantry in the field. Several of her sailors wear the three- coloured badge of the Volunteer Army whom they so well supported.

In the Baltic "Caradoc" has also performed signal service on behalf of those fighting the Bolsheviks.

That she may return to our country and cheer us with her friendly presence is the ardent wish of all loyal Russians".

Jim Alexander, AB

Tom & Mia, ship's pets

HMS Caradoc, 6th light cruiser squadron

Beaty, Malta

HMS Caradoc shelling Bolshevik
gun positions at Ochachov

Hoisting in 21" torpedo

Len Macarthy & Jim, Malta

Nora, Jim's wife

Chapter Nine

At Malta, Caradoc was taken into dry-dock. Blue Watch and the second part of White Watch were given three days leave ashore but the rest of the crew set to scrubbing the ship's bottom under a glaring sun. The topmast was struck and the dockyard workers began "doctoring" the ship.

Jim was sent ashore for grenade and Lewis-gun practise at the Ricasole range. The men were picked up by lorry at Custom House and transported to Ghain-Taffia where the grenade throwing was carried out. There were twenty-two in the party, eleven seamen and eleven marines. Those left on Caradoc continued work on the ship, including fitting up a new topmast.

The bombing party returned to ship the following day and were immediately assigned to work on the topmast. The ship took on fresh ammunition and new P.Vs. Additionally two months supply of stores were loaded aboard. All bags and hammocks had to be taken to Bighi Hospital for fumigation as two of the marines from the ship had reported sick and were found to be suffering from typhus. Since the men had been sick aboard for about three weeks the crew did not very happily receive this news!

HMS Cardiff left for Ismid with a batch of mines aboard her. Jim watched her leave in company with HM Destroyer Seraph. Another batch of the Crew were sent off for grenade practise at the R.M.S.I Camp at Chain, Wiggy with them. Jim was put on loading stores and painting ship. Wiggy and the other eleven Hands returned the following day.

"Didn't blow yourself up then?"' Jim greeted Wiggy.

The next two days were occupied in cleaning up ship after oiling her and getting down all awnings during the dog-watches. She then got underweigh and proceeded out for firing and torpedo running exercises. HM Tug Andrew-King towed the targets. Two runs of sub-calibre were fired and two torpedoes, after which the crews had a swim in the sea before carrying out more runs. At anchor in Mars-Saccanote the crew exercised Night Defence Stations after which the Bolshevik Prize Money was shared out.

The full calibre firing was undertaken the next day with further torpedo firing, and the ship then tied up to a buoy in French Creek as HMS Royal Oak and HMS Resolution were in Malta Grand Harbour, together with the destroyers Vesper and Venetia. They all left for England on July 15th while Caradoc's crew were busy painting the ship's side. They also watched HM Destroyer Tilbury leave for England two days later flying the "Paying-off" pennant.

"Our day will come," Mo said, as the gun crew watched her go.

"Not soon enough for me, that's sure!" Bert Featherstone said.

"Aye!" several of the crew muttered together.

Another man had reported sick and had been taken to Hospital. Jim decided that it was best to keep himself busy during leisure time and not dwell upon the possibility of going down with typhus. He took many more photographs for his collection and then began doing some woodwork to occupy his time. That evening the crew heard the news that one of the marines, Private Ramsey, had died of typhus. There was a stunned silence. It seemed impossible that "the old ram" could have gone; he was too well liked. The crew received official confirmation of the marine's death later at the same time as they were told that Caradoc's gun crews had broken the record formerly held for Practice Firing in the Mediterranean. The latter piece of news would normally have resulted in wild celebrations but no one felt in the mood for them.

Private Ramsey, R.M.L.I. was buried on July 19th. After the burial some hands hoisted aboard a new motorboat, while others loaded thirty mines. The next day Caradoc proceeded to sea at 9.30am. At 5.00pm the Captain stopped the ship and the mines were dropped; she then proceeded towards Port Said where she arrived at 10.00am on July 23rd and joined HMS Calypso in the harbour. Seeing her there and having many friends aboard her, the crew began to talk of having some fun ashore with the Calypso outfit. Their hopes were dashed, however, when the Captain ordered that the ship proceed to the Mouth of the Suez Canal where she tied up stern to a buoy.

The Captain and 1st Lieutenant Critchley left the ship for Cairo with secret and confidential mails, returning to the ship on July 29th. The crew were assigned to painting the ship's side, the gun batteries and clearing out the tanks! During the Captain's absence the senior officer aboard was Captain Cricks the R.M.L.I. Liaison Officer for whom Jim acted as Orderly until Captain Colvin returned. Jim did not mind as it meant his being spared the painting and tanking!

During August Caradoc put in at Alexandria, Soloum and Port Said. A regatta was held at Alexandria with all boats' crews pulling round the fleet. A dance was held aft with the crew entertaining people from the town. The Captain invited British soldiers stationed ashore aboard for a good meal, which the crew served them. Jim said that he had never seen a group of men put away so much food! They were a good crowd and sampled some of the Navy's grog after their meal.

The Captain also invited the crew of HMS Endeavour aboard to a concert. The Caradoc tied up to a buoy, head and stern, which had only just been red-leaded. Jim had the job of buoy jumper and wrote in the Log "another thirty-two shillings for the Royal Navy", his clothing carrying nearly as much red-lead as the Caradoc! Further challenges from other ships were received for whaler and cutter races but Caradoc remained undefeated and the crews celebrated in their usual manner. They lowered the Whaler for a bit of fun after the celebrating and Harry Newsom of 6 Mess had a little too much drink, falling from the Whaler into the sea. He was picked up all right—by the others who thought it a great laugh as the bedraggled Harry was hauled aboard, dripping water. At Port Said the crew were assigned to painting the *port side.*

"Someone's got a fine sense of humour," Little John complained.

HMS Tobago's crew challenged them to water polo but although the Rattlers and Squeakers were ready in full force the game resulted in a draw, so the Rattlers and Squeakers were a little subdued.

The crew of Caradoc were paid the first instalment of Prize Money during the latter part of the month. The first money to be paid out, however, was to all crew with surnames beginning A to G. Jim and Wiggy were delighted.

One day a Siamese Destroyer came in carrying the Prince of Siam. The ship was a former Royal Navy boat that had been "pensioned off" at the end of the war. Most of her crew, however, were English.

"Did you know that the Siamese national anthem has the same tune as ours?" Bert Featherstone asked.

"That's probably why they like to have our ships with our sailors aboard!" answered Little John.

"Can't you be serious for a moment and try to learn something to improve your education?" Bert retorted.

"I already know the British National Anthem!" Little John exclaimed.

"Ah, I'll bet you don't know the words to it in Siamese 'though." Bert affected an air of superiority.

"No and I bet you don't either, Featherstone!"

"Now that's where you're wrong, Little John. If you pay attention nicely I'll teach you."

Little John was intrigued.

"I'll bet the Siamese aboard that ship would be impressed if you were to sing the National Anthem in their language," chipped in Jim, guessing from the wink that Bert Featherstone gave him that Little John was having his leg pulled. The idea of singing to the Siamese in their own language really appealed to Little John.

"Not half so impressed as the English sailors aboard her will be! I'll tell you what, Little John," Bert confided. "You stand up here on this box so that they can see you and I'll whisper the words to you so that you can put them to the tune."

This seemed a good idea to Little John who promptly climbed onto the box and began gesticulating to attract the attention of the crew aboard the Siamese ship.

When he had succeeded in attracting the attention of several of her crew he spoke out of the corner of his mouth to Bert Featherstone who appeared to be suffering some sort of choking fit.

"I'm ready, Bert," Little John said. "Are you all right?"

Bert nodded. "Now listen carefully, Little John. The words are easy. In fact they are very easy as they are repetitive—so listen to them and sing them out loud and clear."

"Stop gassing and get on with it," said Jim. "You'll lose their attention if you don't."

"Ready ... here we go. *"Oh Wah."*

"Oh Wah," repeated Little John.

"Tan Nah."

"Tan Nah," repeated Little John.

"Siam."

"Siam."

"That's it. Now sing out at the top of your voice!" encouraged Bert.

Little John sang out as loud as he could, much to the delight of his shipmates:

"Oh Wah, Tan Nah Siam ...Oh Wah Tan Nah Siam..."

The sailors aboard the Siamese destroyer who had been watching the antics of Little John called out to Jim and Bert and one or two others of the Caradoc's crew who had been attracted by the noise.

"Has he been at the grog?" They were all laughing "fit to bust" as Jim described it later. Little John was still singing "... Oh Wah, Tan Nah ..."

Suddenly Little John's voice tailed off as he realised what a fool he was making of himself. Bert decided to make himself scarce.

"Where's Featherstone?" shouted Little John. "I'll bloody kill him!"

That leg-pull was the favourite topic of conversation not only by the Gun-Crews but also by most of the other crew members too for days afterwards much to Little John's embarrassment!

The crew of HM Destroyer, Tomahawk put out the usual challenge to Caradoc to give the Rattlers and Squeakers their chance!

The Caradoc's bands decided to put on a bit of entertainment for the rest of the crew but got only half way through the first tune when the sea became a bit rough. The crew called out "No wets foreward!"

On September 1st the Egyptians held a sailing regatta that Jim watched in glorious sunshine. The Captain left the ship on the third to visit Cairo again but was away only three days. The Carrier Ark Royal put aboard some naval ratings who were awaiting passage to Blighty and then left for the Persian Gulf. Doug Braun went on patrol ashore in blistering heat with some of the other hands. On their return they came in for quite a bit of teasing when the rest of the crew called them sunburnt heroes!

On September 15th, 1st Lieutenant Hutton joined Caradoc to replace Douglas Fisher. A new sub-lieutenant arrived with him. Khedive's Yacht pulled into the harbour in Alexandria and the Caradoc's gunners fired a salute. 1st Lieutenant Fisher, Lieutenant Hansford Critchley and Sub-Lieutenant Williams left the Caradoc for England on September 17th. The gun crews turned out in full force to cheer their lieutenant as he left.

"There goes one good officer," Mo remarked. Jim was sorry to see their Gunnery Officer leave and thought back to the actions they had fought under his superb direction. He thought too of that time when the Lieutenant had gone scouting alone to locate the Bolshevik shore batteries. Before he had left the Caradoc he had shaken hands with each member of the gun crews in turn and thanked them all for the excellent work done together. The Chaplain also left Caradoc that day, on his way to Malta to get married.

The following day being Saturday, the gun crews decided to have a few drinks to toast their absent officer. Jim led the toasting and as the evening wore on proposed toasts to everyone, being in quite a state by the end of it all. The Captain gave a talk to the crew on the quarter deck on Sunday about not going too overboard with the drink and looking directly at Jim, said "This applies particularly to one man who had far too much!"

After that, it was back to General drill! "Prepare to be towed, forward!" "All boats pulled around the fleet!"

The Consul came aboard and a nineteen-gun salute was fired. Then General Congreve and his staff came aboard. Caradoc got underweigh for Cyprus travelling at 28 knots. Fire drill was carried out. They reached Famagusta the morning of the next day and, after the "top brass" had been landed safely ashore, Caradoc's crew were granted shore leave. Although the gun crews made straight for the nearest bar, Jim decided to heed the Captain's warning. He had only a couple of beers with the lads and then decided to look around Famagusta and pick up one or two things he needed. Bert Featherstone decided to follow Jim's example.

Two days later the General and his staff rejoined the ship and Caradoc proceeded to Lenesol Island where the passengers disembarked. Two days later they came on board again and Caradoc proceeded to Port Said, arriving at 7.00am the following morning. HM Destroyer Tomahawk was already in harbour. Half an hour later HM Sloop Clematis brought in stores. It was Blue Watch who had the fun of unloading them. Some of the stores were for the Destroyer and Jim's Watch had the added fun of taking them across to her much to the delight of Blue Watch.

The Caradoc's marines landed for small arms drill while the crew cleaned up ship. On the last day of September the SS Osterley arrived with England's International Cricket team and were heartily welcomed with cheers from the Caradoc's Company.

During October the Egyptians held a fireworks display one night to commemorate the anniversary of the Italian victory. It was a fine night with a clear sky. The morning after, some ratings came aboard who had become a little too enthusiastic the previous night in their final celebrations and had missed the boat for home. A happier lot of fellows one couldn't wish to meet!

When Caradoc returned to Alexandria on October 8th, Khedivi's Yacht was in harbour and another salute was fired. Jim and some of the Watch rigged up ship's illuminations. With that work completed the Watches were assigned to painting the ship once more.

"What a change!" Jim said.

The crew of an American ship, the Panther, watched them at work. Blue Watch in the meanwhile were busy getting in provisions. There was a Court Martial held aboard for the sailors who had missed their boat!

"Hey! Look at that!" Wiggy Bennett pointed to a square-rigged Warship that was waiting to enter the Harbour. She was carrying the flag of the Argentine Republic and as she drew closer they were able to make out her name, *Presidente Sarmiento.*

The Emperor of India challenged the Caradoc to a Whalers race and Caradoc's lads beat them by one and a half lengths. On October 11th Caradoc left Alexandria for Port Said where she tied up to buoys head and stern, an operation that took two and a half hours to complete.

"Why have we taken so long to tie up?" Little John asked.

"Ginger Swindell was buoy jumper at the head! Handy Alf was the rear jumper!" Jim answered.

"No bloody wonder!" Wiggy said pulling a face. "What a pair!"

A football match between the Blue Watch and the Red Watch teams was arranged for Saturday, 23rd October. Football matches were usually planned for Saturdays as it made the lads feel that they were back in England. The matches were always well attended and the Rattlers and Squeakers always in evidence, making more noise than all the rest of the spectators put together. Blue beat Red by one goal to nil.

"Their first win and last one, no doubt," Wiggy said. Wiggy was an Aston Villa fan back in Blighty.

"How did the Court Martial go with the drunken Blighty Dodgers?" Bert Featherstone asked. "Anyone know?"

"They got thirteen days!" Goodie Goodyear replied.

"Bet that took the smile off the little man's face!" said Jim, alluding to the smaller of the men in the group who had come aboard.

"He was still drunk when they came aboard! The others all looked pretty grim."

"Let that be a lesson to you, Jim!" Frank Butler said. "Oh! I forgot that you are a reformed character since the Captain gave that little talk!"

"He won't be able to keep it up for long!" Little John laughed.

"There's no harm in having a few drinks," Wiggy said with a very serious expression on his face, "as long as a man knows when he has had enough."

"Can a man ever have enough, Wiggy?" Frank Butler asked, trying to effect an air of innocence.

"I always know when I have had enough," Wiggy answered.

"So do I!" Little John announced.

"We've noticed," Bert snapped. "It's when you can't get up off the deck!"

A British India ship carrying marines ran into difficulties with wire fouling up her screws. The Caradoc's divers went out to her in the Cutter and worked for several hours untangling the mess. They finally cleared it and received rousing cheers from the lads aboard.

General drills were carried out frequently, even "Abandon ship!" Caradoc's divers went down to inspect the propeller shafts and work was carried out scraping barnacles. Another weekend football match was played off between the Marines and Blue Watch that resulted in a draw. The Captain went off to Cairo yet again with two of the ship's officers for a couple of days. There was rumour of a strike by the Egyptians and the British ships moved out from the harbour, but it was only a rumour.

"They need the money too much to go on strike," Mo said.

The lads paid money to the natives for coaling the ship. It was a job that the crew did not like much and the natives were glad of the work and the few "coppers" that each member of the ship's crew contributed.

When the Captain returned, he decided to land all seamen and nineteen of the stokers ashore for drill. The men were not very happy about it, which was hardly surprising as the drill was carried out in several inches of sand. Jim photographed them later holding a sign: "John Bull—fallen idol!"

General drills aboard continued. Another "Abandon ship!" A Dutch submarine, K.5 came into view. She had surfaced and her crew were on deck.

Jim and other members of the ship's Company were landed ashore to practise "march past". The Captain inspected the men and congratulated them on their appearance and capabilities. A concert was arranged for the next day on Quarter-deck but it rained quite hard and the lads called it, "literally a wash-out".

All the drilling and "bull" was in preparation for the Admiral's inspection, which took place on December 9th. Rear-Admiral Hope, commanding the 3rd Light Cruiser Squadron, came aboard at 9.30 am. He commenced his inspection immediately, going round ship. He was satisfied with what he saw, lingering awhile with the gun crews and torpedo men, asking a few of them questions about the Black Sea operations. After that he watched the ship's Company at "Panic Stations" "…away all boats' crews!"

"Come on the Whites, don't buss it!"

"Out fire engine! Out stream anchor!"

"Oh, what a picture!" Jim wrote in the Log later. The Admiral's message was that "the Ship and its Company all satisfactory" and he left at 11.30am.

As soon as the Admiral had gone, HM Destroyer Trinidad came in, proceeded alongside HMS Conqueror, paid off, recommissioned and then proceeded out—all in a half hour!

The Caradoc's Concert Party performed at the Corradino Canteen and were given a standing ovation. It all went well as the men slipped into their well-rehearsed routines; one of the highlights being a marriage ceremony between two of the lads, one in drag. Everyone was in high spirits anyway as Caradoc was off to Gibraltar the following day, flying the paying-off pendant.

As they left harbour the next morning to cheers from the crews of the ships they passed, the band struck up refrains such as "Rolling Home" and "Auld Lang Syne".

That night they ran into a heavy storm off the North African coast with heavy seas running but they weathered it all right. The weather was fine in the morning and the ship made up for the lost time, passing a French Cruiser and two American Destroyers and arriving at Gibraltar at 5.00pm on December 14th. HMS Cardiff, their Flagship, was already in and tied alongside the wall. HMS Cardiff "payed off" during the forenoon of the following day and recommissioned, her old crew going aboard HMS Conqueror which steamed off at 5.00 pm bound for England. The crews of the ships in the harbour loudly cheered her and Caradoc's band again struck up "Rolling Home." Then it was "out ammunition" aboard Caradoc.

"Caradoc's being reverted from a fighting ship to a Hip-Hip-Hooray ship," yelled Wiggy Bennett.

"Roll on the day when we cheer ourselves home," said Frank.

After getting all ammunition off, the torpedoes were lifted for returning and other hands were employed making preparation for alterations to the fore-bridge and refitting the fall blocks. The guns from the Forts in Devil's Gap were practising while all the work was going on aboard Caradoc. The Caradoc's guns were lifted after stripping—first A- gun under sheerlegs, ready for lifting, then

Q-gun, Y-gun. Out came the port torpedo tubes, the searchlights, starboard torpedo tubes and so the work went on.

Cleaning, painting, replacing the guns, drills on shore, small arms practice on the ranges; the Crew were always occupied. The Saturday football matches were looked forward to eagerly, giving the Rattlers and Squeakers a chance to let go their pent-up feelings. Christmas Eve a match against the local Football Club was arranged with Caradoc winning by 3 - 0.

"Up the Kapadokas!" Wiggy cried at the top of his voice. "Kapadokas" was the affectionate name assigned to Caradoc's crew by their Russian friends and was the nearest translation the Russians could manage!

Christmas Day the crew were aroused by Leading Seaman Johnson and Leading Seaman Poile and one or two of their friends beating the big drum, sounding the hooters and generally making as much noise as they could. It was a very rude awakening for the rest of the crew. What else could they do aboard but drink? One or two of the lads applied themselves to it with gusto and "drunk themselves silly".

Boxing Day another football match was arranged between Caradoc and the Coronation Club. The result was a 3 -2 win for the Coronation Club but the game was a dirty one.

Then, Christmas over, it was back to painting and the rifle ranges. One of the hands slipped and fell and was taken ashore to hospital with concussion but was released a day later.

The crew were disappointed when the Caradoc team lost 3 - 1 to the Royal Engineers.

Two defeats in a row were too much to bear.

"What's happened to you, you old women?" Wiggy shouted to the team "Where's that sparkle, lads?"

The final crunch came on Saturday, January 7th 1921, a date to go down in Caradoc's history, as Bert Featherstone put it, when the team suffered its third defeat in a row, losing 5 - 0 to Gibraltar Depot.

"Some team!" Wiggy called out at the end of the match. "I give up on you!" With that he threw his Squeaker down and trampled it underfoot.

With all the practise on the firing ranges, however, the gun crews were becoming something of marksmen. *Rapid fire*, *application*, it made no difference. They began to compete with one another and ran a kitty, best score of the day takes all!

On Saturday the Caradoc football team held the Royal Engineers to a 1 - 1 draw. They played better than in the previous three matches but were right off their usual form. It was one thing cheering on a team who were always on top, but quite something else when they were on the downgrade. Wiggy told them in no uncertain terms that he would turn out one more time to watch them and if they didn't win then he really would withdraw his support. Whether his words had any real effect or whether the team was beginning to rally, they pulled off a 3 - 0 victory over the Middlesex's team at their next match!

The fifth flotilla of Destroyers came in after searching for the submarine, K.5, which was missing. The Carrier, HMS Argus had new director-gear aboard which she was testing. The HMS Caernarvon left harbour, followed by the Carrier Argus. Caradoc came out of dry-dock along with HM Destroyers Somme and Restless, who had both been having a face-lift too, but HM Destroyer Speedy still had some work to do on her and remained behind in the dock. Caradoc tied up to the main wharf jetty.

Two days later, HMS Vindictive came in with relief crews aboard. After being paid their money at 9.30am and returning their stores and gear, the Caradoc's old crew stowed their hammocks, trunks and bags in trucks ready for transportation to the *Vindictive*. The new crew for Caradoc left the Vindictive and went aboard their new ship.

"And you are welcome to her!" Bert Featherstone called out.

"You can write 'Finis' in your Log, Jim," Mo said. Although glad to be going home to England there was a note of sadness in his voice which Jim detected and understood.

"We've celebrated company aboard the Vindictive," Frank Butler said. "Prince George is there taking passage to HMS Iron Duke."

The new commission on the Vindictive started with the usual Sunday routine, Church Service. Then it was new ship, old routines, with the inevitable painting the Port side and then torpedo running. The ship was coaled on Tuesday, the first day of February, and the crews returned to painting, Port Side and Starboard.

"Good old Caradoc's, they don't mind! Such good workers with so much experience!" Frank Butler muttered, "Just admire that brush-work!"

They held their concert aboard that night with HM Prince George at the piano.

HMS Caradoc left the wall and tied up to a buoy in the stream. Jim and the others watched as their old ship was ammunitioned. She left the following day for Malta at 7.30am. The Vindictive followed her three hours later.

The Sunday Service at sea. on February 6th was held on the mess deck with Prince George at the "Quaker Organ". The Vindictive arrived at Malta at 10.30am, tying up head and stern. The whole of the Mediterranean fleet was in harbour. Jim picked up a nice quiet number being assigned to standing patrol at Egmont for three days, leaving his shipmates to the usual day and night chores! There was a Carnival being held in Malta with everyone going mad. Jim managed to see Beaty at long last and being Corporal in charge of the patrol it did not prove too difficult for him to arrange. He met her in the Lancaster Bar while his friends covered for him on patrol. It was such a riot everywhere, with the Carnival at full swing, that the chances of his being missed in the overall confusion were remote.

Beaty looked as lovely as ever, Jim thought. He told her so.

He also told her that he was going home to England. They decided to make the most of the three evenings left to them.

The Vindictive slipped her buoy and got underweigh for England at 10.30am on Saturday, February 12th, with the band playing "Rolling Home".

"How did the shore patrol go?" asked Wiggy.

Jim smiled as he thought about the last three days and nights in Malta.

"Oh! *That* last run ashore!" he said, "I shan't forget!"

At Gibraltar on February 16th they tied up to number 3 South coaling jetty. The Atlantic fleet was in harbour—HMS Queen

Elizabeth, HMS Hood, HMS Tiger, HMS Repulse, HMS Lucia, four L class submarines, and the Argus and Centaur.

The Vindictive left Gibraltar at 5.30am on Saturday, February 19th with the band still playing the same old tune. Great cheers came across the water from the Flagship of the world, the *Queen Elizabeth* but on the way out of the harbour the Vindictive unfortunately snapped two of her wires and four more belonging to the Repulse!

The Vindictive stopped at Rosa Bay on February 21st where the first division of the Atlantic fleet were at anchor; HMS Valiant, HMS Warspite, HMS Barham, HMS Canterbury and several destroyers. The reason for Vindictive stopping became clear when the Valiant transferred two members of her crew who were sick, and some Court-Martial prisoners, to the Vindictive for passage to England.

"We'll never get home at this rate," Wiggy complained. "It's bad enough having a ship that full steams at nine knots, without having to stop!"

They entered the Bay of Biscay the following morning at half-past midnight. The weather was good and the Bay quite calm.

"Some difference from when we went through her last time," Mo said.

Jim remembered how Little John had sung to the tune of the National Anthem that day, so long ago. He also recalled that other occasion when Little John thought he was singing the "Siamese" version! What a "buss" that had been!

The sick cases and the prisoners left the ship at Devonport and the Vindictive, at the breath-taking speed of five knots, proceeded to Portsmouth where she tied up to Asia Pontoon at 8.30 am on Saturday, 26th February. The crew were given weekend passes ashore with orders to return to the ship for getting out ammunition and packing all bags for Depot on Monday, 28th February. The bars in Portsmouth were busy that weekend and Jim forgot his resolution— after all, he argued, there is a time and place for all things and it was not the time for sobriety just then!

Chapter Ten

Jim felt disinclined to spend his leave in Norfolk. He had been commissioned to join HMS Pembroke at Chatham at the end of his leave and felt that it would be better to go back to Tunbridge Wells and see if he could spend a little more time looking for his sister. He had decided that the early feelings he had experienced for Dolly were no more than a "crush" and there was no future in the relationship for him. He guessed that his other experiences with women, particularly Beaty, had made him realise that. Dolly had written to him whilst he was on the Black Sea operations and he had replied but he had confined his letters to typical experiences aboard the Caradoc rather than his personal feelings. Letters from her gradually became more widely spaced and eventually he had given up replying. Aunt Esther wrote to him fairly regularly and Jim liked hearing from her. However, she had not had any more communications from Vi. The idea of calling to see Jack did cross his mind but with the passage of time even that had lost its appeal. Jim thought that his own experiences since joining the Navy had probably equalled those of old Jack!

His mind made up, he set off for Tunbridge Wells. The journey passed uneventfully but gave him time to think over how he would set about looking for his sister. He arrived at Tunbridge Wells some hours later. He remembered the town well and made straight for the house in Garden Road where he had previously stayed. Unfortunately, the lady had moved and the new occupants did not take in boarders. He walked back into Camden Road, turning right at the corner of Garden Road, where he found a small cafe. Over a cup of tea he had the opportunity of talking to the woman who served him, asking her where he might get fixed up in digs for a couple of weeks. She was very helpful and scribbled two or three addresses down on a piece of paper for him.

"They are all within short walking distance of here," she explained. "Commercial Road is on the left hand side a little way down the road, Beulah Road is on the right hand side a bit further down, and Granville Road is a turning off Beulah Road at the top of the hill."

Jim thanked her for her help and set off, the piece of paper she had given him in his hand. He found Commercial Road without difficulty, the house he wanted being on the right hand side about half way down. Although he knocked on the door several times quite loudly there was no reply. The occupants were out, the house had that feel about it, so he made his way to Beulah Road. The houses there were larger than the ones in Commercial Road, more widely spaced. He found the one he was seeking, on the left hand side of the road. This time the occupants were at home because as soon as he knocked on the door he heard a woman's voice commanding a dog to stop barking. A woman opened the door. Jim judged her to be in her late forties, early fifties. She was quite short and rather on the plump side. Her hair was fair but greying, and slightly unkempt. She had a pleasant face with high cheekbones, fair eyebrows and grey-blue eyes, which looked large because of the spectacles she wore. Jim told her that he was looking for board and lodgings for two weeks and hoped that she might have a spare room. Yes, she said, she did have a room spare and told him the terms. She invited Jim to look over the room, which was on the first floor at the rear of the house and was really quite pleasantly furnished. He told her that it suited him nicely. The woman explained in some detail that she looked after her father who was a widower and that she also gave music lessons as well as taking boarders in. She was very pleasant if somewhat talkative and sensing that Jim was anxious to go out told him that the evening meal was served at six o' clock, breakfast at eight o' clock but that he would have to get a meal out midday if he needed it as she had piano lessons to give midday.

The following day he bought a map of Tunbridge Wells, having lost the one he had procured on his last visit to the town, and began walking the roads once more. The first week he covered the areas of Upper Grosvenor Road, Park Road, Woodbury Park Road and Queens Road, then Pembury Road, Lansdowne Road, Lonsdale

146

Gardens and the town centre but met with no success. He went to the Church services at St. James's Church on the Sunday, peering at the people who left the church after the service from a vantage point opposite the main entrance, but saw no-one who resembled his sister.

The second week he turned his attention to the Pantiles end of the town—Frant Road, Eridge Road, Warwick Park, Madeira Park and the Pantiles itself where he watched well-to-do ladies and their entourages walking. The weather throughout the fortnight of his leave was fine but the March winds were blowing and once he chased after a hat that had blown from the head of an elderly gentleman much to the delight of some onlookers. The evenings he spent in the public houses he had previously visited but, in deference to his landlady and her father, made do on one or two beers making them last the evening. The people in the pubs were friendly enough and frequently he was asked questions about what ship he was on, what places he had visited. The war victims were embittered about the way they had been treated–he met men with white sticks who had been blinded by gas, men with amputated limbs, one or two who had suffered shell-shock, and others who had escaped with no physical disabilities but had suffered from mental breakdowns, the sheer horror of it all being too much for them to bear. Jim decided that he had been fortunate to have come through it without injury.

At the end of his leave he still had not found his sister. He said goodbye to his landlady and her father and made his way to Chatham to join HMS Pembroke.

The purpose of the commission was to train sailors in the use of small arms and in field combat. In a way it was like being a soldier rather than a sailor. There was plenty of firing practice on the ranges, route marches, manoeuvres, and drill. Each man had his own rifle and steel helmet and inspections were carried out frequently to ensure that all equipment was in "apple-pie" order. Most of the route marches took the men over Rainhem or Cobham. Sometimes they slept out in tents. It was all quite different from being at sea but Jim enjoyed it. Jim was in 32 Company, a part of the NORE E Battalion. The extensive training was given so that sailors could be used in defence of harbours or in offensive operations securing shore positions, so Jim was told. Normal navel routine was also observed on Pembroke.

Aunt Esther wrote to Jim usually about once a month. In September she wrote to say that Vi had been in touch with her and had enclosed a photograph of herself. The letter said that Vi had been moving about a bit in the Kent and Sussex areas but had left Tunbridge Wells at the end of August for Hastings. Aunt Esther had enclosed the photograph for Jim to keep. Jim was excited; it was the first time he had seen what his sister looked like as a woman. He was also pleased that his intuitive feeling his sister was in Tunbridge Wells had been correct; to think that the two of them had been in that town but fate had not allowed them to meet! Vi had still not given any address but Jim knew that she was in Hastings.

On October 17th Jim left the Pembroke and was given a new commission on HMS Tiger and resumed his service as a gun crew operative. He had come to realise that peace-time service was entirely different from his former active service in the War and the Black Sea operations. Simulated battle situations carried little real risks to the crews and towed targets were not likely to fire back! The ship had a good entertainment group, the "Clowns", which provided Jim with an opportunity to display some of his theatrical talent. Whilst with the Tiger Jim received his certificate for the rifle course he had completed and that came through just before he proceeded on Christmas leave for a few days—a leave that he spent in Norfolk with Aunt Esther, much to her delight.

He was pleased to see her too and it gave him the opportunity to discuss Vi. After Christmas he went over to see his other relatives in Norwich but made no attempt to visit Aunt Winifred, the risk of running into Dolly being too great. Whilst at a New Year's Eve dance in Norwich he dated a girl whom he met there, taking her to a pub. She was a nice enough girl, a couple of years younger than himself, but he found her company lacking in any stimulation. He returned to Tiger early in January 1922, remaining with her a further two months before being given another commission with Pembroke at Chatham for two months combat training which he completed on May 3rd.

His next commission was with HMS *Verity* where he reported the following day. It was a happy day for Jim because it meant a return to Malta, Verity being part of the Mediterranean Fleet. After the usual loading of stores and ammunition and general preparation, Verity proceeded out of harbour, destination Constantinople via Malta.

The Bay of Biscay was quite calm and the ship made good progress. Jim's thoughts returned to that day over three years ago aboard Caradoc when Little John had put his own words to the National Anthem. He smiled to himself. His thoughts then naturally returned to that other episode when Little John had attempted to sing in "Siamese" and he began laughing much to the surprise of one of the crew who happened to be watching him.

Verity passed Gibraltar a couple of days later and tied up in Malta in the early morning sunshine three days afterwards. She remained there just over a week, which gave Jim the opportunity to spend time ashore with Beaty. Her dark eyes flashed when she saw Jim, and she flung her arms round Jim's neck and pressed her lips against his. Later the two of them went dancing and had a few drinks together in one of the bars.

"I've missed you, Beaty. It's so good to see you, to hear your voice and to feel your closeness again."

"It is so good to see you again too, my Jim," she said to him several times during the course of that first evening.

Beaty and Jim had exchanged letters quite frequently, of course, but she was not a great letter writer. The letters always smelled faintly of her perfume and whenever he received a letter from her Jim had imagined what it would be like to hold her again in his arms. Her parents were always friendly whenever Jim called at the house. The family were Roman Catholics which could have presented problems had Jim wanted to marry her but he was not ready to settle down with any one woman at twenty-one years of age, he told himself, plenty of time to think of that when his twelve years in the Navy were up. Of all the women he had known, however, Beaty was the one dearest to him in his affections. He regarded her as his regular girl. *The* greatest attraction on the Island of Malta!

The weather throughout the week was really hot. Routine work aboard ship concluded, there were opportunities for swimming and water polo. The Watches took turns in going ashore and Jim was able to see Beaty three more times before Verity left Malta for Constantinople.

On the way to Constantinople the ship's crew held some talent competitions aboard and began to make preparations for a concert. A committee was elected with eight members from the ship's Company, two officers and six ratings. One of the ratings had had some past experience in entertainment management before joining the Navy and was elected as manager, the musical director was one of the ship's band, the scenery arrangement was left to one of the ratings with an artistic flair, and finally the stage and lighting effects were naturally placed in the capable hands of one of the ship's electricians.

Although Jim had taken part in the Caradoc's concerts in both humorous sketches and in singing, he kept in the background as he did not want to give up time to rehearsals. He was busily engaged in collecting material for a book he was writing and needed free time to take photographs, develop and print them, and see as many places as he could during his leisure time. His photograph and postcard album was practically full, containing over five hundred cards and photographs of ships and places he had visited. He decided that he would need to buy a second album. When the ship put in at Constantinople and he was granted liberty leave and shore leaves he set off alone on an expedition to the bazaars and shops, purchasing some postcards and a second album at a reasonable price. Equipped with his camera he visited such places as the Caba Tache, the fortress of Roumeli Hissar, the Summer Palace, and the Kiosque de Flamour. He enjoyed the lonely trips finding much to occupy both his time and curiosity.

Wherever the Admiralty sent him Jim pursued his hobby with zeal. Gibraltar fascinated him with its Moorish Castle at one end of the scale and Wellington's Monument at the other. Catalan and Rosia Bays gave him the chance of watching ships and boats moving unhurriedly across the blue water, and Europa Point was a special delight for him. He crossed the border with Spain one day and went to a bullfight. It was not something he wanted to repeat, Jim decided, he preferred the less bloodthirsty sport of football! At Port Said he was able to get pictures of the harbour, the streets and the people. A trip to Cairo enabled him to visit the Grand Cafe Chicha and, on the second floor, above the cafe, the Photographie Americaine. He visited the Pyramids, took pictures of Arab men and women walking about the streets or engaged in pottery crafts, which they painted when the earthenware pots were dry.

Of all the places he visited, however, Malta was his favourite. Not only because he could enjoy Beaty's company but because he found the people so warm and friendly everywhere he went on the island. The local girls from the villages reminded him of nuns in their dress. He liked walking with Beaty around Palace Square or up the steps of the Strada Santa Lucia. Their visits together to St. John's Church, a breath-taking experience of colour and art such as he had never before witnessed, were a pleasure to them both. They sat in the Piazza Regina where a statue of Queen Victoria, surrounded by flower gardens, was dwarfed by the grand building of the Public Library behind. St. Paul's Bay was one of Jim's favourite views but it was at the Grand Harbour that he could take pictures of so many of the ships he loved, flying the flags of so many different nations. After his visit to the Chapel of Bones he sat pondering on what he had read there:

The world is a stage.
Our life a tragedy.
All is illusion, all a fiction.
Death the close of all things.
It unmasks and solves all.
Thou, who livest, ponder on this.
Pray that perpetual light may shine
on those who rest herein.
Go in peace, remember that thou shalt die.

He thought of Jack Frost, he thought of the victims of the atrocities at Feodosia, and all the young men who had perished in the war. What a price they had paid for supporting their Country or ideology. He thought too about those who had survived but had been maimed. He wondered why man spent so much time in killing his fellows instead of enjoying all the beautiful things that the Creator had provided. Jim thought of some of the places he had seen and how many more there were yet to see. He felt glad that he no longer had to fire the guns at anything but towed targets and prayed that he would see his service through with the Navy at peace. General drills, irksome as they might seem, were infinitely preferable to battle.

He took an educational test in July, which provided him with extra work in his leisure time in the days leading up to it. He had no fear of failing it but decided to review his notes and check up on one or two facts. He took the test and passed it easily, receiving a certificate on July 11th 1922 to add to his collection of documents and medals that were kept in the trunk along with his diaries, notebooks, souvenirs and albums. He had discontinued keeping a Log, for he identified it *only* with Caradoc and the lads he had lived and worked with aboard her

Jim remained on the Verity on Mediterranean Service until July 6th 1923. He was ordered to report to the Pembroke at Chatham, after his home leave, for an advanced rifle course. He decided to spend the leave in the Hastings area. Letters from Aunt Esther led him to believe that his sister was still there as she had received a Christmas card that bore the postmark 'Hastings'. Vi had enclosed a note with the card saying that her present employer moved about a lot and Vi travelled with her as a companion, a much better job than she had held in her previous situations.

When Jim arrived in Hastings in early July he found it very difficult to get fixed up in digs. Holidaymakers filled the town and he encountered either "no vacancies" notices or prices beyond that for which he had budgeted. Eventually he managed to get a room in Ore but the landlady, Mrs Palmer, a thin elderly lady provided only breakfast with the room. The weather was extremely warm and he enjoyed walking into the town, about a mile and a half from where he was staying. The beaches were filled with children and their parents—all seemed to be enjoying themselves. There were plenty of cafes around and he had no difficulty in getting his meals out although most of the places were busy. He thought it possible that Vi and her employer might be out enjoying the sunshine so he walked along the front from the old town to St. Leonards hoping that he might see her. He had the fairly recent photograph of his sister in his pocket and felt more optimistic than on the previous searches in Tunbridge Wells.

The first week of his leave went by and he had no success but he persisted in his walks, carrying out similar searches to the ones in Tunbridge Wells.

On the Sunday he went to Church and afterwards walked to Fairlight along a country lane. He did not expect to find Vi there but his landlady told him that it was beautiful up on the *firehills* and that there were some beautiful views of the sea too. Jim thoroughly enjoyed the walk and agreed with his landlady's appraisal. He remained on the cliff top until quite late in the evening before walking back to Ore.

At the end of his leave, having had no success in his search for Vi, he caught a train to Tunbridge Wells and spent a day there on his way to Chatham. He wondered why he had wanted to return there, it certainly had nothing to do with seeing his sister, but had to admit to himself that the town attracted him in an indefinable way.

On the journey to Chatham, while checking how much money he had left, the programme for *"Up the Arts"* caught his attention. For some reason he had folded it up and placed it in his wallet behind the section for ten shilling notes. It was of a similar colour too and made him think that he had more money than he actually had! As he unfolded the programme his thoughts drifted back to Malta and to Beaty. The lads had put on quite a show and although Jim had not taken part in it he had helped in the designing and duplicating of the programmes.

The programmes had been produced like programmes for London Shows, including "advertisements" which had given he and his shipmates the opportunity of some typical naval humour.

He read them through, smiling as he did so.

BOOKS! BOOKS! BOOKS!

Come and inspect our stock. Read for yourself "Hints on obtaining Rum Tots", "Advice on leave during your watch on board!", "Where in England, what and why?" "Read in *The Woman*, the best work in creation—the edition may be large but everyman should have one!"

ARE YOU EFFICIENT?
If not—join the triple alliance!

THE TOBACCO HABIT

Why waste your money on cigarettes? Cadge them—it's less expensive!

SEAMANSHIP TAUGHT

Have you tried our special correspondence method? If not, write to us at once and tell us what you require! Six lessons for only ten guineas! Testimonial: I can never be sufficiently thankful for the instruction received from you. I can now swing the lead with the greatest of ease at any time.

TOURS IN THE NEAR EAST—FREE! FREE!

The Levant holds a great interest for all. It is noted for its unique cleanliness—not a speck of dirt about anywhere—its sheer beauty enraptures the very soul—Buyuk Dere—Mudros—Chanak and other soul inspiring places visited. All you have to do is join the Third Flotilla!

IN CASE OF FIRE

Cut round the dotted line and escape through the aperture.

The performance itself had been very good, Jim reflected. The band had called itself "the orchestra" and had opened the concert with the Colonel Bogey 'Overture'. Charlie Barnes had sung "Any old iron", Frank Rathall had sung "Come to the Fair" in a soprano voice, followed by Tony Ransom reciting "Mad Carew". Wally Tee had performed some tap-dances to a medley of tunes, and several of the lads had done comedy turns, the best being Stewart Stanley who had a wonderful repertoire. After the interval, when the performers and audience alike had tanked up, the 'orchestra' had struck up "Under the double Eagle" and Charlie Barnes, Frank Rathall and several others had sung the popular songs of the day—*Smiling Through, Ragtime cowboy* and other favourites. One sketch with the twins, Ian Crevy and Harry Mitchell called "I want a boy" had nearly scuppered the ship! The pair of them had then led the audience into the National Anthem, something that inevitably brought back to Jim memories of Little John and probably always would, following which the show ended.

Jim refolded the programme and replaced it carefully in his wallet. Times with the Verity and the Third Destroyer Flotilla had also been good, he reflected. His mind wandered back to the Third Flotilla's Athletic Sports, which had been held at the Royal Naval Ground, Port Edgar. The Naval Ground was just behind the Hospital and had been well attended that day by the Flotilla's crews and their girl friends. Admission had been by programme only unless ladies were accompanied by a Naval Rating in uniform. The events had started at one o' clock and finished at half past six in the evening. There had been races over distances of one hundred yards up to one mile, relay races, three-legged races, a sack race, long jumps, high jumps, tug-of-war, a dry boat race on a pole, veterans races over 120 yards with one yard start for every year over thirty-two, obstacle races and a Ladies' Race. He smiled at the fun they had had in the Ladies' Race, the rules being that every lady who competed chose a gentleman partner, ran forty yards to collect a cake from a stall, then ran back to her partner with it. The partner had to cram the cake into his mouth, sing "Rule Britannia" and then run hand in hand with the lady to the finishing post. Captain F F Rose, RN had presented the prizes.

For some reason his thoughts turned to Aunt Esther. She had written to him quite often when he had been away at sea. Even before he saw the handwriting he could always recognise her letters by the sheer bulkiness of them! She frequently enclosed cuttings from the *Daily Mirror* that she thought might interest him. One batch was headed "Royal Visit to the Atlantic Fleet at Torbay" during the first week of July 1922. King George V, in uniform, was aboard the Royal Yacht "Victoria and Albert" and had taken command of the Atlantic Fleet, leading them in to Torbay. Aunt Esther had thought that Jim might recognise some of the ships in the armada and, of course, she was right. What she had not known was that Jim had been part of that show aboard the Verity, part of the Third Destroyer Flotilla. The paper had listed the big ships by name.

Another letter had with it clippings showing the unveiling of the Tunbridge Wells War Memorial on February 11th 1923. She felt that he might like to see the clipping in view of his interest in the town and the fact that he had stayed there. Jim had kept all the clippings and Aunt Esther's letters. He recalled how he had browsed through them from time to time when he had nothing much else to do. At the post-card shop on the Pantiles he had managed to get two very good post-cards of the unveiling which he would put with his other cards, he decided. He began to turn his thoughts to the course he would be doing at Chatham.

The advanced small arms course with Pembroke at Chatham lasted eleven weeks and introduced the sailors to up-to-date weapons of the time. Jim enjoyed target practise on the firing ranges and did well, having very good eyesight for both short and long distances. The drills and route marches in the heat of summer proved a little arduous at times but the men did their best to make light of everything. There were opportunities to go out some evenings after cleaning rifles and equipment. Sundays usually involved a church service except for the "O.Ds" but after the service the men had the rest of the day to themselves. Jim used to catch up on his correspondence on Sunday afternoons, taking a writing pad and pen with him, and setting off for a place away from the town where he could sit down in the sunshine. Lily no longer wrote to him as she had become engaged to a soldier several months before. Aunt Esther continued to write to him and occasionally he had letters from other relations. Two girls he had met on separate occasions at dances in Norwich also sent him letters from time to time and, infrequently he received a letter from Wiggy Bennett, his old friend from the mad days aboard Caradoc.

Jim looked on those days as being the wild days of his youth. He knew that he had changed a lot since then. He sometimes wondered what he would do when his twelve years with the Navy was up. There was a great deal of unemployment in Britain and apart from a short time as an apprentice carpenter he realised that he had no trade and no skills apart from those acquired during his service which would not be in much demand in civilian life. There was always the Merchant Navy, of course, but he decided that he would prefer to sign on for a longer term with the Royal Navy at the end of the twelve years. He supposed that with the character and ability ratings given him by the Captains he had served with over the years, the Royal Navy would not look unsympathetically on a further term of service. All the medals, chevrons, educational and other certificates must go in his favour, he told himself.

The weeks passed quickly and with the course behind him, Jim received a new commission on HMS Vimiera from September

21st 1923. Jim was glad to return to sea by then, especially to the Mediterranean and Malta. The English Channel was a bit choppy, the Bay of Biscay rough, but it was good to feel the roll and pitch of the ship and the good-natured companionship of the crew. Jim knew that he was popular with the other members of the crew because of his sense of humour and the anecdotes that he was able to relate to them. He decided that he would stay with the Royal Navy for as long as they would have him and having made that decision tackled his work with enthusiasm, General drills included.

The crew of the Vimiera really were good companions and life aboard was similar in many ways to that on Verity. The lads all liked their bit of fun and apart from when the ship was at Malta, where Jim spent all his free time with Beaty, he was pleased to go ashore with other members of the crew at the middle east stops.

Jim told them of Tom and Mia, the Caradoc's pets and mascots. The others thought it a good idea to have a mascot so asked Jim to see what he could pick up the very next time he was ashore.

It was in one of the bazaars that he caught sight of a white monkey with a most appealing expression on its face. The Arab who owned it, seeing Jim's interest in the animal, thought it a good opportunity to make a small fortune. Jim had been in the Middle East many times and knew the signs. He offered a very low price and when the Arab raised his hands as if imploring help from Allah Jim made as if to move away. The Arab began to come down from his original price. Finally they settled on a price and Jim took charge of the white monkey.

He took it back to the Vimiera and introduced it to his shipmates, who decided to call it "Tinker".

It certainly lived up to its name! It climbed up the rigging, made a mess of any of the cabins it went into, stole things belonging to the crew and darted away with its thefts, making noises at any crew member who tried to recover his property. The monkey had a very mischievous streak and seemed to delight in breaking things, tearing up papers, and stealing. Jim thought that it was extremely cunning too. The final straw came when it stole one of the crew's collection of coins and proceeded to bite each coin and then, one by one, from its safe perch on the rigging, fling the coins onto the deck or into the sea.

"You brought the bloody thing on board, Jim," the irate seaman shouted. "You get rid of it! Otherwise I'll chuck the little sod overboard!"

The murmurs of "Amen" from most of the others who had at some time been victims of Tinker made Jim realise that the monkey's original popularity had faded beyond repair. He kept Tinker tied up by one leg thereafter promising to set it free at their very next port of call. It managed to bite through the rope, however, and set off on a final rampage before the ship put in at Constantinople where Jim thankfully made a gift of it to a young Turkish boy.

Chapter Eleven

On January 3ʳᵈ 1924 Jim found himself once more reporting to Pembroke at Chatham for yet another course of weapon training. He had spent the Christmas and New Year holiday at Norwich after leaving HMS Vimiera. His three months or so aboard her had been pleasant enough and he had seen Beaty again, but he could not rid himself of some sort of foreboding that their meeting was to be the last. She had been as vivacious as ever and seemed not to share his pessimism. Yet never in his experience could he recall anything remotely like that strong premonition. His attempts to shrug it off failed—it was like a heavy mantle around him that would not go away, not even alcohol succeeded in dispelling it. He had decided to spend the leave with Aunt Esther in the hope that her cheerful way of life would somehow assist him to recover his optimism.

Aunt Esther had been so pleased to see him. She had made him tea and the two of them had sat down together to catch up on events since their last Christmastime together two years before. Normally Aunt Esther had sent him letters at intervals of about a month but the last letter he had received from her was aboard the Vimiera in late September. She told him that she had been ill at the beginning of the winter with influenza, which had developed into pneumonia, and was why she had not written. Jim learned with some regret that his father had died after contracting influenza in November. Aunt Esther had written to break the news as gently as she could but he had never received the letter. The news therefore came as quite a shock. He wondered whether his own melancholy mood was connected with his father's death. After he had talked about his late father for a while, which Aunt Esther seemed to be encouraging him to do, he asked about his stepmother. He had no real affection for her but felt that his father's death must have been a lot for her to bear. Aunt Esther told Jim that she had left Norfolk soon after Jim's father had died, to keep house for her brother whose wife had also died. Aunt Esther thought that the brother lived in Cumbria but as she had received no communication from Jim's step-mother she had no idea where.

"What about my sister?" Jim had asked. "Do you know where she is?"

"Not exactly, Jim," she had replied.

"What do you mean?"

"Well, she did write to me a few weeks ago, just after your father died, and this last letter from her gave her address at last!"

"Can I see the letter?" was Jim's excited reaction.

"I'm afraid not. You see I enclosed it with my last letter to you, the one you don't seem to have received."

Jim had been devastated. It was not his aunt's fault, of course, she had done what she thought was the best thing. Tracing Vi seemed to be dogged with bad luck.

"Did you make a note of Vi's address?"

"No. There seemed no point—it was only a temporary address anyway. She said so in the letter. She mentioned that her employer was a very wealthy lady and that she liked to travel all over the place. Vi said that they had been to Scotland, Wales, London, Tunbridge Wells, Hastings and Eastbourne and were on the move again."

"Did she give any clue where they were going to next?"

"She mentioned something about spending the Christmas in Devon. Or was it Dorset? Yes, I think it was Dorset." Aunt Esther looked very agitated, as she had tried hard to recollect, she was obviously upset that she had not kept the letter, or at least a note of Vi's last address.

"Perhaps I'll get a Christmas card from her, Jim. She usually does send one."

His aunt had been right. The following morning the postman brought several cards to the house. Aunt Esther had opened the door to take the envelopes from the postman to save his having to put them through her letterbox, which had rather a stiff flap.

Vi's card had a typical Christmas snow scene and contained no message other than "Love from Vi" under the printed verse. The postmark on the envelope was indistinct but Jim had made out Ilfracombe, Devonshire. There had been nothing that he could do about it. He did not think it worth travelling all that distance knowing that he had orders to report to Chatham on January 3rd. It would have been different had Vi given an address but to have attempted to travel to Ilfracombe over Christmas with no clue to her whereabouts was something else! He had not forgotten similar trips to Tunbridge Wells and Hastings!

Aunt Esther had told Jim that his sister had asked for news of him and Aunt Esther had given her some information, including one of the photographs that Jim had sent to his Aunt. There had been nothing for it but to enjoy Christmas as best as he could and pray that news of Vi would be forthcoming in the new year ahead.

Although Aunt Esther had busied herself preparing a small chicken for the Christmas dinner and Jim had bought a few bottles of beer for himself and a bottle of sherry for his aunt, it was a quiet time for Jim. After eating the Christmas dinner Aunt Esther had dozed off to sleep in her favourite armchair. Jim had cleared up the dinner things and washed and wiped up. He had not been able to rid himself of the foreboding and recognised that it was something else besides his father's death, that was worrying him. What it was he did not know.

Aunt Esther had put his moods down to sadness over his father's death and Jim had done nothing to correct her impression. On New Year's Eve she had talked him into going to a dance in Norwich.

"You know you like dancing, Jim," she had said. "Go on out and enjoy yourself and take your mind off things a bit. Don't stay in on account of me— I'm used to being on my own and I'll find plenty to occupy myself. Have no fear!"

He had gone to the dance and joined in the drinking and general fun, seeing the New Year in with Vera, one of the girls who had written to him. She had curly blonde hair and grey-blue eyes and really was quite attractive. She was in high spirits the whole evening. At midnight she had kissed him and wished him a very happy New Year.

"I wonder what 1924 holds in store for us," she had said, giving him a hug. Jim had been wondering about that, too. *What had 1924 in store?*

Well, he had thought, the first thing was to complete the third weapons course and then get back to sea with the destroyer Flotilla.

Things went reasonably well during most of the course. The other men on the course were quite a good crowd. On Jim's twenty-third birthday, 28th April, he decided to go to Wembley to see the Cup Final play-off between Newcastle United and Aston Villa. It was on Saturday and some of the lads decided they would go along too. About a dozen of them travelled up to London with him. The weather was atrocious with heavy rain. This did not stop the teams' supporters and other football enthusiasts, however, because well over one hundred thousand of them turned up to see the game. Jim heard that there had been a tragic accident at Euston and some of the spectators at the Cup Final were saying that, but for that, the crowd at Wembley would have been even larger. Jim wondered whether Wiggy Bennett was there in that huge crowd cheering on Aston Villa. Jim thought that the game was a good one, cleanly played, but was disappointed for Wiggy's sake that Newcastle took the cup, beating Aston Villa 2 - 0. He imagined Wiggy throwing a squeaker on the ground and trampling on it and the thought made him smile. Most of the lads Jim had travelled up with decided to stay on in London for a few drinks but Jim, soaked to the skin, decided to return to Chatham.

A few days after the Cup Final Jim caught a cold. Colds were a nuisance but usually cleared up within a week so Jim carried on with the Course. He was annoyed when he developed tonsillitis. He had had that before when he was at sea and it followed a similar pattern. He knew that he had a fever as he began sweating and shivering alternately.

He tried to struggle on as the Course was practically over but by then had pains in his back. When he noticed that there was blood in his urine he reported sick. The Medical Officer who examined him made arrangements for Jim's immediate admission to the Royal Naval Hospital at Chatham. He told Jim that he was suffering tonsillitis and acute nephritis.

Jim had no idea what nephritis was and said so. The Medical Officer explained that it was a kidney infection and that Jim would need to rest up for a few weeks.

During his time in Hospital he was examined frequently. Blood tests, urine samples, blood pressure and pulse readings were taken regularly and the M.O. listened to his heart and peered into his mouth and throat. At first he was given only orange juice to drink or barley water and a foul-tasting liquid that he was told was cascara. Gradually solid foods were introduced such as bread and butter and egg, then some vegetables and finally fish but he was allowed no meat. He had bed baths daily, being rubbed down with hot dry towels afterwards. As the days passed his urine became clearer and the skin irritation, which he had put down to nerves, also cleared up. The two doctors who had been examining him daily decided that Jim's tonsils had to be removed after his other symptoms had abated. He did not mind having the tonsillectomy. After all, if his tonsils had caused the kidney infection, it was best to be rid of them and ensure that they would never cause him any more problems. After the operation he went back on liquids for a day or two and had a tender throat but that discomfiture soon passed.

The seaman in the next bed had had a burst appendix and peritonitis and had been very ill. However, he seemed to be recovering and told Jim that it had been 'touch and go' with him. He, like Jim, was keen to get better quickly and get back to sea.

One of the doctors asked Jim if he had ever been exposed to severe cold. The only time Jim could remember was after the incident of the fire aboard Caradoc at Constantinople where he had worked for hours pumping out the water from the ammunition hold, waist deep in cold water. He told the doctor this but could see no connection between that incident and his sickness.

Jim was allowed up a week or so later and as some of the other men in the ward were also allowed out of bed they occupied their time playing cards or dominoes, talking together about their service or families, or writing letters home. Jim wrote to Beaty and to Aunt Esther. Now that he felt much better he was becoming bored and was anxious to be released from hospital.

On June 4th the doctor examined Jim and further blood pressure readings were taken, together with blood testing and urine sampling. A second doctor listened to his heart-beat and checked his breathing.

Jim had never worried about medical examinations in the past but for some unknown reason he became anxious about that one. It all seemed a bit of an ordeal. He tried to reassure himself, after all he felt well, so perhaps the medical was a final check-up before releasing him from the hospital. One of the doctors told him that he could get dressed and afterwards to go to another part of the hospital where out-patients were seen. He was told that there was a waiting room there where he should take a seat and wait until he was called.

Jim felt relieved. All that sounded like he was about to be released from hospital at last! He dressed himself in his uniform and made his way to the waiting-room where he had been directed. When he arrived there two men were sitting talking together. He recognised one of the men, a very heavily built man with a florid face and a beer-gut, who had occupied a bed in the ward where Jim had first been admitted. The other man, of medium build with a beard, he had not seen before. The two men looked up as Jim entered the room. The big man nodded to Jim in recognition and then said:

"Been through a bit of a rough time, mate?"

Jim said that he had not minded too much and it was worth it if he was to be released from hospital, as he was keen to get back to sea.

"Released all right," the big man said. "But not like you think! They're looking for excuses to chuck people out. It's something to do with cut-backs in the services. All of us have probably had quite a few bouts of sickness during our service and we'll all be for the high jump, mate!"

Jim was horrified. He had felt concern about the medical but had not thought that the outcome would be so sinister. If what the man had said was correct, what would he do? He thought about his own medical record, the time in hospital with catarrhal jaundice, the accident to his feet aboard Caradoc, the long time in hospital at Edinburgh with diphtheria, an attack of tonsillitis at Malta, and finally the last lot, with tonsillitis and nephritis. The more Jim thought about his record the more worried he became.

The man with the beard was talking about the bouts of malaria he had had. The big man was listening; he then went into his own medical history. The big man was the first to be called from the waiting room. Jim and the man with the beard talked together about their service. The bearded man told Jim that he had served in the North Atlantic during the War but had later been transferred to a cruiser squadron in the far east. He was very interested in the Black Sea operations against the Bolsheviks.

"Of course, after the 1914-18 war was over most of us had nothing much to worry about so far as action was concerned. We had heard that some of you were having a rough time in the Black Sea but you're the first bloke I've ever spoken to who was actually there."

"I was on the Caradoc then," Jim told him. "Captain Munro Kerr was our skipper most of the time. The best Captain I've ever served with."

"Caradoc," the bearded man repeated. "Yes, I know her. She's a light cruiser, isn't she?"

Jim nodded his head.

"I transferred later to the third destroyer Flotilla," Jim told him. "A much smaller crew, of course, and much less to paint!"

The bearded man laughed. "Never fancied them myself," he said. "Still it's every man to his own. Going back to the Black Sea action, what were the Bolshies like?"

Jim told him about the Bolshevik atrocities he had seen.

The man shook his head.

"They sound worse than the Huns ever were."

Jim turned the conversation to what was on his mind.

"Do you think that it's true that we are likely to be chucked out of the Navy, like that big guy seemed to think?"

The bearded man scratched his beard.

"Speaking for myself, yes, I think so. I picked up malaria a few months ago out East. I was pretty ill too. Once you've got it you never really get over it properly. Sometimes it comes back suddenly and you end up with the shakes and fever. A mate of mine worked in Africa before the War and he caught it. He came back to England but still had attacks of it. I doubt that the Navy would want to keep me on."

"What was wrong with the big fellow?" Jim asked.

"Alcohol I should think!"

"Is that what he said to you?"

"He said that he had something wrong with his ticker. That might be but, I fancy, he likes the booze too much."

"I suppose so," Jim said, adding: "Most of us have had too much at times. I know that when I went ashore from the Caradoc with my mates we have often had sessions where we ended up paralytic."

The bearded man nodded his head in agreement, then asked more questions about the Black Sea. Jim was still telling him about it when the man was called from the waiting room.

"Best of luck, mate!" he called to Jim as he left the room. Jim gave a thumbs up sign to him.

Left alone Jim began to feel very agitated. He could not remain seated in the waiting room and began pacing up and down. There was nothing in the room to take his thoughts away from the anxiety, no books, no newspapers. Could it be possible that the big man was right? He knew that the Country's economic situation was bad but could it be *that* bad? Were the "powers that be" really cutting down manpower in the services and looking for excuses to get rid of men like him? True his medical history was not good but it was not too bad either, he argued. The Navy was his life, what would he do if he were kicked out?

Then he heard his name being called from the doorway, it was his turn. He was ushered into a room where several men sat together looking at some papers, which Jim assumed related to him.

One of the men, presumably a doctor, spoke to him.

"We have examined your records," he said in a flat tone. "We also have the results of the tests which you underwent earlier today."

"I trust that they are satisfactory, sir," Jim said.

The doctor looked at him. He then consulted the documents in front of him again. He then looked at Jim once more.

"I am afraid not."

"What do you mean, sir?" Jim asked anxiously. The answer he had been dreading came. The doctor told him that arrangements would be made to invalid him out of the Navy with a lump sum gratuity. There would be no pension as there was no evidence to

166

suggest that his state of health was directly caused by his service. The other men were nodding in agreement.

"But I *feel well*, sir," Jim pleaded.

The silence that followed was broken by Jim.

"I've signed on for twelve years and still have some of that term to do."

"I am sorry," said the spokesman. "Our decision is final."

Jim left the hospital in something of a daze. He just could not face the fact that he had been discharged from the Navy. The sheer horror of it came to him later when he was paid a lump sum gratuity, given four weeks discharge leave and a railway warrant. At the end of his leave, on July 3rd 1924, he would become a civilian, probably an out of work one at that, he thought bitterly.

He had packed all his gear in the trunk and arranged with a carrier for it to be delivered to Aunt Esther's house in Norwich. He dashed off a letter to her telling her that he had been discharged from the Navy and would be seeing her in early July. In the meanwhile, he explained, he had arranged for his seaman's trunk to be delivered to her home as it was too bulky for him to transport about. He added that he knew she wouldn't mind looking after it for him just as he didn't mind having it safely looked after by her!

The last letter he had received from Aunt Esther was at the end of May and told him that Vi had written from the Isle of Wight where she was staying at a place called Niton. It seemed that the address was purely temporary and that Vi and her employer had also been staying at Castle Combe, Wiltshire where her lady, as she called her employer, had relatives. Their plans for the future included Eastbourne and then back to Tunbridge Wells.

Jim decided that he wanted to get away from Chatham as soon as he could. He associated it with his bad luck and thought that anywhere would be preferable to it right then.

It seemed to him that Vi's employer's long-term plans were to return to Tunbridge Wells; therefore he selected that town to settle in himself. He had spent some good times there in the past and had got to know it pretty well. He decided that he would go there from Chatham and secure permanent lodgings in the area, a base as it were. He thought that he should be able to secure work there too, although that was not an immediate problem as he had saved his pay from the Navy since giving up drinking, and he had been paid his gratuity and four weeks leave money.

A couple of hours later he was once more in Camden Road. He had retained the addresses given him on his last stay for some reason and deciding against the Beulah Road address where he had stayed before, made straight for Commercial Road.

He knocked at the door and was successful that time for the door opened and he found himself faced by a girl in her teens with dark hair, some of which had flopped down over her right eye. She had an impish smile on her face as she looked at Jim. He smiled back.

"Do you want to see my mum?" she asked him.

"Yes, please. I'm looking for somewhere to stay."

"You'd better come in," she told him. "Mum's in the kitchen."

Jim was shown into the living room, which he noticed was clean and reasonably well furnished. The girl's mother came from the kitchen into the living room, drying her hands on a towel hurriedly. She was a woman in her late thirties, early forties, Jim judged. She was more heavily built than her daughter but had the same oval shaped face and high cheekbones.

"He's looking for a room, mum," the girl explained.

"That's right," Jim said. "My name's Jim Alexander."

He held out his hand and the older woman shook it in greeting.

"Pleased to meet you," she said. "Did you just want it for a week or two?"

She was looking at his uniform and probably thought he would be going back to sea, so Jim told her that he was on final leave and had thought of settling in Tunbridge Wells if he could find work..

"You're not from these parts then? I thought I detected a slight accent."

Jim told her that he had been born in Norfolk but that both his parents were dead. He added that his sister worked in Tunbridge Wells sometimes but he hadn't seen her for twelve years.

"Well I never!" the woman said with surprise. Jim felt that he had made a reasonably good impression for she then said that although she already had a lodger she could make room for Jim if he didn't mind the small bedroom.

"You'll want to see it, of course. Come on and have a look!"

She led the way upstairs and showed him the room. It was small all right but clean and simply furnished. Jim said that it suited him and as the terms for room and board were very reasonable they settled the matter there and then.

"We usually eat at about six o' clock. Bob and Frank get in about half past five," his landlady said. "Bob is my son and Frank is your fellow boarder. By the way, I'm Mrs Latter."

The young girl was still downstairs; Jim could hear her moving about. Mrs Latter explained that she was her youngest child and that she was between jobs, which is why she was at home that afternoon. Her mother referred to her as my "little girl" whenever she spoke of her.

He felt very comfortable in his new surroundings. Mrs Latter and her daughter were very easy to get along with and he was made to feel one of the family. They asked him about the navy and he told them the names of all the ships he had served on and what places he had visited, during his service. When he mentioned HMS Tiger the girl said to her mother that she would call her puppy "Tiggie". The puppy was curled up asleep in a basket in the scullery, which is why Jim had not realised its presence. They took Jim into the scullery to see the puppy. It was a mongrel but with attractive colouring, white and dark brown, the white fur predominating, beginning with a thick line of white from the top of its head and gradually broadening out below its eyes and jaws and covering its breast, half its back and body; its tail was brown apart from the tip which was white. The puppy was only a few weeks old and Jim was told that, like him, it had only moved in that day.

Mrs Latter and "Girly" were busy in the kitchen preparing the meal they were all to eat later. Jim offered to help but they told him to sit down in the kitchen and carry on talking with them. The door between the kitchen and the scullery was open so the conversation continued whichever room they happened to be in.

Mrs Latter made Jim a cup of tea and then returned to her cooking.

Jim realised that he felt hungry. Perhaps it was the smell of the cooking that was stimulating his appetite, it smelled really delicious.

Mrs Latter was putting the finishing touches to the meal when her son arrived home. He was very much like his sister in appearance with dark hair, dark eyes and the same oval shaped face and wide mouth. Jim judged him to be about nineteen. Mrs Latter introduced Jim to him and the young man gave Jim a grin.

"You're a sailor I see," he said. "Are you spending your leave in this town? Can't think why anyone would choose Tunbridge Wells!"

"I'm on final leave," Jim explained again. "I finish up with the Navy next month. I'm *settling* in this town."

"Were you in the navy during the last war?"

Jim said that he was. Bob wanted to know what it was like in the war at sea. Jim had just started telling him when his fellow lodger came in.

"Hallo, Frank," they all greeted the new arrival in turn.

Frank acknowledged their greetings in an accent that Jim recognised as being North Country. Jim judged him to be about the same age as himself; although about the same height he was heavier built than Jim. He had brown hair with a high forehead, broad nose and generous mouth and eyes that took in everything shrewdly. Like most North Countrymen Jim had met, Frank spoke to the point but he could sense that the man was good hearted and genial, the bluff way of speaking just natural with him.

"And who have we here?" he asked, crossing over to Jim.

"I'm Jim Alexander," Jim said, offering his hand. Frank grasped it firmly and the two men shook hands.

"Pleased to meet you, Jim. My name's Frank Whittam."

Conversation continued over their meal together.

"What brought you to Tunbridge Wells?" Frank asked Jim.

"A train," Jim answered.

The two men looked at one another across the table for a moment or two and then Frank broke into laughter. The Latter family joined in.

Jim explained that he had been to Tunbridge Wells two or three times before, looking for his sister but had not succeeded in tracing her. He told them that he hoped to have more success when he had settled in the town. He added that he had no immediate financial worries but would have to find a job within the next month or so.

"Ever thought of starting a business of your own?" Frank asked him.

"Sometimes it had crossed my mind but it's knowing what to do for the best."

"Can you drive a car?"

Jim nodded.

"Why not buy a cab and start up a taxi business? That doesn't take a lot of capital," Frank suggested.

"I'll give it some thought. It might be the answer if I can't get a job."

The two men sat together over tea while Mrs Latter and her daughter cleared away the dinner things and washed them up. Bob had gone to his room to get ready to go out. Jim liked Frank's company. The man was extremely outspoken and held strong views on certain matters but he had a sense of humour and that was "all important" to Jim. When they had finished their tea the two men decided to go for a walk. It was a pleasant evening and they walked into the town centre, past the War Memorial and into Church Road, talking together as they walked.

"That was a good meal we had," Jim said. "They seem decent people."

Frank told him that when he first came to Tunbridge Wells he took lodgings in Upper Grosvenor Road but was not very pleased with them. Later he moved to Commercial Road having been given a recommendation by someone he had met in a pub.

"I've stayed there ever since. The food is good and she doesn't overcharge," Frank said. "It's not the most fashionable part of town but it is fairly central."

"Where do you work, Frank?"

"At the moment I'm driving a lorry and generally helping out at a friend's place. He's got a greengrocery business and I drive up to Covent Garden with the lorry to pick up stuff to sell. I intend setting up in business myself eventually."

"In the greengrocery line?"

"Yes, but I want to open it in the London suburbs somewhere, not here. What I have been doing is sounding out hotels. There's money to be made in supplying them in bulk, at reduced profit but a quick turnover. All it needs is a little graft loading up a lorry and driving to the Hotels to drop the stuff off. When I have established sufficient contacts in the hotel line I can work out a schedule so that I can deliver with a minimum of travelling."

"You seem to have worked things out pretty well," Jim said. Obviously Frank was a shrewd businessman and enterprising.

"Nobody gets rich working for someone else," he confided to Jim.

"There seem to be few who get rich anyway," Jim said, thinking of the growing numbers of unemployed. "Take this town, for example, there are the rich and the poor. It's a matter of luck whether someone is born into money or not. Like everywhere else this town has its share of men who were in the services and after they had sweated blood for their country they end up on the scrap-heap!"

"A lot of them just sit back, moaning about their bad luck— instead of doing something constructive," Frank answered.

"A few maybe but I think that the Government should have done more for them. Even if a person starts a business of his own he needs some capital. Thank God there's a Labour movement in this Country."

The two then went into a political discussion. Although their ideas on politics were "oceans" apart they agreed that they would not fall out over them. Their walk took them over Tunbridge Wells Common, along Mount Ephraim to the Spa Hotel, down Major York's Road to the Pantiles and then up Mount Pleasant to Monson Road and Camden Road. They called in at the Black Horse on the way back to their digs and enjoyed a few drinks together to round off the evening, over which they continued their conversation. Jim told Frank about his service with the Navy and how he had been kicked out because of his health record. Frank listened attentively until Jim had finished speaking.

"What puzzles me, Jim," he said, with a smile, "Is how you, a Socialist, could have spent so much time fighting the Russian Socialists!"

"If you had seen the Bolsheviks you would soon have realised that they were for the most part nothing more than a crowd of brigands. It remains to be seen what will happen in Russia in the years ahead. The Russians I met were simple and kindly folk who were tired of the war and just wanted to get on with their lives."

"You're probably right, Jim," Frank said. "Mind, I still don't trust these Socialists!"

"Let's leave out politics, like we agreed," Jim laughed. "We could go on arguing until the cows come home. I doubt that anything either of us say is going to make the slightest difference to the other!"

They stayed at the Black Horse until closing time. Jim learned that Frank had a girl friend named Kitty who, one day, Frank hoped to marry. Apart from their difference of opinion so far as politics was concerned the two men were at ease together and a friendship began which was to last many years.

Jim stayed in Tunbridge Wells for fifteen days and then decided to go up to Norwich to see Aunt Esther and arrange for his trunk to be delivered to his new home in Tunbridge Wells. He told Mrs Latter that he would be gone about a week and that he would be arranging to have his belongings sent down from Norwich to her house. She wanted to make some adjustment on his board charge but Jim would not allow that; he thought the terms very reasonable as it was and felt glad that he had found accommodation with such congenial people.

His stay with Aunt Esther was pleasant. She was very upset to hear about his discharge from the Navy and thought he had been treated very shabbily. She wanted him to stay on in Norwich, assuring him that he would be bound to find work there. The stay did produce an unexpected stroke of fortune, however, because one of Aunt Esther's neighbours had decided to sell his BSA motorbike. Jim went along to see it and to check it over. It needed some attention, as the neighbour admitted, but they agreed a price between them that satisfied them both and Jim took ownership of the motorbike. He stripped the engine down in Aunt Esther's yard and worked on it for three or four days, meticulously cleaning, oiling and greasing like he had with the guns. When he had completed the engine overhaul he cleaned the paintwork until it shone like new. The road test he gave it proved satisfactory and Jim announced to Aunt Esther that he would be going back to Tunbridge Wells on it.

Jim had arranged with a carrier to transport his trunk to Tunbridge Wells the day after his arrival in Norwich and had helped the carrier load it in the van that same afternoon. His few remaining belongings were packed into a small bag that he could carry comfortably on the motor cycle. Then he said his farewells to Aunt Esther, promising to keep in touch with her, and started on his journey to Tunbridge Wells. He reached Woolwich that day and decided to break journey there. He stayed overnight in a bed and breakfast place and set off the following morning, getting into Tunbridge Wells some hour and a half later. He was very pleased with the bike's performance and thought that with his own transport he would be able to travel outside Tunbridge Wells for work if needs be.

One evening, after their meal, he took Frank to Fairlight. On the way home they stopped for a beer in Lamberhurst. Frank told Jim that he preferred cars to motor cycles but had enjoyed the run. He asked Jim if he had started looking around for work.

"Not seriously," Jim admitted. "To tell you the truth I want to go across to the Isle of Wight to see if I can find my sister. It isn't much good getting a job until after that trip. No employer is going to give me a holiday as soon as I start work, is he?"

"That's true," Frank admitted.

"I've a few pounds put by me," Jim explained. "More than enough to cover me for the next month or two. The motor cycle set me back a bit but it's a cheap form of travel so I shall save money I would otherwise have forked out on trains."

"When are you thinking of going to the Isle of Wight, Jim?"

"This week. To tell you the truth I want to see Portsmouth again while I'm still entitled to wear my naval uniform."

"You miss the navy, don't you, Jim?"

"Most of the time, yes," Jim admitted. "It's a funny thing but I used to worry about what I'd do if I came out of the Navy and I decided to sign on again when my twelve years were up. Little did I think that I wouldn't even finish the first twelve year stint!"

"You won't have much difficulty in getting work," Frank prophesied. "From what I know about you, that is. You seem to me to be a man gifted with creative ability. I watched you repair

Mrs Latter's clock. How you stripped that down and put it all back together again, beats me!"

Jim had not thought of it like that before. To him anything that man had created could be taken apart and recreated. It was beyond his comprehension how anyone could think otherwise. After all, once one had seen how something worked, it surely was not difficult to rectify any fault and get it working again.

"You ought to apply to the G.P.O and get yourself a telephone engineer's job, Jim," Frank suggested. "That is, if you're not minded to set yourself up in business."

Jim thought the telephone-engineering job might be the answer and thanked Frank for suggesting it.

He explained to Mrs Latter the next morning that he was thinking of going down to the Isle of Wight for a couple of weeks.

"You're a right one," she told Jim. "I guess that after travelling all over the place in the Navy, you must find it difficult to settle down. Well, your room will be waiting here for you. You know that you always have a home here."

Jim thanked her. Once again she offered to take something off his board and lodgings charge for the time he would be away and once again Jim had to insist quite firmly that he would not allow it.

"If you decide to stay over on the Isle of Wight longer than a fortnight, Jim," she said to him on the morning he left. "Just drop me a line. Come back when you're ready."

The ride down to Portsmouth was uneventful, pleasant and unhurried. Jim spent a little time in the Naval Dockyard where HMS Victory's quartermaster was to be found. Victory was anchored just off Spithead. Jim explained that he had done part of his training aboard her eight years ago. The quartermaster told Jim that there would be a Royal Review of many of the ships of the fleet there on July 26th and if Jim happened to be still on leave then it would be worth seeing. Jim had said nothing about his discharge from the Navy, merely that he was on a long leave.

The ferry across to the Isle of Wight took about a half hour but it was good to go up on deck and watch the wake of the vessel. He pretended to himself that he was back on the Vimiera and was so wrapped up in the game that he was quite surprised when the ferryboat shuddered to a halt. The journey was over. Jim had left his motorbike in Portsmouth so travelled by train and bus to Niton. The village was very small and he thought that he would have little difficulty in finding Vi there.

Few places there were offering accommodation and his enquiries about his sister proved negative. No one of her name had stayed at any of them and neither did anyone recognise her from the photograph that Jim produced. It was possible that she might have stayed with her employer at one of the houses, of course. He was unable to find accommodation for himself at Niton or Blackgang but managed to get fixed up with bed and breakfast in the neighbouring village of Chale. This meant travelling or walking but he decided that the exercise would do him good. He walked the few miles into Niton after breakfast and back to Chale in the late evening. He enjoyed the sea views and as the weather was extremely good he did a lot of walking but at no time did he ever see Vi. After three days of wandering about he concluded that if Vi and her employer were still there he would have seen them and began travelling further afield, visiting Ventnor, Shanklin, Sandown in the South-eastern part of the Island and Yarmouth in the west. He bought picture postcards to send to Frank, Mrs Latter, Girly and Bob and also to Aunt Esther. He bought one or two extra cards to keep.

At the end of the first week he shifted his base from Chale to Cowes, staying in a small guesthouse. His room overlooked the Solent and he recalled with nostalgia looking on that same stretch of water from the decks of ships. Gradually he came to terms with the fact that he was out of the Navy, that there was no return to it. If he went to sea in the future it would be as a passenger only. To be a passenger would mean having the money to pay and that would mean getting himself work. Frank's suggestion about a Post office engineering job seemed to be a sensible one, Jim decided. He had felt the benefit of the holiday in the Isle of Wight, felt more relaxed, less bitter and a lot fitter.

He crossed by ferry to Portsmouth the following day, collected his motor cycle from the garage where he had left it and travelled back to Tunbridge Wells.

"Had a good wander around?" Mrs Latter asked him.

"Yes, it was quite enjoyable," Jim replied. "But it's time to find myself a job and settle down to civilian life."

He put his uniform away in the trunk after equipping himself with some civilian clothes. His leave was over.

His application for work as a post officer engineer in Tunbridge Wells was accepted after some aptitude tests, which presented no problem. At that time the area covered by the Tunbridge Wells post office engineers extended to Sussex and it was not uncommon for Jim to drive to Hastings to tackle installations or repairs. The engineer with whom he worked most of the time was older than Jim but easy to get along with and the two men had quite a few laughs together. Ted was a skinny man, blue eyed and with wiry hair that always looked untidy. He smoked a lot of cigarettes on and off duty and Jim wondered how he managed to work with a cigarette dangling from his mouth, smoke drifting about his face and eyes.

On Saturday, July 26th, Ted covered for Jim while he travelled down to Portsmouth to see the King's review of the fleet at Spithead, a sight he was determined not to miss. Forty miles of warships had lined up including Admiral Sir John de Robeck's flagship, the *Queen Elizabeth* with her huge fifteen- inch guns. Jim remembered her well. He also saw HMS Hermes, the fleet carrier. He wondered whether many of his old shipmates were manning the destroyers and the light cruisers. Seeing that array of fighting ships filled him with pride. He had once been a part of that great Navy, "the sure shield" against all our enemies as some reporter had described it in one of the daily newspapers.

Jim was tempted to hang about Portsmouth but forced himself to get back on his motorbike. He was a civilian and had a job to do and a life to live.

The weeks passed and then one day in September he received a letter from Aunt Esther. In it she said that Vi had been staying in Eastbourne with her lady, who it seemed had been ill, but they were anticipating returning to Tunbridge Wells before Christmas and Vi had promised to write to Aunt Esther with her new Tunbridge Wells address. Vi had written a letter for him too, which Aunt Esther had enclosed. It was quite a short letter but said that she was looking forward to meeting him again after their long separation and seeing what he looked like as a man.

Jim took Frank down to Eastbourne several times during the last of the summer and early autumn on the Sundays when Frank was not going up to London to see Kitty. On those Sundays Jim either travelled there alone or took Bob or Girly. Jim, always the optimist, hoped that he might see Vi walking along the front, but much as he hoped, his hopes were not fulfilled.

He wrote to Aunt Esther imploring her to send his Tunbridge Wells address to Vi at the earliest opportunity if she should write before Christmas. He even enclosed a letter for Vi, quite a long one, telling her what had happened to him over the years and ending up by saying that he was looking forward to meeting her again and seeing for himself if she was as beautiful as her photograph.

In early January 1925 he received a letter from Aunt Esther. It read:

"I've had a Christmas card from Vi— no address or letter with it but the postmark is definitely Tunbridge Wells. I expect that she will be writing a letter within a few days". Jim scribbled a quick note to his aunt, thanking her, and asking her to write to him as soon as she had any further news. So, Vi was in Tunbridge Wells; it would be only a matter of days before he would see her! He might even meet her in the town before Aunt Esther had time to write again!

When he finished work that day, earlier than usual, he decided to get a cup of tea before going back to his digs. He wanted a little time alone to accustom himself to the idea of meeting Vi, what it would be like, how well they would get along together after such a long separation. He chose a tearoom, in the town centre, which was practically empty. He sat down at a table near the window. A man sitting at a table nearby nodded to him as Jim sat down. Jim returned the silent greeting. He had no idea who the man was and in any case did not want to engage in conversation with anyone at that time. A young waitress came to Jim's table to take his order. He could not help noticing that she was very attractive. He judged her to be about eighteen or nineteen. She was probably five feet two or three with dark hair, dark eyes and a very lovely face. In fact, he thought her to be the loveliest girl he had *ever* seen. She smiled at him as she took his order. Although his intention had been to sit quietly by himself and think, Jim wanted instead to talk to the girl. Determined to engage her in conversation he remarked on the fact that he had finished work early and wanted a really nice cup of tea to refresh him.

"Do you work in the town?" she asked him, when she brought his tea.

Jim confessed that he did but that his work took him outside the town frequently.

"What sort of work do you do?"

He told her that he worked as a post office engineer but had previously served eight years in the Navy. He wondered why he had said that but she seemed to like talking to him. She gave him a lovely smile and then moved off to serve some other customers who had arrived.

When he had finished he ordered some more tea, although he didn't *really* want another tea! The waitress brought it to his table.

"I only work here part time," she told Jim. "The rest of the week I help out in a post office store near my home. The work here with tips brings in a bit of extra cash."

He asked her if she lived in Tunbridge Wells and she told him that she did.

"What time do you finish work?" he asked her, glancing at his wristwatch.

"Around half past six," she answered. Then added, "We actually close at six but it's usually nearer half past by the time I get away."

Jim thought about Mrs Latter and the evening meal. Bob and Frank would have got home by then and probably be seated at table. He had arrived late before when he had worked some distance from the town or if Ted and he had worked a bit late to finish a job. Mrs Latter had then left Jim's dinner in the oven to keep hot. He thought that she would assume that he was working away and do the same that evening. He made up his mind, dinner or not, he would ask this girl for a date.

"I've my motorbike parked outside. Can I give you a lift home?" he asked her. She was looking at him, weighing up what she saw. She obviously felt that she could trust him for she replied:

"That would be nice," but added with some concern "As long as it won't be taking you out of your way."

"Don't worry about that! My digs are not far from here. Whatever part of the town you live in won't take long to reach on the bike."

She wrote out Jim's bill and then had to leave him to do the same with the other customers. As she left his table Jim told her that he would wait for her outside. He paid his bill at the counter to a woman who was probably the proprietor, and left.

He waited outside for about ten minutes until she came out.

"I'm sorry that I'm a bit late," she apologised. "The old girl kept me talking a bit!"

He drove her to her home, a semi-detached house opposite a row of shops. It was in an area of the town that Jim had never been to before. Conversation had been difficult on the motorbike but when Jim pulled up outside her house they had an opportunity to talk before she went in. She told him that her name was Nora. He learned that her father was a tailor and that besides her father and mother she also had two brothers and three sisters. Jim told her his name, where his digs were, and that he had a sister but had not seen her since he was eleven.

"What do you do in the evenings?" Jim asked her.

"Mostly read or help my father if he has some urgent work to complete," Nora answered. "Occasionally I go to a dance if I can find someone to go with. I love dancing." Jim thought it unlikely that she would have difficulty in finding someone to take *her* to a dance. He imagined that most young men would jump at the opportunity. She seemed to read his thoughts for she added, "Lots of the men around here have asked me out but I haven't wanted to go out with any or them. My brother has taken me to one or two dances. He's a fantastic dancer."

"I love dancing too," Jim told her. "I used to go dancing a lot when I was in the Navy. I haven't been to a dance since I came to this town, seven months ago."

"There's a dance on Saturday I would like to go to." Was she hinting that he should offer to take her? He hesitated a moment then made up his mind to ask her outright.

"Would you consider going to it with me?"

"That would be lovely. Yes, I would like you to take me."

"That's settled then," Jim said. "I'll pick you up here on Saturday. What time?"

"I'm working at the tea room all afternoon and won't be able to get away until half past six, then I've got to get home, change my clothes and make myself look presentable. It would be about eight o'clock."

"How about my meeting you from work?" Jim suggested. "That would save a bit of time."

"Well, if it wouldn't be putting you out too much, that would be really terrific. It would mean your having to wait about while I got ready 'though."

"I don't mind," Jim said. "That's all arranged then. I'll pick you up outside the tea rooms at half past six, Nora."

Jim was in jubilant spirits as he returned to his digs. After all, things were looking up. He had a job, somewhere to live that he could call a home of his own, a good friend in Frank, and a date with a girl who measured up to his ideal. All that remained was for him to find his sister and somehow he felt very optimistic about that too!

When he arrived back at Commercial Road, they had finished dinner. Frank was drinking a cup of tea and Mrs Latter and Girly were washing up the dinner things.

"Sorry I'm late," Jim apologised. "I got held up a bit."

"That's all right," Mrs Latter called from the scullery. "I've kept your dinner hot in the oven. Just sit down, Jim. Girly will bring it in to you. My hands are wet."

"Working late again, Jim?" Frank asked him as Jim sat down and began eating. The dinner smelled delicious and Jim realised that he was very hungry.

"I'll tell you about it later, Frank," Jim said, giving Frank a wink and inclining his head towards the scullery. Frank got the message all right; he was pretty astute.

After Jim had eaten his dinner the two men decided to go for a walk and a few drinks together. Jim had the chance to explain to Frank where he had been and his real reason for arriving late for dinner. Frank laughed and told Jim that he had thought there was some reason for the guilty look on Jim's face when he had first entered the kitchen.

"You looked like a school-boy who had been playing truant."

"It's a good job that the women were busy in the scullery then," Jim said. "If someone like you could sense it, I'm pretty sure that one of the women would have done so!"

Jim knew that Frank would not take the remark as offensive. By that time they had become such good friends that they could say anything to one another in fun.

"I've put some money in my friend's business, Jim," Frank told him. "I'm a partner now. Mind you," he added "it's not my intention to stay in Tunbridge Wells for the rest of my life but Kitty is thinking of moving down here from London to give me a hand. I still want to put my ideas into practise with the hotels. There's money to be made in that idea, I know."

Jim nodded. "I think that you're right, Frank."

"Why don't you have a go at doing something on your own, Jim?"

"I've been thinking about the taxi-cab line we discussed once."

"Don't *think* about it, Jim. *Do* it!"

Jim confided that he had insufficient savings left to buy a decent cab and needed to keep working with the post office a bit longer to make up the deficit.

"I've just put my savings into the business or otherwise I could have helped you out, Jim. If things do as well as I expect I may still be able to help you in a few months."

"Thanks, Frank. I know that you would be glad to help out but if I'm going to do something on my own then I've got to do it under my own steam. I'll save what I need."

"You independent cuss! Anyway, the offer stands if you want it."

On the Saturday Jim felt very excited as he parked his motorbike outside the tea room where Nora worked. He noticed that it was only quarter past six. However, he had not waited long before Nora joined him.

"Have you been waiting long?" she asked him. He told her that it only *seemed* like it.

"As luck would have it I finished earlier than usual. No late customers fortunately so she let me get away early."

When they arrived at her home she asked Jim to wait outside and she would go in and see if it was all right for him to wait for her in the house. She was gone a few minutes.

"It's all right, Jim," she called from the doorway. "You can come in."

He walked along the passage-way to the side door where she was standing. The front room of the house that looked onto the road was equipped as a tailor's shop and was evidently where her father worked. Jim had noticed the man sitting at a treadle machine as he passed. Jim was shown into a small hallway from which a flight of stairs faced the door; there were doors to the workshop and to the living room. Nora took him through the doorway to the living room. There he was introduced to Nora's mother, a tiny lady with black curly hair greying at the temples. Jim thought that he had never seen such a delicate looking person; she was no taller than four feet ten at the most and very thin. She had such a kindly face that his heart went out to her immediately.

"So you're Jim," she said, shaking his hand. "I'm very pleased to meet you. Goodness you are tall! Would you like a cup of tea while you're waiting? Nora told us that you've just come out of the Navy."

She spoke almost nervously, as if she were not used to entertaining people. He thanked her and said that a cup of tea would be nice.

As she busied herself making the tea Jim heard voices coming from the kitchen. They were men's voices and one of them was raised in anger. There seemed to be an argument going on about shoe brushes. He listened, amused.

"Why do you always use the *brown* brush to clean your *black* shoes, Bernie? It's always the same! Too much trouble to sort things out."

"Sorry!" the other voice spoke.

"Just saying sorry is not good enough! Just because you don't take any pride in your appearance doesn't mean that everyone has to be like you! There's mud on the polishing brush too. I'll bet you cleaned your football boots with it!"

"Boys! Boys!" Nora's mother said with a deep sigh, "Stop arguing! Nora's friend is here. I don't know what he will think of us all!"

The two young men emerged from the kitchen. The younger of the two was slimmer than his brother and quite a handsome man, cleanly shaven, black wavy hair and doubtless the one who took pride in his appearance. The older brother had curly black hair, which looked as if it had not been brushed or combed that day, neither had the man shaved by the stubble on his chin and upper lip.

"This is Cecil, my youngest son," Nora's mother announced. "And this is Bernie, my eldest."

"My name's Jim. Pleased to meet you, Cecil and Bernie," he said, shaking hands with each man in turn. He noticed that both men had warm handshakes.

"Pleased to meet you too, Jim!" said Cecil. Bernie nodded his head vigorously in agreement. "By the way, everyone calls me Cec."

"I heard Nora say that you were in the Navy," Bernie said, hardly before his brother had finished speaking. "I was in the army in Germany in the war and after it. I volunteered at the same time as my dad. I was only sixteen then and he was fifty-one!" Jim registered surprise and Bernie, encouraged, went on: "Of course, he was too old to fight in the trenches but he went in as a tailor and made uniforms for the officers."

"He needn't have gone in at all," Cec said. "He might just as well have stayed home and looked after mum."

"Your dad did what he felt was right." Nora's mother sounded defensive.

"I think that it was something to volunteer at all at that age," Jim said. "I was fourteen when I first went for training, in 1915. I went to sea when I was sixteen."

Bernie told Jim that he had been taken prisoner by the Germans shortly before the armistice and subsequently had the pleasure of reversing positions with his guards, staying on in Germany in the army of occupation for a time.

"He had a nice fraulein over there too," Cec chimed in. "He should have married her instead of coming back here. Do you know that this house has only got three bedrooms? My sisters share the biggest room and I have to put up with him!"

"Well, you're fortunate that your brother works nights," his mother said, quite seriously.

"What work do you do, Bernie?"

"I'm a baker. I start work at eight o'clock in the evening and I finish at eight in the morning. Unsociable hours but that doesn't worry me. As long as I can play football on Saturdays and have a drink or two mid-day then I'm happy."

Cec shrugged his shoulders in despair at his brother's statement.

"Well, Jim," Cec said. "I've got to be on my way. I'm going to the dance with a girl I met last week. Probably see you and Nora there later."

"Fine! See you later," Jim answered. He noticed that Bernie had flour in his hair.

When Cecil had left, Nora's mother made Jim the cup of tea she had promised him and poured out three more cups.

"There's a cup of tea for you, Bernie and one for me and one for your dad. Ask him if he wants to come out here for it or take it in the shop."

Bernie left the room, returning a few moments later.

"He wants it in the shop," he said. "He moaned about having a lot of work to do and no-one to help him!"

"Usually Nora gives him a hand when he has a rush job," her mother explained to Jim. "Of course, she's going out tonight so she won't be able to."

"He's in a bad mood," Bernie confided when his mother had left the room with her husband's cup of tea. "He's a bit touchy at times. If you ever want to see his better side take him out for a few beers some time!"

Nora came downstairs. Jim thought that she looked really something. She was wearing a cream blouse and three-quarters length skirt of fawn with a matching jacket. She had an exquisite figure and the clothes showed it off superbly. Her dress sense was very good and she carried herself well, elegantly.

"Have a good time you two," her mother said when they were leaving. "Bring her home safely, Jim."

"I will," Jim replied. "Pleased to meet you and thank you for the tea." He called goodbye to Bernie.

Just before they left Nora popped her head around the door of the shop and called goodbye to her father. Jim caught a sight of the man sitting cross-legged on his workbench stitching the lapels of a dark blue suit. The man looked up and Jim waved to him.

The dance was well attended. When he led Nora onto the dance floor he noticed that her brother was already dancing with an attractive brunette, slightly taller than himself. Cec waved to Nora and Jim.

"That's his girl friend," Nora whispered. "I've met her once or twice. Her name's Win and she comes from one of the villages outside town."

Nora danced very well, Jim thought. Quick-step, fox-trot, or waltz, she had excellent timing. He knew that he danced well as he had been told many times but he was pleased to hear her say so. They talked together as they danced, mainly about her family. She told Jim that both her brothers had passed scholarships but that her father had not been able to afford to let them go to grammar school.

He had grumbled that there were uniforms and books to buy as well as other bits and pieces and most grammar schoolboys were snobs anyway. She felt that it was a shame but being enterprising herself she had got herself a job at weekends helping the sub-postmaster with his accounts and teaching his daughter to read and had paid for her own educational needs. Jim learned that Cec worked first at a dairy and then at a local biscuit factory. Her eldest sister, Mil, worked at a jeweller's in the High Street. Glad, her second eldest sister worked in an art shop and Mabel, the youngest, was still at school.

"You'll meet them all in good time," she promised. That pleased Jim, not because he was eager to meet her sisters but because she was thinking of a long-term relationship.

During the intervals between dances Cec and Win spent some time with them. Jim liked them both. Had Cec not been Nora's brother Jim knew that he would still have enjoyed his company. Cec laughed a lot, was a good conversationalist and a rapport was established between them almost from their first meeting.

186

Cec and Win had to leave before the dance was over because she had to catch the last bus back to Brenchley. Jim and Nora stayed until the end and then he took her home. He arranged to meet her the following afternoon, Sunday, to take her out to tea somewhere if they could find a suitable place open.

Sunday afternoon he took Nora to Fairlight. It was a fine day but not very warm. After walking over the Firehills they went into Hastings. It was a pleasant afternoon and evening spent together talking and Jim felt that he had known Nora much longer than a week. She spoke openly about herself and her family and encouraged him to tell her about his life and plans. When he took her home Sunday evening both her brothers were out but her sisters were in the kitchen talking to her mother. There was no sign of her father and as the shop was in darkness Jim assumed that he was out. His assumption proved to be correct, he had finished the suit that evening and gone out for a drink or two.

Nora's mother introduced her other daughters to Jim.

"This is my eldest girl, Mil." Mil was dark like the others, quite attractive but on the plump side.

"This is Glad." Glad was similar in build to Nora, perhaps a little thinner. Her cheekbones were higher and her eyes lighter in colour than Nora's.

"And this is Mabel, the youngest of the family." Mabel had thick black curly hair and although she was still at school had quite an attractive figure. She had a very unusual smile, her lips moving to one side but it was an attractive smile.

The girls all smiled at him although the eldest one seemed rather shy and it was difficult to involve her in conversation. He had no difficulty with the other two, however. Nora's mother was a quiet person but friendly and Jim thought that she liked him.

As Jim was about to leave, Nora's father returned home. He was in an affable mood, evidently having enjoyed himself at the pub. He had thick white hair and a walrus moustache. His shoulders were slightly bent, probably due to his hunching up over his sewing, Jim decided. He had a Semitic nose and thick, bushy eyebrows. He was smoking a curved pipe.

"Hallo, Alice," he addressed his wife. "Met one or two friends I hadn't seen for a time. Had a few drinks together."

"This is Jim, Nora's friend," she introduced Jim to her husband.

The man turned and faced Jim, scrutinising him closely.

"Pleased to meet you," Jim offered his hand. The man hesitated for a moment, then shook Jim's hand.

"I did catch a glimpse of you last night," he said to Jim. "Couldn't leave my work. Had a rush job on that I had to tackle on my own. Sorry!"

Jim said that he understood. He actually thought that on the previous evening his presence had been resented but he kept his real thoughts to himself.

"Navy man, aren't you?" he asked Jim. "Army man myself. Had a brother in the navy, got himself killed falling from the mast just off South America somewhere."

Jim stayed a little longer by which time Nora's father had asked him whether he read Charles Dickens much and quoted from several of Dickens's novels, also pieces of Shakespeare. By the time Jim left he felt that he had made a reasonably favourable impression on the man. He told himself that he had now met the whole family and seemed to have been accepted by them all. Nora. saw Jim to the door.

"Thanks for a lovely afternoon and evening," she whispered. She kissed him lightly on the cheek. They arranged to meet again the following weekend.

The next evening Frank told Jim that Kitty was moving down to Tunbridge Wells as soon as she had worked out her notice at her London job. He added that he had found digs for her—these turned out to be in an adjacent road to where Nora lived. Frank said that the four of them would have to meet up and have some fun together.

Jim met Kitty a couple of weeks later. She was a tall woman with red hair and an extremely confident air about her. Jim could see that she adored Frank and thought that they were a well-matched couple. He introduced Nora to them both and they took to her immediately, and she to them. There followed some very happy times as a foursome, dances, skating, meals out and drinking together. Frank bought himself a motorbike so that he could take Kitty out with Jim and Nora. Later he bought a sidecar that Jim helped him fit as Kitty did not take too kindly to pillion riding.

One evening, just before Kitty moved to Tunbridge Wells, Jim went out for a drink with Bob Latter. It was one of those evenings when Jim had nothing special to do. Nora was helping her father, Frank had gone to see the landlady where Kitty would be living, Girly had taken Tiggie out for a walk with one of her friends and Mrs Latter had also gone out visiting a friend. When everyone had left the house Bob and Jim played a few hands of cards but both of them became bored with that. In the Navy Jim had often sat in large card schools and sometimes had won quite a bit of money but the excitement in a school was totally different from playing with just one person.

Bob scooped the cards up with an air of finality.

"Do you fancy a beer round the local, Jim?" he asked. "Being a sailor I daresay you enjoy a drop now and again."

Jim smiled to himself, recalling the many times he had been out with Frank, without Bob realising. He also thought of the times he had spliced the mainbrace on numerous occasions with Wiggy, Frank, Bert and the others.

"That's a good idea," he agreed.

They walked to one of the public houses nearby. While they were having their beer together at the bar and talking, a short man with a humorous twinkle in his eye came up to Bob.

"Well, look who's here!" Bob exclaimed, giving the newcomer a bow from the waist. "If it isn't young Charlie taking a night off from courting to join the men!"

Charlie was very similar in appearance to one of the Royal Engineers Jim had befriended. In fact the resemblance was remarkable. Charlie had mouse coloured hair, a high forehead, blue-grey eyes and a wide mouth with thin lips. He was clean-shaven and his hair was cut quite short. The man laughed somewhat nervously, almost as if he were partly apologetic for not being with the men more often.

Bob introduced Jim to Charlie. "This is Jim who moved in with us a while back," he grabbed hold of Charlie's coat sleeve "and this little man is Charlie Hewitt whom I've known for years. One of the best little footballers in St. John's." Jim knew that St. John's was one of the parishes in the town.

Jim shook hands with Charlie. He judged the man to be a little older than himself.

"You put me in mind so much of a friend in the Royal Engineers," Jim said. "The resemblance is extraordinary."

"Extraordinary just about sums Charlie up," Bob said, facetiously.

Charlie ignored Bob's comment. He told Jim that he had been in the army during the war but had never set foot outside England. He said that his football skills had been an asset to him and that he had ended up with a cushy stores job. Jim remembered that Nora's brother, Bernie had told him that he played football locally. When he told Charlie who the brother was Charlie said that he knew him well.

"Bernie's a cracking player," he said. "Everyone knows Bernie!"

"He could have made one of the professional teams if he hadn't liked the booze so much," Bob said. Then turning to Charlie, asked:

"Where's your young lady tonight then, Charlie?"

Charlie shrugged his shoulders.

"Working I guess. She doesn't get much time off."

"That's the trouble with the upper crust," Bob declared. "They never think that their servants should have a life of their own."

"She gets one evening off a week. The old lady she works for resents that, too. Acts like she owns the girl."

"You'll have to marry her, Charlie. Take her away from all that. It's the only way," Bob advised solemly.

"Don't you worry your head, Bob. That's what both of us want and we're saving up so we can get a home together. She can chuck that damned job then."

The evening wore on and the conversation ranged from the war, politics, and the state of the Country and its future, to local matters that included the local football teams. When they had their last drinks at the bar and were saying their farewells, Charlie, a little worse for the drinks inside him, said to Jim:

"Goodbye, Jack! I've forgotten your name!"

"I'm not Jack, I'm Jim ... Jim Alexander."

"Well now, Jack—I mean Jim, that is a coincidence," said Charlie, steadying himself. "That's my girl friend's name too."

"Funny names for a girl!" laughed Bob. "Jim *or* Jack!"

"Not that, you idiot," Charlie snapped at him. "*Alexander*, I mean!"

In spite of the fact that Jim had sunk one or two more beers than he was used to, he was not likely to have missed that information.

"What's your girl friend's first name, Charlie?" he asked.

"Vi!"

"Are you courting Vi Alexander?" Jim asked.

"I am, and why not?" replied the little man, drawing himself up to his full height. He had something of an edge to his voice of defiance and defence.

"Why not indeed!" exclaimed Jim. "She's my sister!"

If Jim had been surprised it had been nothing to the surprise that registered on Charlie's face at that moment.

"Well, I'm damned! She spoke of her brother to me quite a lot. She said that she hadn't seen you since she was fourteen. Fancy us bumping into one another. What an uncanny coincidence!"

"I originally came to Tunbridge Wells to try and find her," Jim explained. "Can you give me her address, Charlie?"

"Of course I can. I'll bet she'll be glad to see you, the way she speaks about you."

Charlie scribbled Vi's address on a piece of paper, using a pencil that Jim noticed had been nibbled at the top. The address was in an area of the town called Broadwater Down.

"How did you meet her, Charlie?" Jim felt curious about their first meeting. It seemed obvious to him that Charlie was not a person who would have been in close contact with Vi's employer.

"I met her several times when she called in the shop where I work," Charlie answered. "She was shopping for the lady she works for. We used to joke together when she came into the shop.

That was months ago and Vi was living in Warwick Park then. She didn't have any friends in the town. I used to meet her on her days off and we went for walks together. Yes, we got on so well together that she even kept in touch by letter whenever she had to go away with her lady. Yes, we got on well together right from the beginning. Of course, I fell for her that very first day she came into the shop but I never dreamed that she would feel the same way about me. I still can't believe my luck!"

Jim was touched by the little man's sincerity. Vi had led a very sheltered life, of that he had no doubt, and in all probability Charlie was the first person she had met who showed her any sympathy and interest.

After work the next day Jim went straight to the address Charlie had given him. He had warned Mrs Latter that he might be home late for his meal and told her why.

The address was in a select area of the town and Jim was aware that he was wearing his working clothes, partially obscured by his overcoat. He rang the doorbell and waited. He could hear someone inside the house. Then the door opened. The young woman standing there was Vi without a doubt.

"Hello, Vi," he said quietly. "I'm your brother Jim."

Chapter Twelve

She stood there for a few moments, her bright blue eyes staring as if in disbelief. Then half laughing, half crying, she flung her arms around Jim. They embraced for a long while, neither of them speaking. After all those years of separation they were once more re-united, that was all that Jim could think as they held each other tightly.

Their joyful re-union was interrupted by a loud voice from the hallway. Across Vi's shoulder Jim could see an elderly woman with a shawl wrapped around her, leaning heavily on a walking stick. The woman was heavily built and her round face was contorted and reddened with anger.

"What are you doing, girl?" the old woman shouted. "I am freezing here with the front door wide open. Come in at once and close the door immediately!"

Jim thought that the woman's tone was angry and petulant. Vi pulled away from him and quickly ushered him into the hall while she closed the front door.

The old lady was glaring at him.

"Who is this *person*?" she snapped.

Vi was evidently embarrassed and confused. The old woman's thin lips were tightly drawn together, her eyes blazing. She epitomised to Jim all that he most disliked. It irritated him that one human being could speak to another in such a way. Vi was his sister, this other creature did not own her.

"This is my brother," Vi said.

The old woman snorted, almost as if she thought Vi was lying to her.

"Tell him to come back another time. It's not convenient now. It's dinner time!"

With that the old woman turned her back on Jim and Vi and returned to the room from which she had emerged earlier.

"I'm sorry, Jim," Vi apologised for her employer's behaviour. She then lowered her voice, almost to a whisper. "She's in a particularly cantankerous mood today. I'll have to go."

Jim made no attempt to lower his voice.

"I think that she is a rude old woman. Who does she think she is, talking to you like that?"

The old woman had returned to the doorway. She glowered at Jim.

"I heard what you said!" she looked at Jim accusingly.

"I'm glad that you did. I meant every word of it!"

"How dare you talk to me like that! Leave this house immediately!"

Jim turned to Vi.

"How long will it take you to pack your things, Vi?"

Vi looked at Jim, then at the old woman and then back at Jim again.

"I haven't got much to pack," she said at last. Jim noticed that his sister was trembling. She hurried off upstairs.

"You have no right to come here like this upsetting everyone," the old woman said, her face twitching. "If she leaves with you now I'll make sure she never gets another job. I'll not give her a reference."

Jim ignored her. He felt sure that Vi would manage to get a job somewhere.

A few minutes later Vi came downstairs with a suitcase in her hand. Jim took the suitcase from her and opened the front door for Vi to make her exit.

"I have told your *brother*, if that's what he is, that I shall not give you a reference," the old woman called out. Jim stepped outside behind Vi and slammed the door shut behind him.

He kick-started the motorbike and then lifted Vi's case onto the petrol tank. He asked Vi to climb onto the pillion and when she had seated herself behind him he set off.

"Where are we going, Jim?" Vi shouted in his ear to make herself heard above the engine's roar.

"To my place," he called back.

When he arrived at Commercial Road Frank and Bob were having dinner with Mrs Latter and Girly. Jim introduced Vi to them all and then told them what had happened.

"Can Vi stay here until I can find her somewhere to live?" Jim asked Mrs Latter.

"Of course you can, dear," Mrs Latter said to Vi. "Here, let's make some room at the table for you and I'll get you something to eat."

Vi told her that she wasn't feeling very hungry but was most grateful to know that she had somewhere to stay. Frank stood up, offering Vi his place at the table but Mrs Latter waved for him to sit down.

"You get on with your dinner, Frank," she said, kindly.

Frank looked at Jim.

"I've been thinking," he said. "There's no reason why Vi shouldn't have my room. I told Mrs Latter earlier that I would be moving soon to the house where I've fixed up for Kitty to stay. Doubtless I could move in earlier if I ask the lady there."

"I'm sure we can manage for a night or two," Mrs Latter said. "Vi can either double up with Girly or we can make up a temporary bed for her in the front room on the sofa."

Jim offered to let Vi have his bed. He was quite prepared to sleep on the sofa. Jim noticed that Mrs Latter had taken to Vi, while Vi, aware of the kindness that she had been shown, was regarding Mrs Latter almost with adoration. In fact, Vi was looking at everyone in turn with gratitude for their kindness. Mrs Latter prevailed upon Vi to have something to eat and she accepted a small portion of dinner. When they had all finished eating Vi said to Mrs Latter:

"I can't get over seeing Jim again after all these years! He was just a little boy when I left home. Look at him now! A grown man and what a man too! The way he stood up to that tyrant!"

Vi related that when she had first left Diss, her job had been as a maid in the house of a wealthy man from Suffolk. She, being the youngest servant, was kept busy all the time by a very stern housekeeper. Over the years, however, younger women had been taken on and the position had become easier for her. Her employer was not an unkind man but had very little to do with the day to day running of the household, which was left in the very capable hands of his housekeeper. The man's wife had been ill with T.B. for many years and was in a sanatorium in Switzerland. Their children, a son and daughter, were at boarding schools and came home only in the holidays. Vi liked them both from the little she saw of them. The son eventually went to a public school and at the end of his time there chose a career for himself in the army. He had been sent to France as a young officer in 1917 but had been killed in action, quite soon after going over there. The loss of his son affected him badly. A few months later he had a stroke and subsequently, after an illness of several weeks, died of pneumonia. His daughter, a young woman in her early teens, had come home for her father's funeral, having been brought home by her uncle and aunt who had taken her back with them afterwards. A few days later the housekeeper called all the staff together to announce that the house was to be closed up ready for its sale.

Vi went on to say that her late employer's brother had given her a very good reference and he also referred her to an elderly widow, a distant relation of his family. Vi said that it was a sort of promotion for her as this lady treated her more as a companion. Vi was quite happy in her new employment but unfortunately it lasted but a few months when her lady became ill and she, too, died. One of the women who had attended the funeral offered Vi a position as a "companion maid"— this was the very person she had just walked out on. At the time of the offer Vi had accepted it gladly but she soon discovered that the woman was autocratic and alienated herself from most people with whom she came into contact. Vi explained that they had moved around frequently, never settling anywhere for long—indeed, she had lost track of all the places they had been to. Sometimes they were hotels, at other times the homes of relatives or people she knew, but invariably ended up the same—with her employer leaving after a row. Sometimes the old woman had rented houses, or on one or two occasions, bought them but she seldom stayed anywhere long, quickly finding fault with the house or the locality. For a time they had been in Warwick Park but the woman sold that, put her furniture in store, and raced off to hotels in Eastbourne and Hastings, then to Ilfracombe, none of which satisfied her. She had gone to the Isle of Wight after that, staying with a cousin with whom she fell out after only a few days. Estate Agents had been instructed to negotiate for the house in Broadwater Down through her solicitor. After which she had returned to Eastbourne until she was able to move into the house.

"She sounds like a nutter to me," Girly said.

"Why on earth did you stay with her, Vi?" Jim asked his sister.

"I hadn't anywhere else to go, Jim," she answered. "I did think of leaving her but I was afraid."

"Aunt Esther was the only person you ever wrote to, it seems," Jim tried to make his statement sound matter-of-fact. He did not want his sister to take it as a recrimination. "If she had known what you were suffering I daresay she would have wanted you to stay with her."

"After I was placed in service by father and his wife, I never wrote to them once," she looked lovingly at Jim. "Don't think that I didn't worry about you, Jim. I did most of the time in those early days and I never stopped praying for you."

He placed his hand over hers for a moment. He felt moved by the sincerity in her voice.

Bob told her that he was a friend of Charlie Hewitt.

"Oh! Charlie," she said, softly. "*Dear* Charlie! He's been such a good friend." She looked at Bob. "Can you let him know where I am, Bob? I don't want him worrying about me."

Bob rose from the table.

"I'll go up to St. John's now," he reassured her. "I'll tell him you're here."

When Bob had left, Frank told Vi that he might be able to get her fixed up with a domestic job in one of the hotels locally if she was interested. She said that she would be glad of any work so that she could pay her way.

The months that followed brought many changes. Vi took a day job at one of the hotels and moved into Frank's room when he vacated it. Frank's business acumen was paying off and he anticipated being in a position to buy the London business that he and Kitty wanted within a year. In September Frank and Kitty became engaged. That month Vi and Charlie announced their engagement too. Jim continued to work with the post office and to see Nora regularly. Charlie was not a man to go dancing and as he had no desire whatever to buy a motorbike or other form of transport Jim and Nora either went out on their own or with Frank and Kitty. Charlie and Vi spent most of their time with Mrs Latter and Bob or in going for walks together. Vi seemed quite contented in these pursuits and Jim had given up asking them to join the others when there was a local dance on.

Of course, it was different with him. Besides the fact that both he and Nora enjoyed dancing, there was little opportunity for the two of them to spend time together in her parental home without also having her sisters or brothers with them. Her mother never went out except to hang washing on the line, even the shopping was done by the youngest girl, Mabel. Cec and his young lady experienced the same problem, of course, so Cec generally went over to her home or took her to the cinemas in town when there were no dances to go to locally.

Frank and Jim bought themselves two pedigree Alsatian puppies in October, Frank called his puppy "Rajah" and Jim accepted "Laddie", the name given on the puppy's pedigree as being all right with him. Laddie's mother was *Yvonne Kruk*, his father *Erich of Wolfsmoor*. Mrs Latter was quite happy for Jim to buy the dog. The young puppy and Tiggie seemed to get on well together from the first day that Jim took him home. Frank, Kitty, Nora and Jim began taking the Alsatian puppies out for walks over the Common. Whatever the weather Frank and Jim would set off with the dogs while Kitty and Nora stayed indoors at Kitty's if there was any heavy rain. Laddie and Rajah, being of similar age, acted like pups from the same litter although that was not the case.

Just before Christmas Jim bought a taxicab and resigned his job with the post office. Mrs Latter told him that he was welcome to use her house as a base for the business. With Christmas only a couple of weeks away Jim thought that it was a very good time to start up. He did very well all over the Christmas and New Year although the work involved being on the road at all times, day and night. Frank had recommended Jim to all his own contacts and with those recommendations and Vi's help in placing some of Jim's printed cards in the hotel lobby where she worked, he had plenty of business. He realised that he loved Nora very much and was concerned about being unable to spend as much time with her.

"I'm sorry that we can't go out like we used to, Nora," he told her. "I've got to make this business work. I hope that you understand. I miss being with you. Sometimes I feel like chucking it all and getting a job again."

"Don't worry, Jim," Nora had reassured him. "I know that you have to make it with the cab business. Naturally I miss you too."

"I'm not doing this just for me, Nora. If I can make it then I can think of settling down, of getting married."

"Anyone in mind?" she asked him, her eyes sparkling.

"You! Who else?"

"Is that a proposal, Jim Alexander?" she laughed. "If it is it's not like the ones I've read about or seen at the cinema!"

"How's this then? Will you marry me, Nora?" He went down on one knee beside her.

"Of course I will, Jim!"

The taxi business went through something of a slump in the early part of spring. One of the problems was that two bus companies had a "cut fare" war raging between them. The bus fares became cheaper and cheaper until eventually passengers could travel miles for one penny! Jim could not compete with such ridiculous prices. He still had a few customers but they were people who wanted to travel at very unsociable hours. Frank was sympathetic but could offer no advice on how to save the business. It was, he thought, damned bad luck that Jim had been caught up in the bus war.

"So, what are you going to do, Jim?" Frank asked.

Jim shrugged his shoulders and then said, philosophically:

"I can't beat them so I'll join them if I can!"

Jim was taken on by one of the omnibus companies as a driver. He was unable to sell his taxicab locally so advertised it in a national newspaper and sold it a week later. The job with the bus company did not pay too well but it was work. In such spare time as he had he did a few carpentry jobs for extra money. He had infinite patience with Laddie and trained the dog to sit, to lay down, to stay until commanded to follow, to walk at heel and eventually, to jump the railings from one side to another between the supporting posts around the cricket ground on the common. He loved the dog and even as a puppy its chastisement was either verbal or a rolled up newspaper, which Jim slapped against his own hand. Every show of obedience from Laddie was rewarded with words of praise and caresses and, occasionally, with a biscuit. Jim did not believe in feeding tit-bits to the dog and trained it quite early to refuse them from strangers. Mrs Latter or Girly fed the dog if Jim was working but if not working he always took over the preparation of Laddie's meal and placed the bowl of food down for the dog.

Frank attempted to train Rajah in the same way but met with less success. Rajah had a voracious appetite and try as he could Frank was unable to stop the dog from accepting food from other people. Indeed, at times Rajah didn't wait for tit-bits to be offered but would snatch bars of candy away from any children who approached. Jim had more success with Rajah and managed to train the dog to leap the rails with Laddie when it felt like it! Jim told Frank that Rajah was wilful. Frequently Rajah dashed off in pursuit of smaller dogs; another favourite passion of the animal was to lie down as if asleep and then nip the hindquarters of any dog that walked by!

In October 1927 Charlie and Vi were married at St. John's Church. Charlie had managed to get a small house on rent and Jim helped them get the house spruced up. The couple spent their honeymoon with Aunt Esther in Norwich.

Jim moved into Vi's room, the room that had previously been Frank's. It was a larger one than Jim's and he needed the extra space in which to store some of the items of furniture he had made in preparation for the day when he and Nora would have a home of their own. Jim was saving as hard as he could and so was Nora. They seldom went to dances or to the cinema but, weather permitting, they either set off for long walks with Laddie, or occasionally on Sundays, went for drives to the sea. Mrs Latter or Girly looked after Laddie at such times.

The following year Cec married Win and the couple moved into a house in St. John's. Jim and Nora used to visit them some evenings and took Laddie with them.

Shortly after Cec's marriage Frank and Kitty also married. Frank confided to Jim that he was in process of negotiation for the purchase of a new business in Putney with splendid apartments over the shop where they would live.

With all the marriages taking place there had been wedding presents to buy on top of the seasonal birthday and Christmas presents. Jim was finding it difficult to save much. Nora was working at the post office stores, the tearooms, and doing some dressmaking with her sister to bring in extra cash and he had nothing but admiration for her. Jim thought that both of them could do with a break and suggested that they should go up to Norwich to spend a holiday with Aunt Esther if she would have them. Nora thought it a splendid idea so Jim wrote to his aunt and arrangements were made for them to have a week with her at Easter. Mrs Latter agreed to look after Laddie for Jim.

Jim and Nora travelled up to Norwich on Jim's motorbike. As they were away for only a week they didn't have to take very much luggage; and Jim told Nora that he would show her round Norfolk so there was no point in packing any fancy clothes. Aunt Esther was delighted to see them both. Jim knew that his aunt would like Nora and he hoped that Nora would feel the same way about Aunt Esther. He was relieved when Nora told him that she thought his aunt was one of the nicest people she had ever met. Nora had no taste, however, for the tripe and onions meal that his aunt had prepared as a special treat, so Jim scooped them off Nora's plate when his aunt went into the scullery to fetch a cloth to mop up some food that she had spilled.

The weather during the week was quite good and Jim took Nora to Happisburgh and to Diss. He showed her the house where he and Vi had lived as children, the Church and the school.

Aunt Esther told them that she liked Charlie, Vi's husband very much. She said that they had spent their entire honeymoon at her home and it was good to have such a loving couple with her.

"Hasn't Vi blossomed into a beautiful woman, don't you think so, Jim?" his aunt asked him.

"She certainly has," Jim assured her.

Aunt Esther turned to Nora.

"And haven't you found yourself a lovely woman, young Jim?"

Jim said that he thought himself very fortunate.

"When are you two getting married?" Aunt Esther asked.

"Soon, I hope," Nora answered. "We're saving hard enough."

Aunt Esther looked at Nora then at Jim.

"Well, now," she said. "Don't think that I'm interfering but I think that you can be over anxious about money. As long as you have enough for a roof over your head and a few sticks together my advice is that you get married. You can save afterwards. They say that two can live as cheaply as one. So long as it remains at two!"

She chuckled, then changing the subject asked Nora if she could see her engagement ring. Nora placed her hand in front of Aunt Esther so that the old lady could see it properly. Nora had wanted diamonds and Jim had bought her a pretty ring with a cluster of diamonds, the centre one being quite a large stone.

"It's lovely!" Aunt Esther exclaimed. "Most elegant, my dear."

At the end of the week they said goodbye to Aunt Esther, promising to consider seriously her kind invitation for them to spend their honeymoon at her home.

"And make it soon!" she called after them as they drove off.

With their holiday over Jim and Nora returned to Tunbridge Wells. They had made good time on the journey back and called in to see Cec and Win. Jim noticed that Win was pregnant. Cec was very excited about it all.

"Do you want a boy or a girl?" Nora asked.

"We don't mind, do we Win?" Cec asked his wife.

"Not really," Win replied, adding: "Although it would be fun making clothes for a little girl."

Jim decided to call in to see Vi and Charlie before taking Nora home.

Vi was excited; for she too had an announcement to make!

"You're going to be an uncle, Jim!" she blurted out as soon as she had opened the door to them.

"Congratulations, Vi!" said Jim, giving his sister a hug. He shook Charlie's hand. "Well done, Charlie!"

Nora asked them whether they wanted a boy or a girl.

"We don't really mind, do we Charlie?" Vi said, but before her husband could reply, she added:"I think Charlie would prefer a boy so that he can turn him into another footballer."

Later, when Jim was saying goodbye to Nora at her home, she said to him:

"Why don't we take your aunt's advice and set a date for our marriage, Jim? The sooner the better as far as I'm concerned."

Jim suggested December that year. He thought that it would give them a further seven months or so to save.

"I was thinking that October would be better," Nora said. "I shall be twenty-one then and won't need my dad's permission. I remember the scene at home when Cec and Win told him they were getting married. I heard the shouting from upstairs in the bedroom."

"I get on with him all right now," Jim said. "Why do you think he would raise any objection to our marriage?"

"He was well past thirty when he married my mother. He thinks that people marry too early in life. He has some very strong views on some things and can sometimes be difficult."

"You know him better than I do. I'm quite happy with October if that's what you want." Jim was not afraid of facing her father, or anyone else. As far as he was concerned "everyone is equal in the sight of God."

With October settled as the month the two of them began saving even harder. Jim opened a Post Office Savings Account and the cash that he had put away in his trunk was deposited in the account. Nora was surprised that he had been keeping money in his room. Jim laughed and told her that it was safe enough with Laddie in the house!

Nora had opened a savings account right from the beginning. Working in the sub post office it had seemed to her to be the sensible thing to do. Jim could see the logic of it but old habits died hard and he had always saved in cash during his days in the Navy. He trusted the other members of the crew with his life; he could certainly trust them with a few bank notes and coins!

At the end of May Jim found himself unemployed. The omnibus company had gone bust! It had been on the cards for some time but the company had struggled on. There was already an enormous unemployment problem and the drivers and conductors had no alternative but to join the dole queue in Tunbridge Wells. Jim felt depressed being one of the men in that line.

The small amount of money that was paid to him was insufficient to cover his board and lodgings. To make matters worse Bob lost his job too. Mrs Latter was very good but Jim knew that she was worried about making ends meet. He appreciated her offer to accept less but his pride would not allow him to reduce payment to her; neither did he believe that it was morally right. In spite of her suggestion that she could get by and he could pay her any arrears when he found another job, he drew some money from his savings and paid her what he owed, week by week. He felt uneasy about his finding another job. The unemployment situation was becoming worse not better.

One evening in early June he told Nora that he had been drawing on his savings and if he were out of work much longer he would have to seek employment elsewhere. He thought that London might be a better proposition for him. Nora seemed very upset about the idea. She implored him to wait one more month and then if nothing turned up to think about looking elsewhere for work. For some reason the idea of leaving Tunbridge Wells really distressed her. Jim thought that it had something to do with her family. She loved her mother very much, he knew that.

The month passed during which time Jim had no success in getting a permanent job. He had a few days doing some carpentry work for a man who was converting a house into flats but the work was poorly paid. Jim's savings went down and down. He had doubts about getting married in October. There was no way that he would get married while out of work and unable to support his wife, he decided. What an awful start that would be, his wife working and he on the dole!

The man for whom he had done the carpentry work had promised Jim first refusal of a flat in Bishops Down when he had completed the conversion there. Jim had seen the flat and he liked it. Being opposite the Common, the views from the windows were excellent. He knew that Nora would like it and Laddie could be exercised without his having to pad through the streets of the town first before reaching the Common. Jim told the owner that he would take the flat, the only disadvantage being it would not be available until December at the earliest. If he and Nora went ahead with their wedding plans for October they would have to find somewhere else for a couple of months or so. He had little doubt that they would be able to live at Mrs Latter's for that time. All he needed *was a job*.

He went up to Putney to see Frank. His friend was delighted to see him. So was Kitty, who was very excited to show Jim their three-month old baby boy. The boy had quite a lot of hair, the same auburn colour as his mother. Frank's business was doing well but he confessed to Jim that he would have had problems at times if it had not been for his idea of supplying hotels. He drove up to Covent Garden early in the morning, loaded his own stock in the back part of the van first and then the bulk purchases for the hotels were loaded. These were dropped off at several hotels that were on the route back. During his absence Kitty served in the shop, while her sister Norah looked after baby Frank, or sometimes Norah served in the shop so that Kitty could spend time with her baby. Jim noticed that the furnishings in the apartment were superb.

"Most of the stuff is antique," Frank told him.

"I really am glad that things are going well for you both," Jim said to Frank and Kitty. "I only wish that I could get a job. I lost my job with the bus company when they went bust. The dole queues in Tunbridge Wells grow daily."

"How's Nora?" Kitty asked. "It's about time you two got married and settled down, Jim!"

"We had planned to get married in October," Jim explained. "That was before I lost my job. I've even got the offer of a really nice flat overlooking the Common."

"Sounds good," Frank said. "It will be perfect for Laddie too. Take a look at Rajah, Jim! He's just one damned fat lump these days!" Jim eyed Rajah over. The dog certainly had put on a bit of weight.

"You look as if you've put on a few pounds too, Frank!" Jim laughed. "You look as elegant as ever, Kitty. I wonder what you see in this self indulgent specimen!"

Later, over a meal, which Kitty and her sister prepared, the conversation returned to the unemployment problem. Frank wanted Jim to stay with them so that he could look around for work in London.

"That's very good of you, Frank. I'll pay my way, of course!"

"You'll do no such thing!" Kitty folded her arms. She could be quite a formidable opponent in any argument and she meant business!

"All right! All right!" Jim conceded. "At least let me give you a hand in the shop or driving the lorry."

"You concentrate on getting yourself a job, Jim," Frank advised. "We've managed the shop and the buying without help and we shall continue to do so. I respect your independence, Jim, but if you're honest with yourself you will have to admit that getting a job is top priority. If our situations were reversed you would be saying to me exactly what I'm now saying to you! Can you deny that?"

Jim was at a loss for words. Tell the truth and shame the devil. He had used that phrase with so many others. He looked first at Kitty, then at Frank.

"No, I can't!" he said.

"Well, now that's settled to everybody's satisfaction," Frank rubbed his hands together. "How about a little drink? I'm for a Scotch, myself. What about you, Jim?"

Jim started his search for work eary the next day. He called at shops, factories, taxicab offices and transport depots but met with no success. His Royal Navy discharge papers gave him an excellent reference but most of the people he showed them to barely bothered to read them. One man in a factory told him that there were so many ex-servicemen looking for work that they just had to take their chances with anyone else.

A friend of Frank's offered him a temporary job putting up some racks and shelves in his shop. Jim accepted the work gratefully. The man liked Jim and they got on well together from the start.

"You work hard, Jim," he said. "I only wish that I could give you a job permanently. The fact is that I can't afford to employ anyone. With trade so poor, the only way I know to make this business pay is by doing the shop-work myself."

When the racks and shelves had been fitted Mr White paid him off. The job had taken him less than a week.

"Some men would have made that job last longer, Jim," he said. "I respect your honesty. I can't afford to pay you any bonus but in that envelope there's a full weeks money. I would have probably had to pay someone else more than that so I'm getting a bargain."

If only other employers would give him a chance, Jim thought, they would see what he could do. On Sunday he went to a church alone and prayed hard for a job, any job.

He missed Nora and he missed Laddie too. Whenever he had felt a bit down in the dumps Laddie had somehow sensed that something was wrong and would nudge Jim with his nose as much as to say, come on snap out of it, let's go out for a walk over the common!

Jim knew that Laddie would be well cared for by the Latters but he missed the dog very much, there was no denying it. He wondered what Nora would be doing. It was strange being up in London and not seeing her. He loved her with all his heart, of that he was certain. He had been fond of Beaty but that was different. They had had a sort of understanding but he reflected that he had gone to dances with other girls when he was away from Malta. He realised that since meeting Nora there was no other girl that he would want to go dancing with—she was the only one for him. Job or no job, he decided, he would marry her in October. He sat down and wrote a letter to her. He also wrote to Mrs Latter enclosing some money to help out, after all she was taking good care of Laddie.

A few days later Jim heard that the London Passenger Transport Board needed some drivers for their Greenline service. He had plenty of experience of driving and was sure that he could handle a bus or coach easily. After his interview he was tested in a Greenline Coach and his confidence behind the wheel impressed his examiner. He got the job! He told the examiner afterwards that he lived in Tunbridge Wells and was told that a Greenline Station was being opened there. One of the popular routes was Victoria to Windsor and Jim began work there the following Monday. He was told that he would have one rest day a week and that his first one would be on the Sunday, followed by seven days work with Monday being the next rest day. To compensate for the seven-day week the drivers and conductors were given two consecutive days off whenever the rest day came round to Tuesday. On those occasions Wednesday was also a rest day. The first week involved day shifts, the second week night shifts, then back to day shifts, and so on.

On Saturday, August 26th he finished work at Victoria in the afternoon and didn't have to report back until Monday afternoon. He decided to go to Tunbridge Wells. He went straight to the tearooms where Nora worked. He had written to her with the good news that he was working again. He waited for her to finish work, as it was nearly half past six when he reached the tearooms. She came out at half past six and flung her arms round him. There was something different about her, which he was unable to define. She looked tired, but he put that down to the fact that she had been on her feet for several hours. No, there was something more than that.

"Jim, I'm pregnant!" she told him.

Jim held her tightly. So *that* was what was different about her. She must have been in the early stages, he thought, because her coat did not appear to be covering any perceptible bulge.

"When is the baby due?" he asked her.

"December. Late December," she said. "I didn't want to worry you. You had enough on your mind trying to get a job. I thought I was pregnant at the end of April but wasn't sure. By the end of May I had no doubts at all."

"What do your parents think about it?" Jim asked, thinking particularly of her father's reaction.

"They don't know yet. Apart from the doctor I haven't discussed it with anyone. I was scared of my dad knowing and I was scared of my employers finding out too."

"How on earth have you managed to hide it?" Jim was amazed.

"I've bound my stomach up," she answered.

"Isn't that dangerous?" He felt very anxious.

"I don't know. I never really thought of that, only of hiding things until I could talk to you properly. I prayed that you would find work and that we would be able to go ahead with the wedding in October. I am so glad to see you, Jim. Somehow it's all right now that you are with me."

Jim felt very protective and tender. He decided that the best thing to do would be to face her father and tell him the truth.

"We can rule out a white wedding," he laughed. "Does that bother you?"

"No, not really. Anyway it would have been expensive and we need the money for our home."

He thought that she sounded a little disappointed but was being practical. It was a shame that the Bishops Down flat would not be available until December. The idea of being a husband and a father was an entirely new concept. It was up to him to find somewhere to live as soon as possible. He could not take her to Frank's place, not that Frank or Kitty would have minded, he knew them too well for that, but this was something that he had to sort out. The idea crossed his mind to ask Mrs Latter if Nora could stay there but he was aware that she too had problems and it would be unfair to burden her with any more of his. There were Cec and Win and Vi and Charlie who would doubtless help out but again, they had their own problems. Jim thought that the first thing to sort out was telling Nora's parents.

When he expressed these thoughts Nora looked alarmed.

"Need we tell them *yet*?" she pleaded. "I think that I could tell my mum but not my dad."

"Let me tell them," Jim said. "You won't be able to disguise your condition much longer and it's better to tell them before they find out. What about your sisters? Do you think they know?"

"I've taken to going to bed early in the evenings. All of them go out most evenings. Mil, my eldest sister has a boy friend in the Salvation Army and the other two go out together. My two eldest sisters get up earlier than me as they have to travel into the town whereas I've only to cross the road to get to work. Mabel, my youngest sister is usually fast asleep when I get up."

"How do you think that they will take the news?" Jim asked.

"Oh! I'm not worried about them. They will probably be excited. It's my dad I'm worried about. He can be so difficult."

Jim thought that however difficult he might be there was nothing much that he could do to change the situation and therefore he would just have to accept his daughter's pregnancy. He refrained from telling Nora that, however.

Nora suggested that they might go into a nearby pub for a drink before he took her home. He was quite prepared to have a drink but wondered whether or not Nora should be having any alcohol. He had heard that it was bad for an unborn baby. She told him that she didn't want any alcohol anyway, a soft drink would be fine; all she wanted was somewhere where they might talk together for a little while.

Jim bought Nora a fruit juice and a pint of beer for himself. It was early in the evening and the pub was not full. They found a corner table where they could sit together.

"Your family set-up puzzles me," Jim said. "Your mother seems afraid to go out. Your youngest sister does the shopping for her. Why do you think that is?"

"I think that over the years my mum has become more and more withdrawn from the outside world. That she loves us all I've no doubt. She's fifteen years younger than my dad although you wouldn't think so to look at her. She's so frail. I suppose that having six children in ten years hasn't helped. She seems resigned to being dominated by dad."

"Why do you think that is?"

"My dad was well educated and came from a good family. After his marriage the rest of his family had very little more to do with him. They thought that he had married beneath him!" Nora gave a toss of her head. "My mum might have come from a different background but she is the kindest, most loving person you could ever wish to meet. He was fortunate to marry her, I think!"

Jim reached over and took hold of Nora's hand.

"What about your father's drinking?" he asked her. "Tell me about that."

"As a young child I remembered his coming home drunk. Even when my mother was doing her best to keep us all fed on the pittance he gave her for housekeeping he still found the money to go out drinking. Do you know what Scotch broth is, Jim?"

"I've heard the expression but I don't really know what it is."

"Well, the Scotch broth we had as youngsters was hot water with salt and pepper in it! I have seen my mum mix potato with butter to make it go round. We all had hand-me-down clothes until I was old enough to make my own or buy them from my earnings. Once I remember my dad discovering a five-pound note in the lining of a suit which had come in for alteration. There we all were, hungry and in rags. What do you think he did? He went out and blew it on booze, every penny of it!"

"Do you think that he blames you all in some way for his own problems?" Jim asked. "It must have been a bitter blow for him when his family cut him out of their lives. Perhaps he blames your mother in a sort of mixed up way and unconsciously punishes her?"

"Yes, I think that there is something in what you say. Mum takes it all, that's the real problem. If I ever had to put up with treatment like she has I know how I would react!"

Jim laughed. "I don't think you ever need worry about that from me. I used to drink when I was in the Navy but nowadays I can take it or leave it. Besides, I love you far too much to ever make you suffer in any way."

"I know that, Jim."

"Leaving your family aside for a moment, let's talk about us," he suggested. "We'll have to have a Register Office marriage. Can you see the Registrar to start the ball rolling?" She nodded in assent, so he continued. "We will have to try and fix a date for the ceremony, if that's what it's called. It's probably too short notice to fix up for Tuesday, September 12th but if it were possible to get that day I would have the Wednesday off too. Anyway, see what you can fix up. If necessary I'll see if I can do a swap with one of the other drivers. The other thing is that they are going to extend the Greenline service. A man I was talking to said that they would be operating from Tunbridge Wells to Victoria. That means that we could live in Tunbridge Wells, that's what you prefer, isn't it?"

"Yes, but if you have to work away then I'd go where your work takes you. My jobs aren't very important now because I shall have to give them up anyway when the baby arrives."

"I wonder whether our baby's a boy or a girl," Jim said.

"What would you prefer it to be, Jim?"

"I don't really mind. A boy would carry on the Alexander name!"

They laughed when Jim added: "And the family fortunes!"

He took her home about half past eight. Her mother and father were alone. Bernie had gone to work and all three of her sisters had gone out. It was a good opportunity to have a talk, Jim decided. Her father looked up when they entered the room.

"You're late, Nora. We wondered what had happened to you."

"I met her from work," Jim said. "We had a drink together as we had some things to discuss." Jim noticed that Nora was looking very uncomfortable.

Her mother asked Jim if he would like a cup of tea. She reminded him of Aunt Esther sometimes, not in appearance but in her mannerisms.

"We're going to get married," Jim announced. He had decided that the best approach was the direct one. Nora's mother looked at her husband, waiting for his comments. Jim thought that she did not look displeased. He had not expected any trouble from her anyway. There was silence from Nora's father, he looked at Nora, then at Jim.

"Well, aren't you going to congratulate us?" Jim said, forcing a laugh. "Why don't we go out and have a drink together and we can leave Nora and her mother to have a talk?" He looked her father straight in the eyes as he spoke.

The man raised himself from his chair.

"That sounds a good idea to me," he said, reaching for his coat and trilby hat, which were hanging on pegs by the door. Jim gave Nora a kiss and said: "See you later, darling."

He asked her father where he usually went for a drink and was told that sometimes he went to High Brooms and sometimes to the *Greyhound* in Upper Grosvenor Road.

"Would you like to walk or would you prefer to ride?" Jim pointed to the motorbike that was propped against the kerb.

"I've never been on one of those things," the man spoke with a mixture of doubt and curiosity.

"Well, there has to be a first time for everything." Jim sat astride the bike and started the engine. "Come on! Jump up on the pillion, we're wasting good drinking time! Hold on to your hat!"

Jim opened the throttle on the drive to the Greyhound. He noticed that Nora's father held on tightly to his waist, both arms encircling Jim. He smiled to himself as he brought the bike to a halt outside the Greyhound.

"Well, how's that for time?" Jim asked him.

"Good! It goes well, doesn't it?" he added "I can do with a drink!"

After Nora's father had downed several pints of stout and mild and a couple of tots of whisky, during which time the two of them had discussed the war, Charles Dickens's novels and politics, that Jim was treated to samples of the man's repertoire of jokes. He had mellowed a lot after the first couple of drinks, Jim noticed.

"I told you earlier that Nora and I are getting married," Jim said, in a matter-of-fact tone. "I wanted to have a chance to talk to you on your own which is why I suggested that we came out for a drink or two."

"Glad you did, glad you did," the man said, draining the last few dregs from his glass. "Is it my turn to get the next round?"

As he had not bought any of the drinks up to that point Jim told him that whoever's turn it was didn't matter as he would buy them! That being settled, Jim ordered another stout and mild, and a pint of mild for himself. He carried the glasses over to the table, setting the stout and mild down in front of Nora's father.

"So you and Nora are getting married?" the man said, wiping the froth from his moustache with the back of his hand. "Young Cecil married and now Nora. I wonder who'll be next. I wonder who'll be next."

"Children have a habit of growing up," Jim said. "Does it bother you when your family leave you?"

"When you're older, Jim, you'll understand. It seems that you spend most of your life struggling to bring them up and the next thing they get themselves married. What have you got left, what *have* you got left?"

"You have your wife!"

The man thought about that for a moment or two.

"Yes, that's true, *that's* true!"

"You can enjoy your grandchildren too!" Jim thought it a good opportunity to turn the conversation to his advantage.

"Yes. It won't be long now before Alice and me are grandparents. Cecil's baby will be along any time now."

"Nora's expecting too," Jim said. "That's what I wanted to talk to you about."

Jim watched the man's reaction. He expected an angry outburst but it didn't come. Instead, the man sat quietly sipping his drink. Jim wondered if the announcement had fallen on deaf ears. Several moments elapsed during which neither of them spoke. At last the man set down his glass and said:

"They say that history repeats itself," once again he wiped the froth from his moustache. "Well, I'll say one thing for you, Jim. You are straight to the point. As long as you two love each other, that's what matters. Yes, I guess that's what *really* matters."

Jim felt relieved that the truth was out. He thought that Nora's father had taken it well. Of course, the drink might have helped, Jim thought, silently thanking Bernie for the advice he had once given.

"We're getting married as soon as we can fix a day with the Registrar," Jim explained. "Nora and I love each other. We were going to get married anyway. It just means that we won't be having a church wedding."

"So what does *that* matter?" the man asked with a snort.

When they left the Greyhound Jim noticed that Nora's father was swaying about a bit and felt concerned about him on the pillion.

"Would you rather we walked back?" Jim asked him. "I can leave the bike here and pick it up later."

"You don't need to do that," the man said. "You drive home and I'll walk. I'll see you later."

"Are you sure you're all right on your own?"

"Of course I am! I've walked from here enough times. You go on ahead, Jim. I'll see you later!"

Jim set off, arriving at Nora's home a few minutes later. Nora and her mother looked surprised to see that he was alone.

"Your dad's walking home," he explained. "I took him up to the Greyhound on the back of the bike but he decided to walk home."

"How did he take *our* news?" Nora asked.

"Very well," Jim replied.

"That's good." It was Nora's mother who spoke.

"I've told my mum about the baby," Nora explained. "She wasn't really surprised, were you, mum?"

"I'm not blind," her mother said. "I've suspected it for some time. I was waiting for you to say something. It was how your dad would take it that worried me." She looked at Jim. "You're a decent fellow, Jim. I know that everything will work out all right."

Nora gave her mother a hug. Her mother smiled at Jim.

"She's a good girl, Jim! So loving and kind. She'll be a good wife and a good mother, I know."

Some quarter of an hour later Nora's father returned.

"I walked home," he explained to his wife. "Jim took me up there on the motor bike but I decided to get a bit of exercise and walk back. We had a darned good evening together, didn't we, Jim?"

"I really enjoyed it," Jim answered. "We must do it again soon."

"As soon as you like," Nora's father exclaimed, the idea obviously appealed to him.

Jim left soon after. He shook her father's hand and kissed her mother lightly on the cheek, Nora went out to the gate with him.

"Thank God that's over," she whispered. "It won't worry me telling my sisters. In fact I'm quite looking forward to it!"

"What about Bernie?"

"Oh! He won't care. He's so easy-going it would take more than that to shake him!"

They kissed goodnight. Now the evening was over Jim wanted to get back to break the news to the Latters. He decided that he would take Nora to see Vi and Charlie and Cec and Win the next day. Perhaps if the weather was good they could walk and take Laddie along.

* * *

Jim's shift work had its compensations. It gave him time to fit in a few carpentry jobs to earn some extra money. He needed every penny he could earn with a home to furnish and a baby on the way. The Register Office wedding had been arranged for October 24, a Tuesday, at eleven o'clock. Jim had managed to swap his original Tuesday and Wednesday in September with Ernie, one of the other drivers, as the September dates were too early for the Registrar's books without special licence. Ernie's double rest days in the latter part of October were later than Jim and Nora would have liked but the best that Jim could arrange.

The ceremony was quite a simple affair, not quite like Jim had imagined. He guessed that he had been conditioned by the weddings that he had attended as a choirboy, and had wanted his to be just like them.

The flat at Bishops Down was not ready so Jim had to take his wife back to Mrs Latter's. Nora had resigned her job at the tearooms but had decided to remain working at the sub post office as long as she possibly could. Although Mrs Latter was prepared for Nora to share Jim's room she did not feel that she could cope with a home confinement so Nora's parents had insisted that the baby should be born there.

Jim became an uncle to Vi's baby in early November. His nephew, Donald, was a fine looking baby and Vi and Charlie were very proud to show him off. When Vi placed Donald in Jim's arms the baby seemed to him to be so small that he was frightened to hold it. Vi laughed.

"You'd better get in practise, Jim," she said. Then turning to Nora, added "Just look at Jim, I never thought that I would ever see *him* looking so nervous!"

The flat in Bishops Down became available just before Christmas. Jim took possession of the keys on Tuesday, December 19th. His double rest day on the Tuesday and Wednesday was spent in getting the place in order and arranging for moving his belongings there, which included quite a lot of furniture that he had made. He bought the other things that were needed from furniture shops in the town on the strict understanding that the furniture was delivered *immediately* so that he would be at home to receive it. There was so much work to do, laying lino and fitting carpets, putting up shelves in the kitchen, fixing curtain rails and hanging the curtains which Nora had made, using her father's sewing machines. Jim was able to work right through each of the two days without bothering to stop for lunch but at six o'clock he was glad to get his evening meal inside him, which Mrs Latter had prepared. After the meal he dashed off to pick Nora up from her parents' home and in spite of her advanced state he took her on the pillion of the motorbike along to Bishops Down. He drove slowly and joked with Nora about having to sit so far forward on the bike. She wanted to help in getting jobs done but Jim was nervous about her doing any work involving her in any lifting or stretching.

"We don't want the baby coming before it needs to!" he told her. "I've done a lot of things in my time but I never got round to a course in midwifery!"

By the end of the second day the flat was looking really good. Jim was pleased with it. Nora was looking tired but not so tired that she was unable to appreciate their efforts.

"What a lovely home we've got, Jim," she said. "I can't wait to move in here."

"I'm taking you back to your parents' place right now!" Jim informed her. "Don't get any ideas in your head about staying here on your own with the baby due any moment! You'd better give up your job at the Post Office too."

"We're pretty busy there with Christmas," Nora said. "I shall pack the job in on Christmas Eve."

"I wonder if you'll go that long," Jim said, looking at her doubtfully.

"I think so," Nora said. "I'll probably give birth on Christmas Day! That should make a good Christmas present for everyone!"

Jim had Christmas Day off but had to work on Boxing Day. Nora had finished up at the post office on Christmas Eve as she had said that she would. The Boxing Day shift was paid at a higher rate and Jim volunteered for it. He needed the money and Nora told him to take the work. On Boxing Day morning she felt fine and helped her mother in the house. Jim carried out his Boxing Day shift in an anxious state. He knew that the baby was due at any time and wondered how Nora was, how she was coping. After work he called in to see her but things were just the same. She told him that she felt fine. Jim's next rest day was due on Thursday, 28th December but on Wednesday, December 27th he was on late shift. On that Wednesday Nora started to have some pain. She told Jim that she thought that the baby would arrive some time that day but that he was not to worry as her mother was there and the midwife would be calling.

Reluctantly, Jim had to leave for work. Again he went through a day of anxiety. By the time he had worked through his shift and motored back to Tunbridge Wells it was the early hours of Thursday, 28th. He had eaten very little that day and felt tired and hungry. However, he called in to see how Nora was to set his mind at rest. It was in the early hours of the morning when he pulled up outside the house. Snow was beginning to fall quite heavily. He propped his motor cycle against the kerb and banged on the front door. He could hear people moving about in the house and fancied he heard the cry of a baby. Nora's sister, Gladys, opened the door.

"Nora's had the baby," she told him.

"Is *she* all right?"

"She's fine! The baby was born at mid-day."

Jim realised that he hadn't even asked whether he had a son or a daughter.

"How's the baby? Is it a girl or a boy?"

"The baby's fine too. It's a boy. He weighed seven and a half pounds at birth."

Nora was tired but so pleased to see Jim. Her father had moved into the small bedroom, which Bernie used during the day so that Nora could have her confinement in the best bedroom. Her mother had helped her during the birth and was sleeping with her that night in the double bed. Jim looked at his son for the first time. It was quite an experience for him and he was unable to express his feelings. Instead he kissed the baby gently on its head and then kissed Nora.

Her mother seemed very excited and told Jim what Gladys had already told him about the baby's weight. He wondered why people talked about the weight. As long as mother and baby were all right nothing else really mattered.

Nora and Ken, the name they had decided to give the baby if it were a boy, stayed with Jim's in-laws until New Year's Eve when Jim took them to Bishops Down in a hired taxi after he had finished his day shift. When they were safely in the flat Jim gave Nora a big hug.

"Welcome to our home!" he said, addressing both her and the baby.

"We've a new home and a New Year just starting," she whispered to him. "It's wonderful! Thank you, Jim."

"What more could anyone ask?" Jim said to her. "A home, a family, and a job!"

"It's not quite complete," Nora told him. He wondered what she meant and why she was looking at him in that way.

"Go and fetch Laddie," she said. "He should be here with the rest of us!"

Epilogue

Jim, Nora, Ken and Laddie remained in Tunbridge Wells until the Spring of 1933 when Jim was transferred to the Windsor Garage. The years between 1930 and 1933 were not all happy ones. In 1931 Vi and Charlie lost their two-year old son, Donald. The little boy caught whooping cough and died. The death of her son put Vi into a state of shock and it took weeks of love and devotion from Charlie and Jim to bring her through those difficult days. During Christmas 1931 Ken fell ill with double pneumonia and nearly died. By some miracle, perhaps engendered by the earnest prayers of Jim and Nora, Ken slowly recovered.

The maisonette, which Jim rented in Windsor, was large. Adjacent to the entrance door was a superb workshop area where Jim was able to fit a workbench, vices and tool-racks. The carpentry work he was able to do brought in additional money so that Nora had no need to work outside the home. Jim wanted her to be at home with their son and Laddie, seeing his own role as being the family breadwinner.

The family were very happy at Windsor. Nora took Ken and Laddie on long walks in Windsor Park and on his rest days Jim took them all over to Old Windsor, weather permitting, where he enjoyed sitting on the banks of the river doing a spot of fishing. Jim had saved hard and bought himself a car. It was a Triumph Sports model but he purchased it quite cheaply as its previous owner was disappointed by its performance. Jim stripped the engine right down, virtually rebuilding it, after which the car performed superbly.

Ken started school in 1935, the school being just around the corner from the maisonette. In 1936 Jim took Laddie to a vet as the dog had become ill, losing the use of his back legs. The vet diagnosed that Laddie was suffering *Bright's Disease* and asked for Jim's consent to give the dog an injection to end its life. The decision was a difficult one to make although Jim knew that he had no real choice in the matter, he could not bear to see Laddie suffer. He took the loss of his faithful friend very badly and was unable to sleep properly, or to eat for nearly a week. Nora, too, was distressed at the loss of Laddie but even more distressed at the effect it had on Jim. She suggested that he bought another Alsatian but he told her that he could never find another one like Laddie. It was fortunate that Jim received notice of transfer to the Chelsham Garage at that time, which involved moving home again.

He bought a house in Sanderstead, using his savings and the money he was able to earn building wardrobes, fitting banisters and the fences and wooden coalbunkers for all the houses on the Estate. The family moved into their new house in March 1937. Jim built a workshop behind the house soon after moving in. The house had a fair sized garden and Jim developed an interest in gardening, planting plum, pear and apple trees as well as varieties of both flowers and vegetables. His work, his carpentry, his gardening and his fishing filled his time.

Nora had tried for another baby when they were living at Windsor but she had had a miscarriage. Later she conceived again and that time went through her pregnancy only to lose the baby at the end of it all. However, on 25th June 1939, Nora presented Jim with a daughter. They decided to name her June Rose-Marie. Jim was delighted to have a son and a daughter. They had feared that they would never have another child so the birth of June Rose-Marie was a wonderful event for them both.

Less than three months after the birth of the baby the war broke out. Many of the neighbours joined the armed forces and Jim watched them enlist one by one. George next door went into the Army, the man opposite joined the Royal Air Force, and another friend a few doors away went into the Royal Navy. Jim had been discharged from the Navy on health grounds and was unable to get back in.

Frank Whittam called to see Jim one day. He was wearing the uniform of a Warrant Officer in the Royal Air Force. He told Jim that Kitty was running the business with her sister, Norah and Kitty had even taken over driving the lorry up to Covent Garden! Jim became very restless, telling Nora that he wanted to take some part in the war against Hitler's Germany. Following the collapse of France in 1940 the Local Defence Volunteer army was formed and Jim volunteered immediately. He was the only member of the local group of the L.D.V who had a rifle! It was a Mauser .300 rifle that he had kept as a souvenir of the 1914-18 war. He had a licence for it and had displayed it on the wall of the sittingroom as a decoration along with the Cossack sword, the dagger and the bayonet. The Russian revolver however was not licensed and Jim always kept it locked away in his seaman's trunk. When the L.D.V was reformed into the Home Guard, Jim was promoted to Corporal. His uniform was kept pressed, his boots polished up like black mirrors, and his leather gaiters and rifle sling polished to a deep mahogany. The rifles that were first issued to the men came from a grammar school O.T.C unit and none of them was equipped with a firing pin. Jim spent some hours in his workshop with the rifle and emerged later triumphantly with a rifle that was capable of firing bullets. To make sure that Nora and the children would be as safe as possible during the Battle of Britain he took delivery of an Anderson shelter, digging out a trench for it and erecting it at the bottom of the garden. He rigged up sleeping bunks inside and built a wooden door with a ventilator in it. In front of the door he erected a blast wall to give maximum protection. The earth, which covered both the shelter and the blast wall, made excellent marrow beds!

In June 1941 Nora collapsed with pains in her stomach and was taken into hospital to have her appendix removed. Jim cooked the meal for Ken, June and himself that evening. He arranged with Cec and Win in Tunbridge Wells to look after the two children while Nora was in hospital. That same weekend Germany attacked Russia. Jim knew a little about the Russians from his Caradoc days and remarked "He's bitten off more than he can chew this time!" referring to Hitler, of course.

Jim spent a lot of time with his son, Ken. He taught the boy Morse code and the two of them used equipment that Jim made to transmit and decipher code messages. Later they experimented with more elaborate light signals, adapted from the original equipment. Jim rewarded Ken with a little pocket money for helping in the garden, assisting in the collection of firewood and sawing it up.

He also encouraged Ken to collect waste paper for the war effort. When his son gained a scholarship to a grammar school Jim was very pleased, the only disadvantage being that the boy had to travel to Old Coulsdon daily—which involved his getting up early to catch a bus into Croydon and another one from Croydon to the school. Jim bought his son a cycle so that the boy could continue doing a paper round before setting off for school. Jim respected his son's independence as the money he earned enabled him to buy the things he needed to pursue his own hobbies and interests.

In spite of Jim's preparations and care of his rifle and equipment the German invasion never came. Apart from practise firing, the only time Jim had cause to fire his rifle was when a gang of drunken French Canadians tried to break into the Canteen Jim was guarding. He challenged them but they laughed and told him that he wouldn't dare use the rifle on them. The first bullet was so close to the first Canadian's ear that he and his companions realised that Jim meant what he said when he informed them that the next bullet would *not* be merely a warning and they left the Canteen at the double! On the lighter side, Jim and some of his friends arranged concerts for the servicemen and put on various sketches and songs. Jim's bass voice was described as being very like that of Paul Robeson and Jim sang *"Trees"* and other numbers which had been Paul Robeson's favourites. Jim also found a spot in the concert for his son.

Kitty and young Frank came to see Jim and Nora one weekend. Visits, including holidays, between the two families had been frequent occurrences before the war. Weekends in the cars at Brighton, Little Hampton and Hastings were also a regular feature. After the war started and Frank enlisted in the RAF, the two families maintained only postal contact. The visit was therefore a rare thing and there was a special reason for it. Kitty told Jim and Nora that an unexploded bomb had fallen right outside their shop in Putney High Street. The police and air raid wardens had cordoned off the area and evacuated the families. She said that Frank had come home on a forty-eight hour pass the following morning. He had brushed aside the warnings from the police and taken his greengrocery lorry right up to the front of the shop beside the unexploded bomb. He had then proceeded to load his antique furniture into the lorry. The police had tried to force him to leave but he would have none of their interference. Kitty said that she could watch him struggling alone no longer so she had helped him with the heavier items of furniture. Frank had said that 'if the bloody Germans had ruined his business he would be damned if they would ruin his belongings too!' They had loaded the lorry and driven off and within minutes of their leaving, the bomb exploded destroying the shop and their apartment completely. Undaunted, Frank had taken another shop in Wandsworth with accommodation and had spent the rest of his short leave in moving his furniture in and getting the shop ready for "business as usual". Kitty said that the whole thing had been a real ordeal. Jim said that although he admired Frank's guts he felt that both he and Kitty had taken a risk, which could have left young Frank an orphan.

Jim had excellent eyesight but driving a bus in the blackout was quite a strain and he was always glad when his late shifts were over and he went back on day shifts for a week He had suffered quite a lot with back pain during 1942, which the doctor had told him was due to lumbago brought on by driving under stress. Although Jim never complained to anyone and continued to work, to dig his garden and allotments, and to turn out for guard duties and drill with the Home Guard, Nora began to worry about him. He could not hide from her the pain he suffered. She implored him to see another doctor and get a second opinion but he told her that he was all right.

In late October he returned home early one day. He told Nora that he had been in severe pain all morning but had carried on driving the bus until he started to get coloured lights in front of his eyes whereupon he had stopped the bus, not daring to risk the lives of his passengers. The Garage had sent a relief driver out and Jim was told to go home and see his doctor immediately.

Jim told Nora that he had called in to see the doctor on his way home and had been told that he was suffering eye strain and that the severe back pains were either lumbago or a chill caused by sitting at the driving seat of a bus and being in a draught. He had told Jim to go home and rest in bed and to place a hot water bottle on his back and take some aspirin to relieve the pain. Jim did as the doctor had instructed but the aspirins failed to shift the pains in his back. He struggled out of bed to go to the toilet but the coloured lights in front of his eyes were making it difficult for him to see where he was going.

Nora helped him back to bed. He refused any food but gratefully accepted the fruit juices that she had prepared for him. Rather than see him trying to struggle to get to the toilet she told him to use a chamber pot if he wanted to pass urine. She was horrified when she went to empty and clean out the pot. The contents looked more like blood than urine. She sent Ken up to the doctor's surgery on his bike with a request that the doctor should call immediately. The doctor was out on his rounds but the receptionist promised to arrange for the doctor to visit Jim the moment he got back. He called during the afternoon. He examined Jim and looked at the contents of the chamber pot. Jim had been ill in bed three or four days by then. The doctor asked Nora what Jim had been eating or drinking. She told him that he had refused food but that she had made him up some fruit juices, which he had enjoyed. He asked her what sort of juices and Nora explained that she had used orange juice, blackcurrant juice and apple juice to give some variety. The doctor told her that the blackcurrant juice doubtless had caused the discoloration of urine. Nora was not happy with the doctor's diagnosis and asked him to test the urine. He told her that she was obviously over-stressed and that he would give her a sedative and call back to see how Jim was doing within the next forty-eight hours. The next day Jim was worse and slipped into a semi-delirious state. He was calling out things that she could not understand:

"It's Jack Frost!" and later "It's like looking for a needle in a haystack." Jim was obviously very distressed and his forehead was wet with perspiration. She asked her son to stay with Jim and to look after June Rose-Marie and ran along to the doctor's surgery herself. She refused to leave there until he gave her a guarantee that he would call to see Jim *immediately* he had finished his morning surgery. Nora waited for the doctor to call. She knew that Jim was very ill and needed care beyond that which she could give.

The doctor called after his morning surgery as promised but after one look at Jim summoned an ambulance.

Jim was taken into Croydon Hospital on Saturday, October 31st.

The neighbours were very kind and took Ken and June Rose-Marie into their homes so that Nora could spend as much time as possible at Jim's bedside. The delirious state had gone and Jim slipped into unconsciousness. The doctors at the hospital had rigged up blood transfusions and drip feeds. On Saturday, November 7th, 1942 they told Nora there was nothing more they could do and Jim passed from this life with Nora beside his bed holding his hand in hers.

* * *

As for Jim's first love, *Caradoc*, she survived the 1939-45 War but made her final journey to Briton Ferry, South Wales, for breaking-up in March 1946.

…And what happened to Jim's family in the ensuing years? Well, that's another story but one that is in process of preparation.